What youth leaders around the country are saying . . .

"THE MOST COMPREHENSIVE, ARTICULATE AND PRACTI-
CAL PRESENTATION I'VE SEEN ON YOUTH WORK IN THE
PAST TWO DECADES. What you have here is not mere theory,
but gut-level wisdom wrenched from miles upon miles of
work with kids. Jim Burns has lived each of these pages . . . .
PERHAPS THE FINEST BOOK EVER WRITTEN ON YOUTH
MINISTRY."

—Tim Hansel
Founder and President
Summit Expedition

"FANTASTIC . . . SO INSPIRING . . . as a youth minister it is
such a practical workbook. I RECOMMEND IT FOR EVERY
YOUTHWORKER."

—Keith Waldrop
Frazer Memorial United Methodist
Montgomery, Alabama

"JIM BURNS KNOWS TEENAGERS and understands what it
takes to effectively capture their attention and involve them in
the life and ministry of the church. His breadth of experience
and depth of commitment to the task come alive on every
page of this important manifesto of relational youth ministry.

"I plan to recommend *The Youth Builder* as one of a handful of
'MUST HAVES' in any volunteer or professional youthworker's
library."

—Rich Van Pelt
Associate Staff
Youth Specialties
Denver, Colorado

THE
YOUTH
BUILDER

THE YOUTH BUILDER

THE YOUTH BUILDER

"This book is an EXCELLENT RESOURCE for anyone doing youth ministry. It communicates an attitude of excellence and enthusiasm even as it communicates a wealth of practical instruction and strategy."

—Steve Murray
Minister of Youth
St. Andrew's Presbyterian Church
Newport Beach, California

"Jim has provided a practical volume that doesn't insult the intelligence of the professional youthworker. It is particularly helpful in developing models for ministry application, financial planning, and development of youth ministry teams. I EXPECT THIS TO BE A SOLID RESOURCE FOR YOUTH MINISTERS."

—Byron Klaus
Director of Graduate Studies
Southern California College

"There aren't many of us around who have survived the challenges of doing youth ministry for over 15 years. Jim Burns has! But he hasn't just survived, he's learned and now shares in this book the nuts and bolts of doing effective youth ministry. I RECOMMEND *THE YOUTH BUILDER*. READ IT!"

—Dan Webster
Willow Creek Community Church
Lexington, Massachusetts

THE
YOUTH
BUILDER

Today's Resource for
Relational Youth Ministry

THE YOUTH BUILDER

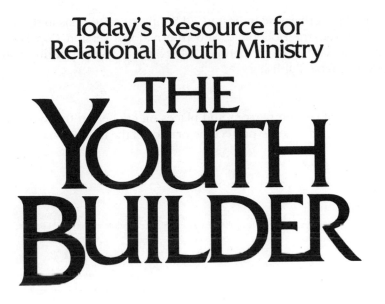

JIM BURNS

HARVEST HOUSE PUBLISHERS
Eugene, Oregon 97402

THE YOUTH BUILDER

Copyright © 1988 by Harvest House Publishers
Eugene, Oregon 97402

Library of Congress Catalog Card Number 87-081664
ISBN 0-89081-576-3

Printed in the United States of America.

To Cathy . . .
. . . the most influential person in my life.
Your support, sacrifice, and consistent
Christian behavior inspire me.
Your faith, commitment, and accountability
motivate me to focus on Christ.
He is the reason for our life together,
our shared ministry, and this book.

CONTENTS

Preface and Acknowledgments

I love youth ministry. I believe that people who spend a part of their lives working with youth are participants in one of the most challenging and valuable walks of life. I hope this book is an affirmation to your calling. You *are* making a difference in the world.

This book is a culmination of my life in youth ministry for the past 16 years. My goal in this writing is to give you a comprehensive look at relational youth ministry. I have tried to mix the philosophy of youth ministry with practicality. I have written as a youth ministry practitioner, not a theorist. This book comes out of the years of my life "in the trenches" with kids.

As I considered the acknowledgments for this book, they are simply too numerous to mention. Youth ministry and my entire life are very intertwined. At the risk of not mentioning people who have had a profound influence on my life and ministry, I do want to acknowledge a few people.

Cathy (to whom this book is dedicated) has put up with my fanaticism for youth ministry. She is the greatest influence in my life, and I am deeply grateful to God for her. Mike Yaconelli and Wayne Rice, as well as Tic Long and the entire Youth Specialties Organization, brought me on as a 25-year-old "kid" and taught me how to train youth workers. I will forever be indebted to them for their belief in me, their influence on me, and most of all their friendship toward me. John Watson and Tim Timmons were pastors who gave me great support in my ministry. A special thanks to Rich Van Pelt for his friendship and concern for Kids in Crisis. Thanks to Doug Webster for his comments on the manuscript outline. Noel Becchetti, editor of *Youthworker Journal*, gave me invaluable help in putting together this material. He is a co-creator of this book's form and style. My regular column, "High School Ministry," in *Youthworker Journal* was the catalyst for some of the material presented in this book.

My colleagues at the National Institute of Youth Ministry took on extra tasks and walked the second mile in order for me to write this book. Katie Temple's reading of the manuscript, sacrificial time, and insightful comments were extremely helpful. Karen Heeley and Linda Gray did an excellent job of typing.

Lastly, a very special thanks to the wonderful people of Harvest House Publishers, who are a joy to work with. Thank you, Eileen Mason, Bob Hawkins, Sr., and Bob Hawkins, Jr.

—Jim Burns
Dana Point, Calif.

THE FOUNDATION

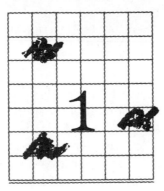

WHAT IS
RELATIONAL
YOUTH MINISTRY?

Y our young people are making major decisions that will affect the rest of their lives. Adolescence is a time of transition that brings long-lasting effects. As a youth worker, you play a powerful role and influence in the life of your students. In a recent survey, students on a secular high school campus were asked, "Who would you turn to in time of trouble or for help in life decisions?" The number one choice was parents, but the second choice was youth workers. Many years ago, youth ministry in the church was either a glorified babysitting service or an insignificant event on the church calendar. Today, youth ministry is viewed as one of the key elements of service within the church.

But what is effective youth ministry? In the past, good youth ministry was often seen as program-oriented—rallies, events, and other elaborate, orchestrated gatherings. However, today we realize that long-term influence with lasting results comes from significant relationships and role models. Of course programming has its place in youth ministry, but the long-term positive influence on the lives of students comes from people, not programs.

I recently asked one thousand youth workers at a conference to list the five most influential sermons or programs in their life. One minute later, no one had come up with five sermons or programs.

In fact, the vast majority of the workers could remember only one or two sermons or programs at best. Then I asked them to list five of the most influential people in their life. After one minute, most of the people in the conference had listed four or five people who had influenced their life in a significant way. My guess is that you are where you are today because of a few significant individuals who cared for you on a personal basis.

In order to have an important influence in the lives of young people, you do not need to be a dynamic speaker, know all the latest rock musicians, or even dress in the latest fashions. You must, however, love kids and be willing to spend time with them, which is basically what relational youth ministry is all about. Effective youth workers may never be polished communicators, but they will surely need to have a listening ear and a willingness to get to know the students in their youth group. *Caring for your students is the primary prerequisite for working with them.*

The Incarnational Ministry

I was speaking to a group of youth workers in Kansas. After I had finished, several people came up to talk. The particular issues varied, but the question was the same: "What program can I use to keep my group enthusiastic about their faith?" My answer was probably disappointing to some people: There are a variety of proven methods; many different youth ministry organizations, denominations, books, and individual churches use every type of program imaginable, and they all seem to work. Yet at the same time, any method can also fail!

However, there is a way to build a youth group spiritually and numerically. (Contrary to what some might say, youth go where other kids are, so numbers can at times be important.) There is one word that stands out above all others, and that word is *relationship*.

Our Christian faith is sealed in a personal relationship with Jesus Christ. Theologically, Jesus is the *incarnation* of God. He is God in the flesh (Colossians 1:15). As the ministry of Jesus was incarnate in the Gospels, so our life must be incarnate in youth ministry. If we are ever to have a positive influence on our young

16

people, we must build relationships with them and live out our faith in front of them. Young people tire of phony programs or manipulative methods. They can see through false pretenses. By building genuine relationships with them and allowing them to see healthy staff relationships, young people will consider the adults as friends and confidants. I believe that the students who remain active in the group will stay in the group because of healthy and genuine relationships.

The old adage "More is caught than taught" rings true in the world of relational youth ministry. Here are the six basic ingredients of an effective relational youth ministry.

Team Ministry

Young people are looking for role models to imitate. The adult staff (whether comprised of scores of youth workers or a husband-and-wife volunteer team) must build toward a loving *team* before any young person will stand up and take notice. I believe that the first commitment which a new youth worker should make in the church, even before developing a ministry with the students, is to develop a ministry with other youth sponsors. Relational youth ministry starts with a relational youth staff. Jesus told His disciples, "A new command I give you: Love one another. As I have loved you, so you must love one another. All men will know that you are my disciples if you love one another" (John 13:34,35). In other words, the youth in your church and community will often judge the attractiveness and validity of the gospel by the relationships which the staff members have with one another.

Take time to build significant relationships with your staff, and encourage affirming friendships between them. You will be creating a wonderful role model for your students. You will also be cementing the volunteer staff's involvement in youth ministry. The youth group is watching, listening, and at times imitating the relationship role models of the staff.

A unified staff is one which prays and shares with each other. A unified staff plays together. Some of the most quality times for building staff unity can be done in the very same manner as with students: through playing athletics together, shopping, or other "fun" outings. As your youth staff develops a mutual love, support, and respect for each other, then your young people will notice and respond.[1]

Modeling

Most likely, your greatest influence will not be in what you teach through your words. Rather, it will be through your actions, reactions, and lifestyle.

The most effective teaching that takes place is usually not in the formal teaching times, but rather when the students get to know their youth worker and *imitate* some of his or her actions. Imitation is perhaps the greatest gift someone can give you. The apostle Paul even went so far as to say, "Join with others in following my example, brothers, and take note of those who live according to the pattern we gave you" (Philippians 3:17).

A number of years ago I came to our youth group wearing a pair of multicolored suspenders. (Earlier that day I saw a wild pair of suspenders in a local department store. I hadn't seen anyone wear them in years, so I decided to purchase a pair and wear them to the youth group.) When I arrived that evening, the kids mobbed me with questions and opinions on my new suspenders. The next week five students arrived at our meeting wearing suspenders. The following week 12 students came in suspenders. Imitation is powerful. A good relational minister is aware of the powerful influence of modeling his or her Christian faith. When I first started in youth ministry it dawned on me that my Bible studies, my special events, and even the way I treated kids was an imitation of my Campus Life leader in high school. I respected him so greatly that I unconsciously imitated his behavior.

Unconditional Love

The truth of the gospel says, "God loves you not for what you do but for who you are." God loves you unconditionally. His love is sacrificial and deep. Grace permeates our relationship with our Lord. We also must love our students with an unconditional, "no-strings-attached" love. We must accept the fact that kids will fail. When they miss the mark, they need our love and encouragement to keep trying.

Your actions of unconditional love will often be the determining factor in solidifying the faith of your students. How can they know God's grace and love if they don't see it firsthand from significant others? The apostle John's wise words are so important for youth workers: "Let us not love with *words or tongue* but with *actions* and in truth" (1 John 3:18). In other words, actions do speak louder than words.

A few years ago while chaperoning a party for one of the local high schools, I watched one of our leadership core kids literally being carried out of the party because he had passed out from drinking too much. I was hurt; he was embarrassed. Of course, on Sunday he didn't come to our group. I decided I had to go to him and let him know I loved him and still wanted him in our group. (You can disapprove of actions and still deeply love your students.) He had to learn that even though he made a mistake he was still accepted by our group and leaders. Even through this negative experience, he would understand the *grace* of God in a stronger, more meaningful way. Recently this young man told me that if we had not loved him with unconditional love, he probably would never have come back to church. Don't miss the opportunity to demonstrate God's grace to your teenagers.

Nurturing

There is no such thing as "instant spiritual maturity." Sanctification is a continuing process. Just as newborn babies need constant care and nourishment, so young people need our consistent attention, time, and presence. Good youth ministry with a real impact takes time and nurture.

I'm convinced that the reason we have so many young people with an impeded spiritual life is because we have not given them the nurture needed to produce healthy spiritual lives. One of the major goals of youth ministry is to move the students from dependence on you, the youth worker, to dependence on God. Yet the process takes time. Many youth workers have been guilty of manipulative methods to produce "instant spiritual maturity" only to see in the long run that this tactic didn't produce healthy and genuine spiritual fruit. Students need to know that their youth leaders will *stick with them* and nurture them to become all that God desires them to be.

Meeting Students on Their Territory

We live in a fast-paced, exciting culture. If the church stands

19

still and waits for the kids to come to her, then the church will have a long, quiet, empty, and frustrating wait. Meeting students on their territory is vital because it breaks down the often-imposing walls of the church. To get a response it is important to go out to the schools and hangouts and *meet them on their territory* in order to relate to them. For many youth workers this means watching a high school soccer match or helping with decorations for the school play rather than spending time in the office.

By going into the young people's world, they will know that you are interested in them as people, not just as church participants. One of the most important aspects of ministry is to let them know you care.

Invading "their" world can become a great tool for evangelism. Young people will introduce you to their friends, and eventually as friendships evolve they too will want to see what "youth group" is all about.

Contact work (meeting them on their territory) is one of the most rewarding aspects of youth ministry. When we show up at a school game or event or even lunch, the kids will usually react with enthusiasm because they know that we were willing to take time out of our busy schedule to take interest in them.

While working with Young Life I remember going to soccer games and practices. Eventually the coach asked me to help with the team for the last few games. Actually I was more like an adult water boy. At the time we had two guys on the team coming to our Young Life club. Before the season was over a majority of the team had come to one of our club meetings. There was nothing more effective that entire year than spending a considerable amount of time on the soccer field.

You can learn a great amount about the youth culture when you invade their territory. If you want to really understand the youth culture, spend a day on a local junior high or high school campus. Your life will never be the same.

Spending Time with Your Students

Students need significant adults to give them time and attention. It takes both quality and quantity time to do effective relational youth ministry. Not too long ago I called up two high school guys one Saturday morning and asked them to go shopping with me at the mall. I already knew what I wanted to buy, but I thought it might be good to spend some time with those two guys. After finding what I wanted to buy, we walked around the mall for an hour and went over to the local hamburger stand for lunch. During lunch we had a very nonthreatening, open conversation about the faith. As I look back, the investment of those few hours and the conversation that took place was far more productive then all the Sunday school classes I had ever taught those two students.

Educators today talk about the idea of "hidden curriculum." By this they mean that we must look for every opportunity outside the classroom setting to teach our students. When you spend time with kids in your groups, you are showing them they are important and that you really care. A friend of mine plays basketball with a group of guys every week. He told me recently that he talks more about God before, during, and after the weekly basketball game than at any other time during the week.

Jim Rayburn, the founder of Young Life, used to say, "It's a sin to bore a kid with the gospel." The gospel of Jesus is the most exciting news the world will ever hear, yet young people often drop out of the church because "it's boring." I believe that one of the major reasons kids drop out of church and call it boring is because no one was willing to take an interest in them or spend time with them.

Reaching Out

We can't compete with the latest technology in media to keep kids' interest. Producers and advertisers spend millions of dollars to keep the attention of young people riveted on the television set. However, there is one thing that TV or the other competitors for kids' attention cannot give: a real flesh-and-blood relationship. Young people will respond to someone who genuinely cares about them and is willing to spend time with them. *Relationships are the key to effective youth ministry.* The greatest programs will fail and the most interesting curriculum will never be absorbed if the primary focus in youth ministry is not building solid, encouraging, positive relationships with young people. The good news for most of us is that it isn't necessary to be an excellent communicator or to produce incredible programs; rather, we need a willingness to spend time with kids and let them know we care.

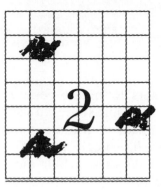

PREPARING YOURSELF
FOR RELATIONAL
YOUTH MINISTRY

O ne of the major concerns of my life is the high turnover of youth workers in youth ministry. The odds are high that most of the youth workers in churches today will not be in the same church two years from now. Furthermore, the majority of the volunteers won't be involved in the youth group next year. Burnout and frustration are chronic handicaps in our mission to reach young people.

I believe the high turnover rate in youth work is often due to a lack of personal preparation for youth ministry. How can we who have been called to work with kids prepare ourselves to be effective for the big haul?

Devotion

I once heard it said, "Untended fires soon become nothing but a pile of ashes." One intern involved at my church said, "I can't afford to take the time to have a quality devotional life with God." My reply was simply, "You can't afford *not* to have a quality devotional life with God."

Many youth workers are high on energy and enthusiasm. We can wing a program and Bible study with some degree of success. However, in the long haul we often run out of gas and burn out spiritually because we have neglected to fuel the fire of our faith.

Most Christian leaders have their most effective ministries after they are in their forties or older. They are mature and have set a foundation for their faith. Unfortunately, many youth workers never become effective ministers in their forties or older because their lack of personal time with God catches up with them. They fade away before God can use them in the greatest ways possible.

Paul's advice to Timothy was to "train yourself to be godly" (1 Timothy 4:7). A disciplined devotional life is not an option for spiritual growth; it is a necessity. As I read the biographies of great men and women of God, there is one common thread visible in all of their varied lives: They all met with God on a daily, personal, devotional basis.

I had read many times about marathon runners "hitting the wall." They experience intense pain, nausea, exhaustion, and even at times loss of primary bodily functions. This year, after only halfhearted training in too short a time, I ran my first marathon. At mile 17, I hit the wall! It was as if my body quit working. After walking dizzily for a few miles, I regained enough energy to finish the marathon and tell my wife to remind me never to attempt something like this again without proper training. Many of us in ministry don't take time to do the proper preparation for ministry, and we "hit the wall." We leave the ministry before we can be used in the greatest way by God.

With proper priorities, there should be no excuse strong enough to keep us from a daily, disciplined, devotional time with God. I don't believe length of time is as important as regularity. We Christians wonder why we feel powerless and spiritually drained when less than 1 percent of those who call themselves Christians spend 30 minutes or more a day with God.

Rejuvenation

Most youth workers are undertrained for their work with adolescents. Not only are we undertrained, but our culture and the needs of adolescents are constantly changing. Study leave provides people with the opportunity to strengthen skills, gain needed education, and be spiritually refreshed. I strongly believe that the church should give a youth worker two weeks a year for continuing education and should pay for the expenses. (Of course, we must keep it reasonable. Study leave to cruise the Caribbean Islands is probably not wise stewardship of church funds!)

As you look for study-leave experiences, search for types of study that will fit your particular needs best. I have found four different types of study leave helpful.

Continuing education. There is now an abundance of high-quality continuing-education experiences emerging in all shapes and sizes. Many Christian colleges and seminaries offer short-term classes, summer sessions, and weekly classes in youth ministry or counseling. There are excellent organizations putting on conventions and conferences. With the onslaught of video, we now have access to video training films. Even sprucing up your cassette tape library can be a real educational boost.[1]

Visiting other ministries. If you are tired of seminars, conferences, and conventions, then an excellent idea is to plan your own study leave by visiting successful youth ministry programs. Plan your trip carefully so that you can visit with successful youth pastors in a single area of the country. Try to visit their youth meetings as well.

Spending time alone. I have found that for me one of the most efficient uses of study leave is to find a motel or a friend's cabin away from the phone and other interruptions. I bring my curriculum needs for the quarter as well as commentaries, idea books, and a calendar. In a few days alone I plan my talks, work on scheduling, come up with ideas, and study for curriculum. Two to four days of uninterrupted time frees me up to spend more time with students when I'm back home.

Bringing in an expert. You may not be able to afford to pay for an expert to be your personal consultant, but many people today are bringing together a number of churches to fly in an expert to train and equip their youth workers. When a few churches come together, it really reduces the cost of the program. If you offer to drive to the airport to pick up such experts (or, better yet, invite them to dinner), you'll find that the special one-on-one times will be well worth "picking their brain."

Solitude

I'm excited about the sudden upsurge of interest among Christians in taking a Sabbath. The Old Testament Sabbath is a form of rest, reflection, and change of pace. Even God rested one day out of seven! A solo is a time away from the office for extra time with God. When I go on a solo, I try to be away for five hours. I bring my Bible, journal, and pen. I spend my time reading, praying, journaling, singing, worshiping, and walking. I've even been known to take a short nap! I want my solo to take place in nature. I will go to the beach, a park, a lake, or somewhere else where I can be away from people and in God's creation. It's a time of reflection, worship, and refreshment. The purpose is to refresh me so that when I'm with people they will have all my attention. If you've never taken a solo, try it. You may get hooked, and I believe it will help you become a more effective minister.

Administration

Administration does not appear to be the main spiritual gift among most youth workers. Often the strength of a youth leader is that he or she is flexible and spontaneous. Sometimes the strength of spontaneity can become a weakness when it comes to administering a youth program. Yet in the long run a well-planned ministry will provide more valuable time to spend with your young people. Here are a few suggestions.

1. Plan a calendar for an entire year. There is no reason why you can't know in September who will be in charge of the February car rally.

2. Organize certain times of the week for certain projects. Every Tuesday morning plan your talk, with no other interruptions. Make Thursday a study day, etc. (See the Sample Schedule for an example of this point on page 29.)

3. Before your week begins, plan it out on paper.

4. Begin each day by knowing what you plan to accomplish that particular day.

5. Leave room in your schedule for flexibility.

6. Plan out meetings in advance. It will save you hours of wasted time. I even plan out phone calls in advance.

7. Read a good book or attend a seminar on time management.

8. Seek the advice of men or women who appear to be organized. Ask them how they do it. (People love to share their stories and ideas.)

Prevention

The deadliest sins of the youth worker are perhaps the sins of *overcommitment* and *fatigue*. I heard the comedian Flip Wilson once say, "If I had my life to live over again, I don't think I would have the strength." I can identify with him, and you probably can too. Youth workers burn out because they tackle too many responsibilities and commitments without enough rest. Professional football coach Vince Lombardi used to tell his team, "Fatigue makes cowards of us all." Many youth workers burn out because they can't say no.

The sooner we learn that most of us tend to have a "messiah complex" and that we must say no to insure long-range success, the sooner we will have a more productive ministry. Look at overbooking your schedule as a sin, not as a sign of success. People in ministry are prone to becoming workaholics. Workaholism is an addictive sin in our lives similar to any other addiction. Leave room in your schedule for rest, flexibility, freedom to be available, and fellowship. The best advice I ever received in seminary was from a friend who upon my graduation wrote these words on a card to me: "If the Devil can't make you bad, then he will make you busy."

Fellowship

Supportive fellowship is not an option; it is a necessity. If you are not in some form of a support group, I question how long you will last in youth ministry. These are strong words, but I believe them to be true. Working with students is both a joy and a strain. We need the support and accountability of peers who love us and encourage us but aren't afraid to question our motives. In my own life I try to be in relationship with an accountable *support group* in order to share my hurts and joys. I need to feel a sense of community. I also need a *mentor relationship*. I've had to find more mature and wiser Christians from whom I can learn and grow in a mentor capacity. I also need a *Timothy* in my life—someone to whom I can give myself in a ministry of discipleship and training and someone to whom I can be a mentor. Your own personal preparation for ministry and the longevity of your ministry often relates to this important area of support more than you realize. Unfortunately, I find most youth workers to be lonely, isolated people.

Rest

If you are not taking at least a 24-hour period of rest in your week, most likely your primary relationships are out of order and you are not functioning as a cutting-edge Christian. Even God rested on the seventh day, yet many youth workers consider themselves to be "bionic Christians." Rest heals; rest soothes; rest gives us perspective. Without a definite time of rest each week, our lives become more and more confusing and disordered. If you can't finish all you need to get done in five or six days, then you are doing too much and are most likely not listening to the Spirit of God in your life.

Family [2]

After the first year of our marriage, Cathy and I decided to review the year. We talked of our joys and discouragements. Cathy's biggest complaint hurt: "You give all you have to the youth and their families, and you have nothing left for me." What made

SAMPLE SCHEDULE

MONDAY: Solo; personal prep; ministry prep; get ready for the week physically & spiritually; speaking prep; special lunch; appointments after 2:00.

TUESDAY: Elders' meeting; staff meeting; one-on-ones; continuing weekly prep; afternoon appointments.

WEDNESDAY: Morning for writing or outside-of-the-church ministry; finish Sunday school; afternoon appointments.

THURSDAY: Spouse time; pastors' staff meeting; staff or student appointments; evening Bible study.

FRIDAY: Preparation for youth staff meeting; 9:00 to 11:00 youth staff meeting; afternoon contact work.

SATURDAY: Off (if you work Saturday, take at least another full day off).

SUNDAY: Church and evening work.

matters worse is that she was absolutely right. Through the years I've had to make adjustments to insure a healthy, solid marriage. Here are a few suggestions.

1. A weekly date night is a nonnegotiable item in your calendar.

2. If you must work morning till night, make up for the time on another day during the week.

3. Your spouse should have veto power over your schedule.

4. Daily phone calls are a must when you are traveling and are away from each other.

5. Take periodic overnight trips with your spouse.

6. Take vacation times for building up your relationship, and not always for visiting the relatives!

7. Give your family your *prime* time, not just the time when you are exhausted.

If your family life is suffering, then it is certainly time to reevaluate your ministry and make the necessary adjustments before your family and ministry dissolve.

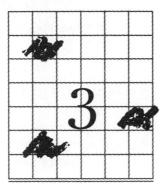

UNDERSTANDING TODAY'S YOUTH

The adolescent world is changing rapidly; it is virtually impossible to keep up with every new fad and movement of the culture. The pressures of today's culture hardly compare to those of previous times. To accentuate the challenge of ministry in today's culture, let's look at some frightening information. In 1940 the top offenses in public schools were as follows: running in the hallways, chewing gum in class, wearing improper clothing (which included leaving a shirttail out), making noise, and not putting paper in wastebaskets. In 1980 the top offenses in public schools were as follows: robbery, assault, personal theft, burglary, drug abuse, arson, bombings, alcohol abuse, carrying weapons, absenteeism, vandalism, murder, and extortion![1] Not a great deal of comment is necessary, except to say that times and conditions have changed.

The Revolution of Change

The young people that you and I work with today are different from those of any previous generation. They are smarter, better-looking, and filled with greater potential than people of any other time in history. This same teenager is filled with more stress, anxiety, and pressure than teens of any previous generation. Their world is a maze of continuing transformations. In order to meet the important needs of this generation of young people, we must keep our ears and eyes carefully tuned to the rapidly changing beat of the culture. There is a revolution of change taking place in the youth culture. Youth workers can help make a positive influence amid the frightening changes taking place.

The Family Revolution

In 1986, a general sampling of youth workers taken by Youth Specialties indicated that 35 percent to 75 percent of the adolescents in any group were not living with both of their natural parents. The stable under-pinning of the family is not just buckling—it has col-lapsed. Even those young people whose parents are not divorced are not free from anxiety. Every time their parents have an argument, they wonder: *Is my family next?* The adolescent of today has been deeply affected by this family permutation. In the past, the family was stress *re*ducing; now the family is stress producing.[2]

Many studies tell us that the greatest place of violence in America is inside the home. It's no secret that the home is no longer a happy place to be in the majority of teenagers' lives. Physical abuse and neglect are at the top of the list of problems in the home. We can't assume that the kids in our groups are doing okay at home.

Much of our youth ministry must be geared at helping the family make it. The family is, by God's design, the center of life and even of the young person's Christian education. Youth workers cannot neglect the fact that one of their major goals must be to help families succeed. Your job is to promote the family.

The Sexual Revolution

In 1967, 85 percent of the teenagers surveyed believed that

premarital sex was morally wrong. In 1981 only 26 percent felt it was wrong. Nearly six out of ten 16- to 18-year-olds have had sexual intercourse. The average age for the first sexual experience is 16 years.[3]

A conservative estimate of teenage pregnancies in a year is *one million*. At least a third of those pregnancies will end in abortion. Only one of every ten teenagers who get married because the woman is pregnant stays married, meaning that nine out of ten get a divorce. Teenage pregnancy is the number one cause of school dropouts for females. The suicide rate among teenage mothers is ten times that of the general population.[4] Who says there is not a price that is paid in the sexual revolution?

Where the Puritans did not want anyone to know that they had sexual feelings, our generation is ashamed if it does not show its feelings. Sexual stimulation is not new, but the overwhelming sexual barrage from every aspect of our society is a relatively new phenomenon in our country.

The church must take a strong stand for morality. In a world of phony, instant intimacy, the church must teach and live the values of commitment and fidelity taught in the Bible. Because sex is a dominant issue in the minds of young people, the church can no longer remain silent. We must let our kids understand that God is not the great killjoy; He cares about their sexuality. God created sex, and within His biblical guidelines He sees it as *very good* (Genesis 1:31). It's time for the church to provide a healthy view of sexuality and a wholesome respect for relationships with the opposite sex.

The Relationship Revolution

The Robert Johnson Company conducted a study for Junior Achievement all across the United States in 1960 and 1980 on the "teen environment."[5] In this study they discovered a radical shift from the 1960's to the 1980's. The question was asked, "What is the most dominant influence in your life?"

Most dominant influence in *1960*	*1980*
1. Mother/father	2
2. Teachers	4
3. Friends, peers	[1]
4. Ministers, priests, rabbis	6
5. Youth club leaders, advisors, Scout masters, coaches	9
6. Popular heroes, sports, music	5
7. Grandparents, uncles, aunts	10
8. TV, records, movies, radio	[3]
9. Newspapers, magazines	7
10. Advertising	8

The shift in major influence is really quite startling. In this study, mother and father were replaced by friends and peers as the most influential relationship, with the friends moving from number three to number one. Notice also that the greatest shift occurred in the area of television, records, movies, and radio. In 1960 this area of influence came in at number eight, but by the 1980's it was number three in influence.

Unfortunately, at the same time that the family influences seem to be disintegrating, the mobility factor is increasing. People are moving more often and farther away from home and their extended family. Youth workers must seriously consider the fact that in our mobile society some young people are retreating from making significant friendships. The result is a sense of loneliness. Many analysts of the teenage culture call this decade the "decade of loneliness."

The church youth group can fill the need for positive influence and intimate relationships. One of the major goals of any youth ministry is to provide an opportunity to form a healthy, Christ-centered community of peers influencing each other in a positive way. One 14-year-old expressed it this way to me: "Until I found this youth group, I had moved so many times that I just gave up on making friends anymore. Every day after school I retreated to my TV set in my bedroom."

The Media Revolution

Television

Television is much more influential than most of us realize. Modern television holds teenagers' attention through sophisticated technology. Visual stimulation is a "high" to the mind similar to that of a chemical high. Today a young person's morals, values, and thought process are molded as much by media as by relationships. Television profoundly affects our society.

Jennifer's parents separate. Instead of feeling any grief, she represses her emotions because on the latest television drama (which she watches with religious fervor) everything turns out okay. Her mind is programmed to see 45 minutes of murder, divorce, and robbery, but by the time the show ends everyone is happy again. Jennifer doesn't realize what she is doing, but she is living with a mixed agenda of the expectations of television and of the real world.

Television is so real to its viewers that no less than 250,000 Americans wrote to TV's Dr. Marcus Welby seeking medical advice, as if he were an actual physician. Markiewicz (past president of National Public Radio) and Swerdlov (free-lance writer) cited the results of a two-year study in which a college researcher asked children ages four to six, "Which do you like better: TV or daddy? Forty-four percent preferred television."[6]

Music

I'm not one who advocates record-burning parties; however, I'm very concerned about the emphasis shift in music today. Let's get something straight: *Kids listen to rock music.* The latest statistics available tell us that teenagers listen to four hours a day of rock music and ten hours a week of MTV music videos. There is no way to calculate what that kind of exposure does to an adolescent, but it's *scary.*

According to a study from the University of Tennessee at Chattanooga, almost 60 percent of MTV music videos contain sex or violence.[7] Tasteless, graphic, and explicitly sexual songs saturate the airwaves and bombard our homes. Many of the songs are nothing more than rock pornography.

35

What is unique about the rock songs of today is not the blatant sexual language; there was music like this before. What is unique about this music is that it is not unique: These pornographic rock songs tend to be the rule rather than the exception. Aristotle wrote, "Music has the power to form character." Music forms and influences our imagination.

Is all media evil? I'm not convinced it is. However, youth workers have two important roles to play when thinking about the media. First, they must be willing to keep up with the changes in order to know what is influencing the people in their own ministry and community. To think that the church's weekly one to four hours of influence is overpowering the media's 30 hours is to be naive. Second, youth workers must help their teenagers learn how to view the media with proper suspicion. Since young people are and will continue to be influenced by media, a good youth ministry program will help students learn to filter what comes into their lives. We must teach them that they have a choice; they do not have to be unduly influenced by the media.

You Can Make a Difference

Given the reality of the influence and transformation of our culture, many youth workers feel paralyzed: What can I do in our little church? That is precisely the feelings of the Israelites when they encountered the Philistines, and particularly Goliath. The Israelites were paralyzed with fear. The young shepherd boy David came out to the battle, at his father's request, to bring supplies to his older brothers. When David observed Goliath mocking the people of Israel and the living God, David decided to do something about it. Armed with five smooth stones, a sling, and his faith in the living God, he killed the giant Goliath. When other people's philosophy was *He is so big that we can't win,* David's belief was *He is so big that I can't miss.* With God's help, David prevailed. We look at the realities of the culture and often see them as too big to overcome. Yet in actuality, with God's help we can make a difference that lasts for eternity.

What can we do? For starters we can begin to help kids view life on a different level.

Help Your Kids Experience Life

Many leaders believe they have to entertain their group to have a successful program. Wrong! Young people must experience the work of Christ if they are to grow in their faith. For example, we can never just talk about missions and expect our young people to understand. Kids must *experience* missions, whether it's painting a widow's home, working at a rescue mission, or visiting a rest home.

Help Your Kids Learn the Joy of Service

Our society says "What's in it for me?" and "Look out for number one." On the other hand, Christ calls His people to *serve.* We can instill a sense of servanthood in our young people. The ones who find the joy of serving stay in the church.

Help Your Kids into Community

We need to teach and practice a sense of community in our youth groups. Young people will stay in the church because they are drawn into the community by faith. They are socialized into a community that affects their actions, beliefs, attitudes, and values—even their dating habits.

Students' Needs

The young people of this culture will not be dazzled in the church through good programming. They can stay home and watch programming on TV that is 100 times better. However, as our technological society continues to become more and more impersonal, the church can meet the more important needs of students and make a difference in their lives.

Love

Young people today need to know that they are loved unconditionally. We must love our people with the "Jesus style" of love. He loved unconditionally, with no strings attached. Kids today need to be loved even when they don't produce or don't look good or aren't successful. We can learn so much about working with students by observing how Jesus related to people. Consider, for example, His meeting with the woman caught in adultery (John 8). He didn't agree with the sin, but His love and forgiveness were evident in the conversation. He knew that greater change takes place through demonstrating love than through inflicting guilt.

Challenge

Too many Christians are never challenged to go farther, dig deeper, or walk the second mile. Your students need to be challenged to leadership and service. They must understand the high calling from God to serve. Living out the Christian faith is so much more than coming to youth group only when they feel like it. Young people are continuing to join religious cults at epidemic levels, and I'm convinced that this is because the cults provide a challenge that the church has failed to offer. Don't soften the words of Jesus: "If anyone would come after me, he must deny himself and take up his cross and follow me" (Mark 8:34).

Accountability

Along with challenge comes accountability. If your students don't follow through on something, they must understand that it matters. When it comes to following through on assignments or even discipline, expect results in a loving way. We bail them out too quickly, and they lose the opportunity to feel needed. At one time we started holding our leadership core students accountable for attending leadership meetings and the worship service, or else they would be asked to step off leadership. Our attendance doubled.

Tough Issues

We learn and grow through tension. We must prepare students for the future by dealing with difficult subjects and bringing up uncomfortable questions. If the struggles of the faith aren't brought up in church, where there is love and security, then the difficult issues will be brought up somewhere else. It's a matter of with whom and where you want these tension issues dealt with. My youth group didn't like me bringing up the fact that our little four-year-old neighbor was dying of cancer, but it was the best meeting we had that year on the subject of prayer. Difficult life experiences must be dealt with, especially in a culture that tends to repress the struggles of life.

Affirmation

Most of today's young people are starved for affirmation and encouragement. Unfortunately, few people take the time to affirm. Affirmation and encouragement are possibly the central ingredients when battling the impersonal culture. There is power in affirmation. I realized this truth when I developed a relationship with Tom. I really liked him, but he was different from most of our group. He was quiet and extremely intellectual, and he was dealing with faith issues that very few high school students would ever think about. He was very politically minded even though most of our students never thought about politics. During our times together I affirmed him for his intellectual searching in his faith and his political interest. He wrote me a letter from the mission field recently that said, "Thank you for encouraging me to use my interests for the kingdom of God. The affirmation of challenging *me to be me* was what I needed to find my call to the mission field."

Gift Recognition

One of the major roles of a youth worker is to help his or her young people realize their God-given potential and giftedness. Whenever we place our giftedness alongside the superstars of our culture, we lose. Our job is to instill a knowledge of the fact that all of God's people have spiritual gifts and abilities. He has created each person unique. Not only should we help our young people discover their gifts, but we must encourage them to use their gifts, abilities, and talents for the glory of God.

Hope

Kids today need someone to trust them and give them hope. They need to see light where there is only darkness. We must refuse to let go of our dream for them. Christ is the hope that keeps us going in the midst of a changing and confusing culture. As you give young people hope in Christ, they too have the power to become all that God desires them to be.

39

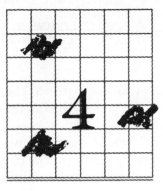

A BRIEF OVERVIEW
OF ADOLESCENT
DEVELOPMENT

I once heard it said that the only thing about adolescent development that is normal is that there are very few norms. Just when you think you have the wonderful world of teenagers figured out, you meet someone who doesn't fit the pattern. One 14-year-old girl is four-feet-eight, weighs 86 pounds, and measures 26-24-26. Her best friend, also 14, is five-feet-eight, weighs 125 pounds, and is 34-26-34. John at age 14 was the most serious Bible scholar in the entire church. He was so together that you considered firing the senior pastor and hiring John. Now at age 16 he seldom comes to church, has lost complete interest in the youth group, and has been heard to say, "This Christian stuff is a bore." He would much rather stay away from church and play with his computer.

Anyone who spends very much time with teenagers has often asked, "Why do they act the way they do?" Unfortunately, most youth workers, teachers, and parents have forgotten the changing developmental world of the adolescent. *Adolescence is a time of transition and change.* It is very easy as adults to simply forget what it was like to be a teenager.

Teenagers move rapidly from childhood to adulthood. Not only their bodies but their minds, emotions, friendships, and even their faith are making major transformations. The adolescent years are turbulent because change is usually difficult to handle.

It's no wonder that many adolescents struggle during their teenage years. Each day brings them a new round of unexpected and sometimes bewildering changes. The chemical makeup of our students changes almost daily; they can be significantly different from week to week.

Many youth workers do an excellent job of working with their students, but they could do an even better job if they took the time to understand the important areas of adolescent development.

Body Under Construction

The advance of puberty carries with it the difficulty of coping with all the physical changes that are occurring. The adolescent's body grows in rapid spurts and then slows and finally stops growing. Even muscles and bones are growing at an uneven rate. Coordination problems sometimes exist. Jerry was the outstanding leader in the junior high group. During the summer between junior high and high school Jerry grew seven inches taller. He now slouches in class with a bored look on his face. Is it a spiritual problem? Probably not; Jerry is tired. The other aspects of development haven't caught up with his bodily growth spurt.

Your young people are very much aware of the physiological changes taking place in their lives. At times they will be totally self-absorbed in the transformations happening regularly in their body. *You* know that the ordinary skin problems of adolescence will eventually disappear and be forgotten, but try explaining that to a 15-year-old girl who now refuses to come to the youth group because she has a fresh case of pimples on her chin, forehead, and nose.

Both young males and young females are extremely aware of their sexual development. Hair is growing where once only skin lived. The size and shape of their sexual parts are very important to all teenagers. After a talk I gave at a conference center years ago, a beautiful young girl came to me after the talk and asked to speak to me in private. She was sobbing uncontrollably. I wondered what horrible event had happened in her life. Finally she gained her composure and shared with me what she had never shared with anyone else: "I'm frightened. You see, I have one breast that is larger than the other." Not understanding adolescent physical development and having only brothers in my home, I had absolutely no idea what to say. Finally I asked her if she would be willing to tell her "trauma" to my wife. When she told Cathy the story, Cathy smiled and explained to her that this problem was extremely common and assured her in a short amount of time that everything would be normal again. The young girl left jubilant!

Another very important matter in physical development is to remember that *teenagers have an extreme concern that their physical appearance measures up to the cultural norm*. As much as kids want to be different from their parents, they do not want their physical appearance to be dissimilar from their peer social group. The implication for youth ministry is that young people are painfully aware of the physical changes inside their body and of their outer appearance. We can help them begin to accept themselves as we teach them that their body is the temple of God.

Social Development

All adolescents are affected by their peers. They are social by their very nature. During the teenage years, the social life of young people often becomes the most important area of their life.

The need for acceptance and belonging drives some young people into lives of moral compromise. They view the compromise as worth it if they will be accepted by the peer group. If we are to effectively minister to our students, we must understand their social world and influences.

It is important to note that today's campuses, and often our youth groups, are broken up into *friendship clusters* (discussed at greater length in Chapter 7). The average high school lunch area is a maze of "friendship clusters" within the student body. Each cluster has its own section of the lunch area. The jocks and jockettes eat together in the same section of the lunch area. The band members eat inside the band room, where it is a safe friendship cluster environment. It doesn't matter if it is ethnic minorities, "brains," cowboys, surfers, preppies, or the Christian clique; they all have their set space, lingo, and friendships. The majority of students receive their greatest influence from their social peer group

TYPICAL SCHOOL FRIENDSHIP CLUSTERS

(Lunch Area)

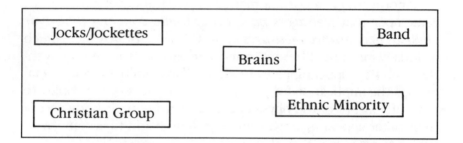

Sociologists tell us that kids build their social world around these friendship clusters, and that their most important influence comes from a still smaller, more intimate group of two or three best friends. It is no secret that you become like the people you spend the most time with.

In 1980 I started a new youth ministry at a church in Newport Beach, California. Six freshmen came to my first Bible study—three guys and three girls. The next day I took the three guys out for a Coke after school to get acquainted. I tried every possible way I could, but I couldn't get these young men to talk. Finally I asked them, "What do you do here in the summer?" They all shouted at once, "We fish!" Immediately the conversation opened up as we talked about fishing. Since I had been fishing only once in my life, luckily they did the talking. I found that their peer group at the high school centered around fishing. A whole group of guys and a few girls ate in a certain section of the lunch area and talked about fishing. On weekends and holidays they all fished together. Their social group and influence centered around their mutual love for fishing. I had to adjust my youth ministry programming to include fishing trips.

The implications for youth ministry in the area of social development means that we not only need to be a friend to the kids but also to understand the social friendship groupings at our schools and our youth group. As youth workers we must do all we can to help unify the different friendship clusters within the youth group. We will also need to develop our student leadership out of a variety of friendship clusters, because students from the same friendship cluster will tend to have a greater influence on their own group. We will not be able to tear down the strong friendship groupings that make up the social setting, but we must strive to do everything we can to help the students see that there is life beyond their own small sphere of social influence.

The Emotional Roller Coaster

Until Lois turned 13 she felt fine about letting Mom make most of the major decisions in her life. Yet it was almost as if on her thirteenth birthday she changed. Her parents put it to me this way: "Lois has no self-control; she lives her life in extremes. Sometimes she is the loving daughter we have always known, and the very next minute she is sobbing uncontrollably for no good reason at all."

The emotional or affective life of an adolescent moves from parents-regulated to volatile to self-regulated. Few young people come out of adolescence without a time of intense emotional responses. For many teenagers this period of life's emotions can be summarized by an increase in chaotic extremes and contradictory, intense inner feelings. Emotions like anxiety, worry, anger, inferiority, passion, and fear can really get a grip on teenagers.

Sometimes, if we are not careful, youth workers will overlook the strong emotions of teenagers and not channel them. In a time of emotional intensity like they have never experienced before, they need role models of emotional stability and consistency. An effective youth worker cannot be perturbed by the emotional instability of youth. We need to listen to their hurts and feelings because they are real, but we also need to help balance out their tendency toward emotionalism. I spent five months on an interim basis working with a large youth group who believed they needed

45

to work themselves into an intensely emotional frenzy on a weekly basis to feel close to God. My job was to follow their high emotional experiences with rational, concrete activities to give them balance. The emotional experience was not necessarily bad *if* it was balanced with other, less emotional meetings.

Intellectual Development

One of the greatest areas of change from preadolescence to adulthood is in the area of cognitive or intellectual development. The people in your youth group are moving from *concrete* thinking to a more *abstract* way of thinking. The students in your group who are always asking the question "Why?" or at times seem argumentative are testing their new intellectual development in the world of abstract thinking.

During this stage adolescents tend to be curious, adventuresome, open to new ideas, inventive, and often a bit idealistic. Jean Piaget is the father of cognitive development, and he defines these two stages as concrete operations between 7 and 12 years and formal operations (abstract) after age 12.

This new period of intellectual development has important implications for the church because kids are beginning to ask questions like "Who am I?" "How can I know?" and "What is life all about?" In elementary school, the teachers could get by with mostly just talking to the students. However, in the adolescent years discussion becomes a necessity for good learning. Youth ministry is a time of enabling the students to learn on their own. We must *ask* rather than *tell*. It's a time to unleash creativity and develop leadership.

One of the best youth ministry preachers I know asked me to evaluate and consult with him about his youth group. I watched a magnificent speaker preach an excellent message to his students. After the meeting he shared his concern that he was losing numbers in his group. My response was that his preaching was fine for a younger group, but he never gave his high-school-age students the opportunity to interact and dialogue. A spoon-fed discipleship program or a message without interaction will leave the students empty. In order to stimulate their newfound abstract thinking we must find a Christian education approach that involves the students, isn't afraid to ask questions, and even accepts some differences of opinion.[1]

Faith Development

There is much literature today which addresses the issue of faith development. James Fowler's *Stages of Faith*[2] is probably the foundational work in this area. Oversimplifying Fowler's six stages can be misleading, yet it may be important to do so in order to help youth workers comprehend at what stage of faith development their students may be involved.

Fowler's Stages of Faith

Stage 1: *Intuitive*. At this stage the people have simply taken on their parents' faith.

Stage 2: *Literal*. The literal stage moves from only their parents' faith to their extended family and perhaps their church's faith.

Stage 3: *Conventional*. This is still an "unowned faith." The conventional stage is their church or denomination's faith. They have still not personalized their faith. This is often the stage for students entering junior-high youth groups.

Stage 4: *Individual*. Their faith is now their own. They have moved outside the faith of their significant others. However, it is usually very close to the faith of their family. It is a simplistic yet serious commitment.

Stage 5: *Consolidating*. The consolidating stage is relatively complex and reflective and is aware of paradoxes. This stage of faith does not shatter at the apparent suffering and evil in the world, unanswered prayer, etc. There is a consistent commitment.

Stage 6: *Universalizing*. This is a more complex stage. They have developed a world vision. They have a mission in life. Their life, faith, and call from God make sense.

We live in an instant society in which we tend to move toward instant spiritual maturity. This is definitely not God's way. Faith develops in stages. Sanctification is a lifelong process. *Our goal in youth ministry is to help young people own their faith and enable them to grow in Christian maturity.*

Since adolescents' intellectual development comes at different stages, we must present the faith in both concrete and abstract methods. Young people need spiritual experiences that will give them the opportunity to do "reality testing."

Adolescents often see the world as a problem. They are struggling to establish an identity, and yet they are unsure what identity they desire. Youth have strong convictions about the existence of God, and yet they are at a point in life where they become uncertain about the necessity of organized religion.[3]

Parents and significant adults play a significant role in the faith development of adolescents. Stephen Jones says, "We have the right to influence our youth with our own values, prejudices, and faith. There is no such thing as a sure environment in which youth can choose on their own what is important for them. Inculturation and socialization of young people are not exploitative acts."[4] We can no longer allow the two great institutions of the church and family to assume that their tasks are mutually exclusive. The youth worker's biblical role as an equipper must focus on the parents as well as the teenagers because both live in a relationship together. In a society that continues to put stress on the traditional family structure, the youth worker must remain committed to recapture the family as the context in which faith is primarily formed.

Given the reality of faith development, what does it mean in practical terms for the youth worker?

1. *We need to lead kids to experiential faith.* A firsthand faith, one that is experienced and is not just their parents', is essential. This is why mission and service projects are so necessary in youth ministry. Also, we must use terms when teaching that are understandable and can be practiced.

2. *We need to help kids learn how to integrate their faith in their daily lives.* Many adolescents have great difficulty relating their spiritual life with the other important areas of their life, such as home, school, work, relationships, and dating life. One of our main jobs is to give our people the opportunity to comprehend how their faith belongs to every area of their life. It is not a compartmentalized faith.

3. *We need to help kids act on their natural spiritual interest.* Because their moral, intellectual, and faith development is in a stage of constant change, we sometimes wrongly suppose that there is no interest in spiritual things. This is a misconception. Even though there is a great deal of doubt and even lifestyle inconsistency, adolescents are very interested in spirituality. Our goal is to facilitate movement from an unowned faith to an owned faith that is maturing in Jesus Christ. In fact the reason I stay in youth ministry is because I believe that when adolescents are given the right kind of opportunity, they will make lifelong decisions to faith and discipleship in a stronger manner than any other age group.

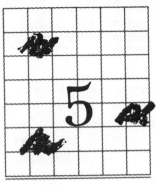

LEARNING TO COMMUNICATE WITH TODAY'S YOUTH

B arney was a mediocre preacher at best. However, he was one of the finest communicators I've ever met. His love for his congregation and staff was evident. He was extremely personal and caring. When in his presence, I felt like the honored guest at a party. His influence in many of our lives is still extremely strong even though he has gone to be with the Lord.

When we think of the word "communication" most of us immediately think of dynamic speaking. Yet communication is much more than just speaking. I'm convinced that you can be a mediocre speaker and still be an excellent communicator to young people. Effectively communicating to young people is essentially the ability to create an atmosphere or environment that will be conducive to the learning process. Two ingredients are absolutely necessary in creating an environment that is conducive for communication with young people: *acceptance* and *love*.

Unconditional Acceptance

Kids need to be accepted for who they are and not for what they can become. They need to be taken seriously. Frankly, if kids do not feel accepted by the church, they will not feel accepted by God. The church youth group needs to be a place where kids can be kids. We sometimes forget that adolescents don't have to act like adults. One night after a very frustrating youth group meeting in which a whole group of freshmen guys were being squirrelly and disruptive, I came home to share my frustrations with my wife, Cathy. Her response was, "They shouldn't be rude, but don't forget what you were like when you were a freshman!"

The church youth group should be an environment of honesty and transparency, where even doubts are accepted. We often make the mistake of pressuring kids into conformity and of not respecting their unbelief. I'm convinced that accepting, yet not agreeing, with young people's unbelief is the most positive witness we can have with them.

The Love Connection

Kids need to know that they are personally cared for and loved. The degree to which we are effective in communicating love is the degree to which we will be effective in touching and changing lives for Christ. An atmosphere of love will be the strongest motivation for change in a person's life. Unfortunately, many people try to change kids' behavior through guilt. While guilt has a short-term change effect, love and acceptance is what can bring long-term change in kids.

A question we must ask is, "Am I expressing love in a language that the kids can understand and feel?" We can't be like the husband who, when asked by his wife if he still loved her, answered, "Twenty years ago, on the day we got married, I told you I loved you; and if I change my mind, you'll be the first to know." Students need reassurance of your love and care for them in ways they can understand.

How can love be expressed?

Time. Your presence and time with the kids says that they are significant. When you invite someone to dinner or shopping or to an athletic event, you are telling this person by your invitation that he or she is significant in your life. When you attend his game, band concert, or drama event, you are showing that you care.

Touch. Even touch is an important source of showing that you care. Although we definitely must be aware of the way we give affection to young people, our nonverbal touch will speak much louder than most words. Linda was a very heavyset, unpopular, melancholy eleventh-grader who was on the fringe of our youth group. She was quiet, shy, and unresponsive, and her home life was less than desirable. One day I went up to her and told her how much I appreciated her presence in our youth group. I then felt by her response that it was okay to give her a hug. It was an awkward hug, but nevertheless a hug. At a senior dinner a year-and-a-half later we were sharing important youth group events. Linda stood, and with tears in her eyes she shared with the group that the time she felt loved and cared for the most was when I hugged her. Frankly, I had forgotten all about this experience until she brought it up.

Phone calling and notes. A three-minute phone call or a post-card often speaks louder and communicates more than all your youth group devotionals. In these days of superficial relationships, significant adults are not calling or writing notes to teenagers. Yet the teenagers will be appreciative and will respond to your thoughtfulness. Acceptance and love are the best means of communication with young people.

The Ministry of Affirmation

The most effective ministry is not found in special programs and events. In the past we have placed altogether too much importance on tangible events and not enough emphasis on long-term, difficult-to-measure, life-transforming results.

Anyone who has worked with young people for more than two hours would agree that one of the major problems among youth is a poor self-image. Today young people suffer greatly from a lack of proper self-image, and this affects every area of their lives. Unfortunately, at times the church has been just as negligent as everyone else in helping young people enhance their self-image in a biblical way.

As youth workers, we must view our young people the way God views them: as His special children. Since it is our goal to open up their lives to what God has in store for them, it is important for us to help them view themselves in a proper manner. In order to grow spiritually, they must understand that God loves them unconditionally. They must also accept the fact that they are loved. One of the best methods to let them experience God's love and your love is through what I call the *ministry of affirmation*. For every critical comment we receive, it takes nine affirming comments to even out the negative effect in our life. Most young people receive more critical comments a day than encouraging ones. You can have a very positive, life-transforming effect when you develop a ministry of affirmation.

Believe in Your Kids

While attending seminary, I worked as an assistant to the chaplain at a prison in Yardville, New Jersey. As I took time to listen to men who had been incarcerated for every crime imaginable, I kept hearing the same story over and over again: "Everyone told me I'd be a flop; no one took the time to believe in me." There they sat in prison, dejected and disturbed, with little hope for the future. In contrast, I would return to the seminary campus and see men and women filled with zeal for life, striving to be what God desired them to be. I realized that one major difference was that these men and women had someone who believed in them.

Jesus had the power to draw out the best in people. He met a clumsy, big-mouthed fisherman named Simon. He looked Simon straight in the eye and said, "So you are Simon, the son of John?" Simon nodded. Jesus then said, "You shall be called Cephas" (which in Greek means "the Rock"). Most of Peter's friends and family had a good laugh at his nickname. No one would have believed that one day this fisherman would be the leader of the church in Jerusalem. Jesus looked beyond Peter's problems, personality quirks, and sin. *Jesus saw Peter not only for who he was but for what he could become.* Even three years after their conversation, when Peter so blatantly denied Jesus, Jesus stood by him and Peter was changed. Simon became what Jesus knew he could become. Who are the

Simon Peters in your life? What positive steps are you taking to believe in them?

Shower Your Kids with Praise

Mark Twain once said, "I can live two months on one good compliment." Young people can too. To be liberal with praise is not vain flattery; praise is a gift which everyone needs to bestow freely and often.

There was a woman in one of my congregations who was a "note writer." She would continually take time out of her busy schedule to write encouraging notes to people. Her simple ministry of affirmation was important. Every time I received a note from her I was encouraged to continue my ministry, even in the midst of frustrating circumstances. Young people are hungry for praise, whether for a positive act at church or for a role in the school play. Find every possible reason to share your gift of praise with your youth. Be creative in your methods.

Be Available for Your Kids

Parents brought little children to Jesus, and the Bible tells us that "the disciples rebuked the people." After all, Jesus was a busy man! But Jesus was available even to the little children, for He said, "Let the children come." Wherever Jesus went, He took time to help, lead, and minister to those around Him.

Our young people need to know we are available to them—available to sit and talk as well as spend time doing things with them. Some of my best conversations with kids in my youth group have been after a tennis match or while shopping at the local mall. Just the thought that they are special enough for you to make your time available to them will often be a great boost to them.

Although it is sometimes difficult to be spontaneous and available, it is necessary in order to show that we really do care. I program a time of availability into my schedule. Seldom do I book anything on Friday afternoons, because I want to be free to be available for whatever is happening that particular day.

The "divine interruption" policy has helped me in the past few years. "Divine interruption" is a phrase that Charlie Shedd coined to describe the time in your week when God uses you to help someone you hadn't planned on helping. I don't know about you, but sometimes God has to use the "divine interruption" method to get through to me and my busy schedule.

Being involved in youth ministry means being available to young people to meet their needs. Being in ministry also means using your time wisely. I am not pushing the idea of 24-hour-a-day, seven-days-a-week availability at the expense of personal and family time. There is a fine line between always being available and knowing when to say, "Let's get together to talk about that tomorrow."

Discipline and Accountability

There are times when all the acceptance, love, and affirmation you can give still needs to be tempered with a dose of discipline. In fact, discipline and accountability are often a part of true love and affirmation. One of the people I admire most in youth ministry is Wayne Rice. Rice's Ten Tips on Discipline in Youth Ministry are worth repeating here:

1. First, let kids be kids. Don't expect perfection.
2. Avoid disciplining kids in front of the rest of the group.
3. Look beyond behavior to what is at the cause of the behavior.
4. Establish rules ahead of time, not after the fact.
5. Don't get mad and lose your cool, pout, threaten, lay guilt trips on them, call their spirituality into question, or lock the doors and pass out Bibles.
6. Don't always be looking for trouble. If you expect something bad to happen, it probably will.
7. Try to lead by example. When it's time to settle down, *you* settle down.
8. Give them opportunities to blow off steam. Give them a chance to talk, yell, run, be with friends, and goof around, so that when it is time for your meeting they will be ready to settle down.
9. Try to retain your sense of humor.

10. Learn to go with the flow.[1]

You may be wondering how discipline fits into communicating with young people. Actually the way we discipline our people will sometimes have a greater ministry effect than any other method of communicating.

Kyle was a very disruptive kid. His parents didn't stand up to him, and all of us on the youth staff tended to let his obnoxious behavior slide. One day I realized that by allowing Kyle to continue his disruptive behavior I was actually telling him that I didn't care.

We had a meeting after school. I told him I cared for him and I was not going to put up with his behavior. If he chose to continue being disruptive he would have to take a four-week break from attending the group. The very next week he tested me. I pulled him aside and told him that I loved him and that he was not allowed to come for a month. I told him I would talk with his parents and that I wanted to get together with him personally once a week for that month. He begged and pleaded to return to the group. When I talked with his parents they also caused a fuss. But I held my ground, and we met all four weeks. His behavior changed, because following through on discipline communicates commitment and love to a person.

PRACTICAL
STRATEGY

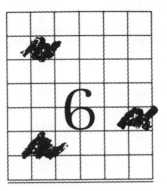

DISCIPLESHIP—
GETTING KIDS
INVOLVED

J ohn and Donna are cousins. Their families had similar involvement in the church. Both were active in their high school,
received good grades, and had lots of friends. John and Donna both
made commitments to Christ at the same age and attended the
same church.

John is now an active leader in the church, but Donna dropped
out of church after high school. Why? What happened? Of course
there are theological reasons, but I would like to give an answer
that is less complicated but just as important: *involvement*. John
was *involved* in the ministry while Donna was a spectator.

Moving to Involvement

The question facing anyone serious about discipleship is how
you get your students to move from a spectator role to one of
involvement in the faith. I'm not so much for "discipleship programs" as for getting students *actively involved* in the life and
ministry of Jesus Christ through His church. *The bottom line in
youth work is not how many kids are coming to your youth group.*

The bottom line is "Where will my kids be five to ten years from now? Is our church preparing them to be Christian leaders?"

Good discipleship involves developing a ministry that lasts. Contrary to some prevalent philosophies of youth ministry, mature discipleship does not come by memorizing a "discipleship manual" or graduating from a discipleship program. Discipleship is a long-term, character-building relationship that challenges people to take what they have been given by our Lord and give it to other people.

How can you develop a stronger sense of involvement and discipleship in your youth? You must see yourself as a discipler, enabler, and model.

Discipler

If you see your role as that of a teacher, a dispenser of knowledge, you don't have high enough goals. To nurture youth involvement, use the method that Paul suggested to Timothy: "The things you have heard me say in the presence of many witnesses entrust to reliable men who will also be qualified to teach others" (2 Timothy 2:2). You teach first, but for the purpose of helping people transfer what they have learned to other people.

One of the questions you must ask as a discipler is: "Am I preparing my young people to be *hearers* of the Word or *doers* of the Word?" A discipler is constantly motivating his or her people to live out their faith in actions. Two verses sum it up best: "Dear children, let us not love with words or tongue but with actions and in truth" (1 John 3:18) and "Do not merely listen to the word, and so deceive yourselves. Do what it says" (James 1:22).

Enabler

Youth workers who desire to see long-lasting results must see themselves as enablers. The I-will-do-it-all mentality might be great for the smoothness of the program, but it can be horrible for growth within the lives of your kids. Always look for ways to train and equip your young people.

One of the most difficult areas of ministry for many youth workers is the area of delegation. When it comes to delegating, Dave Stone's "Four Phases of Ease" is really helpful:

1. I do it, and you watch.
2. I do it, and you do it.
3. You do it, and I watch/assist.
4. You do it, and I'll do something else.

The first time I asked Doug to help me with a retreat, he was nervous about being in a leadership position, and I was nervous that he would not do as good a job as I would. I took responsibility for most of the retreat preparation, but he was by my side observing. (I do it and you watch.) During the next retreat I gave him more responsibilities. (We led the retreat together.) He gained both confidence and enthusiasm (I do it and you do it.) On our third retreat I handed the leadership to Doug. I became his assistant. My job was to watch, observe, and make helpful comments. I remember helping him when he needed a Plan B, because the snow retreat had become a "mud bowl." This retreat didn't run as smoothly as if I had been the leader. After all, I had put on scores of retreats. This was only the third retreat in which Doug had taken over my leadership. (You do it and I assist.)

The fourth time Doug and I tried this process was a very memorable experience for me. He was totally in charge. In fact, he had a new assistant. I was in charge of a cabin of the rowdiest twelfth-grade guys in our youth group. Doug's leadership ability was excellent. His talent in administration far exceeded mine. At first I felt awkward about not being in on the decisions of the camp. However, it gave me the opportunity to pour my life into the guys in my cabin and it gave Doug the opportunity to see that he was capable of doing a great job of leading a retreat. Now there were two people in the church who could lead a youth retreat, with more on the way. (You do it and I'll do something else.)

As you enable your young people to do the actual work of the ministry, the results will be evident in their enthusiasm for their faith.

Model

One of the most memorable experiences in my Christian life happened while I sat in what I thought would be a dull chapel service at the Christian college I attended. A thin, short, bald-headed missionary stood up to speak; he looked out at the crowded auditorium and shouted while pointing his finger, "You are the only Jesus somebody knows!" He kept repeating the same phrase, and on the tenth time he looked straight at me, pointed his index finger at me, and again shouted, "You are the only Jesus somebody knows!" It was as if God turned on a light inside my brain and heart. It dawned on me as never before that I represented Jesus Christ to some of my friends and family who knew very little about Him. They seldom if ever read the Bible or attended church. Through my life, actions, and lifestyle I was modeling Jesus Christ to them. *You are modeling Jesus Christ to a number of young people in your youth group.*

Kids find heroes among musicians, film stars, or athletes whose lifestyles are contrary to Scripture. When it comes to the faith, kids also imitate their leaders. That's why ministry which emphasizes relationships is so important. The best way to model the faith is through a consistently open and honest lifestyle. When your students see in you a person who loves God but isn't perfect and still has problems, they will identify with your Christian faith.

There is nothing more fulfilling than watching your young people respond to Christ's call, become involved, and continue to mature as Christians. The time and energy you invest in your young people is worth it.

My life verse for youth ministry summarizes our call to discipleship and modeling the faith. It was Paul's philosophy of ministry, and he shares good insight into his life and ministry with these words to the people living in Thessalonica: "We loved you so much that we were delighted to share with you not only the gospel of God but our lives as well, because you had become so dear to us" (1 Thessalonians 2:8).

Yes, we are called to give our young people the gospel of God, but we are also challenged to give them our very lives as well. Your actions, your lifestyle, your openness, and your vulnerability will teach your students more than any curriculum lesson you will ever give them.

Person-Centered Ministry

Throughout the life and ministry of Jesus we see a person-centered discipleship ministry. Jesus spoke to large numbers, but the majority of His time and energy was focused on a few people. I've found that the single greatest success in my ministry is when I get my eyes off the big numbers and focus on individuals. Developing a one-on-one ministry is a must for discipleship. Four aspects of a one-on-one ministry are essential to its success.

1. *Get acquainted.* Arrange a time with each kid in your group when you will spend an hour simply getting acquainted. This is not the time to bring out the Bible and preach; instead, use this time to find out as much as you can about the young person, and let him or her get to know you better. You might end up talking about soccer, drama, or whatever the young person happens to be interested in. Young Life calls this "earning the right to be heard." Even in a one-hour conversation you can learn a lot about the youth, and you've probably made a friend for the rest of the year. Sometimes your new friend will even share his or her family struggles, dating problems, or other concerns. As far as location goes, whenever possible take him out to the local hamburger stand or a similar comfortable hangout. Stay away from places that might intimidate him.

2. *Be a pastor.* We can sometimes forget that we as youth workers are also pastors to our groups. We are their spiritual shepherds. It is important to periodically assume our pastoral role and find out how our kids are doing

I remember a get-acquainted time with a kid I'll call Norm. He mentioned that his father and mother were thinking of splitting up. I could tell that he wanted to talk but wasn't ready yet. A few weeks later I saw him in the hall at church and asked him specifically how things were going at home. He ended up telling me that his dad had left home. This conversation continued off and on during the year. I learned to discern when he needed to unload, even if only for five minutes or less.

Students need follow-through and ongoing nurturing. Take the initiative to periodically invite students to get a soft drink just to talk. Many times you'll see the conversations turn to some very valuable dialogue. Even if you feel the conversation is getting nowhere, the fact that you initiated a meeting with a kid may be a very significant event for that young person and lead to future, more productive discussions.

3. *Be a counselor.* Like it or not, every youth worker is a counselor. You may not be "professional," but the fact remains that you will counsel kids in your group and have a great effect on them. Research indicates that most counseling is done by peers or adults, not certified counselors. Also, many professional counselors contend that the *best* counseling takes place in a nonclinical setting. Counseling is listening, and listening is the language of love.

A good counselor is a good listener. Let the young people talk. They need to verbalize their problems before they understand your input. Don't jump to conclusions too quickly; many kids will not tell you their real problem until the very end. Also keep in mind, when listening to a kid's tale of woe about his or her tyrannical parents, that there are two sides to every story.

There will be many times when you'll be called upon to be a counselor. After a youth group meeting someone will ask to talk with you; a family will ask for your input into their problems. Your one-on-one counseling ministry will play an important part in your overall effort.

If you haven't already, get some basic education in counseling skills. Many community colleges and seminaries offer basic counseling courses. Read books on counseling. Talk with a professional counselor or your pastor for helpful ideas. But at all costs, get some basic counseling skills.

When counseling, it is crucial to know your limits. Some situations are too complicated for an amateur. Develop relationships with a few good counselors in your area whom you can utilize for referral. Find out about their philosophies and approaches. Most counselors will welcome periodical calls from you with questions about situations you are involved in. If they aren't willing to give you some time and attention, find someone who will.

Even after you have referred someone to a counselor, stick with your pastor/shepherding role. Don't just dump the young person onto the counselor. Your support and encouragement will complete his or her counseling experience.

4. *Meet for study.* One of the more effective discipleship methods is a one-on-one study program. Select a growthbook or workbook together with your young person in a local Christian bookstore or in your own youth resource library. Choose something that is both of legitimate value and of genuine interest to your student.

Then commit to one hour of study per week for a fixed period of time (such as six weeks).

As you work through the material, try to avoid a teacher/student relationship. When the two of you study *together,* the atmosphere is much more conducive for learning. Leave time in your hour together for sharing and prayer. After you have completed the length of time agreed upon, evaluate your progress and decide whether or not to continue your sessions. Usually you will find that this is such an exciting experience for both of you that you will want to continue. It's thrilling to be a close part of the rapid growth of a young person, since that's what one-on-one ministry is all about.

Making It Happen[1]

For years I have had the audacity to ask my adult volunteers for an extra hour-and-a-half of ministry each week. I've always felt that the more ministry involvement which adults have, the longer they will stay as volunteers. I ask them for one hour a week of meeting with a student to study a growthbook together. During this time they will study the Word of God, but they will also talk and build a relationship. I then ask the adults for 15 minutes of phone calls to students a week. One week they may only talk to one student; the next week they may reach five students. I figure they will average around three calls a week. Lastly, I challenge them to take 15 minutes a week and write a positive, affirming note to three students. You can write three short notes, address the envelopes, and put them in the mailbox in 15 minutes. Within an hour-and-a-half your volunteers have had a significant influence in the lives of seven students.

90-Minute Influence

1 hour in growthbook	1 student
15 minutes for phone calls	3 students
15 minutes for notes	3 students
	7 students total

Small Is Better

My wife, Cathy, loves small support groups. Over the years she has led several support groups and has always had the same successful results. In a small-group atmosphere there is more open sharing, vulnerability, encouragement, and community. The groups become the high point of each person's week. It's a time of intimacy and acceptance. Small groups go deeper and often have a greater impact than any other ministry. Cathy's expertise is not in front of a large crowd, yet her small-group ministry has had a greater impact on kids' lives throughout the years than any of our large-group activities.

In a world that shouts "Big is better!" small is more effective when it comes to discipleship. The ingredients of an effective small-group ministry are: 1) three to six kids meeting regularly for a set period of time; 2) a time of heartfelt sharing, encouragement, and support; 3) a time of prayer. Other options may be a Bible study or worship time. However, if these needs are being met in another area of your ministry, you may want to focus more on the personal sharing as the main part of the small group.

If you are just starting a small-group ministry, don't be alarmed if there is little interest at first. Jesus had the same problem. The greater the cost of discipleship, the less people turned out.

Although I'm not for a totally homogenous youth group, sometimes the more the kids have in common, the easier it is to start a small group. You will want to take into consideration age, sex, spiritual maturity, and location. You will want to start with a commitment to meet regularly for perhaps only six weeks, and then reevaluate. The longer you meet together, the deeper the sharing will tend to be. Some small groups end up taking on a ministry project together; other groups dissolve after a few meetings. Some groups meet specifically for prayer, others for Bible study, and still others for a set purpose (such as meeting the needs of the children of alcoholics or of kids from divorced homes). Small groups can be the most effective discipleship tool in your ministry. They can be time-consuming, but the results are definitely worth it.

Making Sunday School Enjoyable

Most Protestant churches still have some form of Sunday school. Although many students and adult youth leaders view Sunday school as a necessary evil, this weekly hour of ministry may be one of your most important discipleship methods. The truth is that if you have kids coming to Sunday school because they choose to come, then you have kids deeply committed to discipleship and the church.

Some youth ministries put all their creative ideas into other youth group activities, and Sunday school is nothing more than a boring hour of mediocre input. *Make your Sunday school program enjoyable.* No one ever said that it had to be boring. Prepare interesting lessons, ones that are experimental and relevant. If your group has more than ten kids, then you may want to divide them into elective seminars.

Electives work well because you can separate the more serious-minded disciples from the ones who don't care about growing. I strongly believe that the youth ministry department should be in charge of the Sunday morning program. If the kids have a completely different program with different faces at each meeting, then you are in reality creating separate youth groups. If the head of the youth ministry puts time and attention into the Sunday school program, then one of the best built-in tools for discipleship is already in place.

Male and Female Role Models

Since role modeling is the most important aspect of Christian education and discipleship, I believe we need positive male and female role models in leadership. The typical American Christian church still gives students the impression that in most youth groups men lead and women bake cookies. Frankly, I'm excited at the fact that more women are becoming visible in youth ministry. For far too long I've heard teenage girls say, "I want to marry someone like Bill, my youth worker" rather than say, "I want to have a ministry like Cathy has had with me." Since good discipleship is good role modeling, one of the basic ingredients of discipleship is to have positive role models of both sexes in front of your kids.

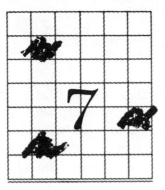

RELATIONAL EVANGELISM

F ollowing my high school Bible study a few weeks ago, I was talking to one of our adult sponsors who had been a missionary overseas. I was telling her that sometimes I feel guilty for not being a missionary to another culture. She shot back, "You *are* a missionary to a different culture. These high school kids"—she pointed to a few kids who were still left after the youth group meeting—"live in a different world. You've chosen to infiltrate that world to give them the message of Jesus."

Outreach in the Blackboard Jungle

I had never before looked at ministry to high schoolers as missionary work, but she was right. We're working with kids who are different from the way we were when we were in high school and junior high. As one youth worker put it, "We were never their age. Yes, we were 14, 15, and 16, but we were never their age." Life has changed for high schoolers since our adolescent days, and if we're going to reach them with the good news of Jesus Christ, it's time to take on a missionary perspective.

People ask me periodically why I continue to work with students instead of getting a "real job," like the senior pastorate. I always tell them, "I work with high school students because they're

making major decisions now that will affect the rest of their lives."
In fact, every staff member working with me at the National Institute of Youth Ministry made his or her commitment to Jesus Christ
while in high school. If that's typical, then youth ministries should
make quality outreach and evangelism a top priority.

I recently heard a story about a young boy who received an
archery set for his birthday. One day he asked his father to see
where he had been shooting arrows into the side of an old barn.
There on the side of the barn were several targets, and dead center
in the bull's-eye of each target was one of the boy's arrows. The
father was naturally impressed and very proud of his young Robin
Hood. He asked the boy how he was able to shoot so accurately and
to hit the bull's-eye of every single target. The boy replied, "Easy—I
just shot the arrows first and drew the targets around each one."

Very often, we in the church do the same thing with evangelism. We shoot first and draw the people around our programs,
regardless of whether we are meeting their needs or not.

The sad reality, however, is that too many of us spin our wheels
when it comes to evangelism. As I evaluate my own programs, I see
that I've often wasted time, effort, and money on activities that
didn't accomplish the goal of reaching unchurched kids in our
community. Instead, I held evangelistic meetings for Christians.

A few years ago, for example, our high school group sponsored
a concert that attracted well over a thousand kids. Our paid and
volunteer youth staff invested weeks putting the concert together,
and our student leadership poured out an incredible amount of
time and energy into making it a success.

Was it a success? Our hard work helped the concert to come off
smoothly. Our senior pastor was ecstatic at the numbers, and our
kids enjoyed themselves. Our goal, however, had been outreach.
And to my knowledge, *no* unchurched kids became a part of our or
any other church because of that concert. We had an evangelistic
concert without evangelism. I don't believe the evening was worthless, but we came to the conclusion that we could have reached out
more effectively with those 200 + hours and the 2600 dollars the
event cost us than by putting on a one-night concert extravaganza
for the saints.

It is statistically staggering how few people respond to Jesus

Christ and the church through mass evangelism. Most people become Christians through influential friendships and family relationships. People respond to mass evangelism appeals usually because of a positive relationship with a Christian person.

You can call it what you want—lifestyle evangelism, earning the right to be heard, or relational evangelism—but good, influential, and responsive evangelism is based around a relationship with someone or some group of people who are modeling a healthy Christian lifestyle.

The Friendship Cluster

Besides the family, the most effective outreach takes place through peer relationships. Given that our kids are the best evangelists to their peers, one of our chief tasks is to equip them to become those evangelists. Evangelism is scary, so they'll need lots of encouragement and modeling from us as we reach out to our peers as well as to other students. As our young people learn to share their faith, we will see great spiritual growth in them as well as an increase in the size of our youth group.

In order to create a healthy atmosphere of peer evangelism, we must understand the world in which they live. Canadian youth ministry expert Donald Posterski says, "The majority of teenagers are *clustering* together and enjoying their small circle of friends."[1] As you know, the typical student's life is centered around his or her social group. For teenagers there is nothing more important or significant than their friends. On each campus today there are hundreds of small friendship clusters which constitute the sociological makeup of any school. Groups of three, four, or five students loiter in the hallways before going to classes. They meet for lunch in the same spot every day. They pass notes between classes and wait for each other to walk home together. Out of this "friendship cluster" comes much of what is influencing students' decisions.

When an adult authority asks a teenager the question "Why did you do that?" the answer is often "Everybody does it." "Everybody" is the friendship cluster. *We cannot overrestimate the value which students place on their friendships.*

Posterski put together a very important study on Canadian adolescents which has startling information that is extremely important for the world of youth ministry. Imagine a "ladder of values." The highest rung of the ladder represents values which young people consider very important in their lives, and the lowest rung represents those of lesser importance.

Here are Posterski's findings:

91 percent ranked *friendship* on the top rung of their value ladder. (Nine out of ten high school students ranked friendship as their highest value.)

87 percent ranked *being loved* next on the value ladder (looking for friends and family who will love them).

Family life was only ranked at 65 percent on the ladder. This survey shows that high-schoolers are replacing traditional family relationships with their own "family of friends."

Rather surprisingly, only 21 percent considered being popular as very important on their ladder of values. General popularity has been replaced by being accepted in a friendship cluster.

The bottom line for your youth ministry program is that if your students don't make friends in the group, they won't stay in the group. As we develop a relational evangelism ministry, we can never stray very far from the idea of the friendship cluster.

Contact Work

Contact work is one of the most productive evangelism tools in youth ministry. *Contact work is meeting young people on their territory, outside the walls of the church.* Contact work is identifying with young people where they are and penetrating their culture.

Throughout the New Testament we see Jesus identifying with people on their own territory. Even the well-known words about the incarnation of God found in John 1:14 help us understand the power of a contact ministry: "The Word became flesh and lived for a while among us. We have seen his glory, the glory of the one and only Son, who came from the Father, full of grace and truth." Jesus was not afraid to be seen with "sinners" (Luke 5:27-32; 15:1,2).

Similarly, the powerful effect of the apostle Paul's ministry was based on his willingness to identify with the people. We see Paul as a minister who lived among his people. He even urged his followers to imitate his actions.

Paul truly shared his life with the people he had a ministry with. Contact work is merely following the example of those before us who understood and penetrated the culture of those they wanted to influence with the good news of Christ.

The possibilities of being on a teenager's territory are almost limitless. Wherever teenagers congregate should be considered as a possible setting for contact work. Typical examples of places for contact work are athletic events, school plays, choir and band concerts, pep rallies, recreation centers, shopping malls, and lunch hour at the school. You can also use your imagination to plan or attend events conducive to contact work, such as water- and snow-skiing trips, pizza parties, professional athletic events, chaperoning school events, slumber parties, or Broadway-style plays.

One of the greatest Christian youth ministry organizations of our generation is Young Life International. They have developed a relational-contact style of ministry that is second to none. The following are some of their principles.

PRINCIPLES FOR CONTACT WORK

1. Practice the discipline of learning names. Use whatever system will help most.
2. Look for ways to serve young people—taking them home, keeping charts for games, giving Cokes to cheerleaders, etc. (Caution must be used to prevent giving the impression of "buying their friendship.")
3. *Do not attempt to "be one of the kids."* We are leaders, aware of our age yet loving and genuinely interested in the kids and in their affairs.

4. Through established friendships, seek to know others. Sometimes we can receive a lot of help from those we know.
5. Do not force your way into certain social situations where you would not be welcome, such as some parties or group discussions.
6. *Avoid making fun of young people* (unless you are very sure of the situation). *This is the most dangerous kind of humor.*
7. Be careful about talking too much about your own accomplishments, such as college athletic experiences.
8. Be yourself. Do not try to impress with overdone or clever antics, or by imitating others. You don't have to be a comedian, athlete, or personality-plus in order to love them.
9. Ask questions about school life when in conversation with high-schoolers. Most enjoy talking about these things.
10. Ask God for a sincere interest in young people. They can spot the feigned interest. We might not like all they do, but we can appreciate them as people.
11. Be casual. Don't work too hard at being friendly, with a lot of handshaking or rapid patter, unless this is natural to you.
12. Develop a sense of humor. Find what fits you best.
13. Be adaptable. Expect to have to change pace from time to time. We cannot predict the adolescent behavior.
14. Keep close personal records of significant contacts. Some sort of diary is of great value, especially in your prayer life.
15. Seek to gain friendships with all types of young people, both school leaders and followers. Many of them will have great potential for leading their friends or their particular activity group. As with foreign tribal work, it usually makes sense to spend much time with the "chief" as well as the tribe.
16. Cheerfulness and enthusiasm are contagious.
17. In many areas, adults are not welcome in the halls of a school. Study the situation carefully. Have a valid reason for being there. Probably you will have to forgo any contact work in the buildings.

18. Every school situation or neighborhood is unique. Work out a plan or strategy that fits your local picture.
19. Pray for those you have met or want to meet. Enlist prayer support from interested adults or Christian young people.
20. Contact work is never finished. There are always new people to get to know. It is this continued effort to be their friend that "wins the right to be heard" with the message of Jesus Christ. Once the right has been won, work on the right of continued hearing.
21. Realize that contact work is identification with people in a real way in the sense that Christ, the Word, "became flesh and dwelt among them."
22. As you walk around the neighborhood or school, pray for kids as your eyes touch them. Ask God to lead you to those He wants you to meet. Make it a trusting experience.
23. Keep in mind that every relationship should become deeper. Ephesians 3:18 "...that you, firmly fixed in love yourselves, may be able to grasp how wide and deep and long and high is the love of Christ and to know for yourselves that love so far beyond our comprehension."[2]

Call On Me

Many studies in church growth show that the reason people don't stay at a church is because they don't know anyone in the church very well. The dramatic increase in interest and numbers in several of the cults is because they have an extensive calling, visitation, and follow-up program. Every Christian youth group needs calling and visitation as an important part of its evangelism program.

As you create a calling and visitation program, it is always best to begin with an easy-to-follow plan. Listed below are three principles that I believe should be incorporated into any plan.

1. *Visit each person on your church's youth group roster at least twice a year.* The most effective way to have a ministry with

someone is to get better acquainted with him. Despite the size of your group, everyone should have at least two one-on-one contacts a year. If your group is small, then you are fortunate because you can do much of the visitation on your own. If your group is large, then other leaders will need to be in on the program.

Some nonactive students will wonder why you are getting together with them. My suggestion is to state up front that you are trying to get together with everyone on the church roster in order to get better acquainted with them.

2. *Have a quick and easy method for visitors to your group to fill out pertinent information.* We ask visitors to put their name on our "junk-mail mailing list." In a nonthreatening atmosphere, encourage the visitors to sign a card. Tell them up front that you will be sending them "junk mail" from the group to keep them informed on upcoming activities. The card should have all the needed information, such as name, address, and phone. I suggest strongly that you also include grade, school, church affiliation, and birthdate. Also give the visitors an opportunity to indicate that they would like to talk with someone about the Christian faith. If you have never used an "Info Card," you may be surprised at the amount of young people who ask to speak to someone about the Christian faith.

3. *Follow up on the visitor within a week.* Far too many young people slip through the cracks of the faith because no one responded to them at church. If they are willing to visit the church or youth group, then the overwhelming odds say that they will come back if relationships are built and they are asked back. Within a week of their visit they should receive a handwritten note from one of the leaders. The note should be short, positive, and personal (mention the student's name they came with) and should tell them you hope to see them again. Also within the week they should be contacted by phone or personally at school and invited to attend the next youth group event. Many churches have effectively used peers to make the phone or personal contact. When you invite them, be sure to offer them a ride. Sometimes students don't come because they don't have transportation.

These three timeless principles are simple, yet profoundly important. When people take the time to apply these principles to their ministry, visible results are usually not far behind.

Evangelistic Happenings

Students can still be drawn to the "significant event." Kids love to be in the middle of a happening. For a number of years, organizations such as Youth for Christ and other parachurch organizations have shown us that non-Christian young people will come to special events if we are willing to put the time into making it a significant experience for them. Many churches make the fatal mistake of putting together "the world's greatest event," only to be disappointed because it turned out mediocre at best.

If you are going to try evangelism through special events, then make sure you have the time, energy, finances, and manpower to pull off a very successful program. My suggestion is to make the event high-quality or else don't do it. Honor the students with thorough preparation and an exciting program, and don't forget a well-planned follow-up program.

When you decide to put together a community outreach or special event, combine forces with other churches and organizations. Many youth groups never get together with the other churches in their community because of insecurity on the part of the leadership. Unfortunately, the greatest evangelistic opportunities in many communities have been missed because no one ever came together to do something worth raising the attention of students in the community. Here are some ideas that will draw a crowd.

1. *Christian concert.* Music draws students better than any other activity. A well-done Christian concert can be an excellent outreach.

2. *Multimedia presentation.* Our young people have been brought up in a multimedia generation. They enjoy and will respond to quality media presentations.

3. *Special speakers*. Non-Christian students will not usually attend a seminar unless the subject draws them or the speaker is a famous personality. A sports figure, musician, or actor will usually be your best evangelistic draw. If you bring in an unknown Christian speaker to the kids, make sure you talk up the subject. Have your speakers talk on sex, dating, rock music, and other subjects important to young people.

4. *Special events*. Community-wide events such as car rallies, parade-float decorating, broom hockey, or rental of roller-skating rinks (or health clubs) can also be an exciting event to pull in students. How you relate to the kids once they have come will often determine the success of the event.

Campus Ministry

In the 1970's I accidentally started a campus ministry. Fresh out of seminary and a Young Life ministry, I went to work at a church with a handful of students and a desire to develop a strong youth ministry. Every Thursday I visited the same campus after school. I played tennis, went out for Cokes, watched football games, and was the only person who sat through the band's rehearsal for homecoming. Every Thursday the few kids in my church would look for me, and it ended up that I met their friends as the weeks turned into months. We eventually started getting together "to talk" every Thursday afternoon. The second semester I suggested that we start a Bible study after school. Most of the students said they were too busy—they had not realized I had taken their Thursday afternoons for months! We ended up with a great Thursday afternoon Bible study. In fact we started *four* Bible studies at four different high schools that year.

When youth workers decide to have a campus presence, the first thing we must do is meet with the principal of the local school. It is a time to leave our Bibles in the car and spend the time getting acquainted. I even dress up for the meeting! I want them to know who I am and that I care for students. We can offer our services as chaperons and in any other way we can serve the school. I let the principal know I will be attending games and events. I then ask if he or she minds if I eat lunch with a few of the kids on campus as long as it is not a Bible study. Principals are usually nervous about "religious hassles." However, as you get acquainted and then never take advantage of the system, you will usually be openly received on campus.

The interpretation of the law of equal access on public school campuses will continue to be debated, but you have every right to make your presence known on the campus. Listed below are a number of suggestions.

1. Hold a campus Bible study.
2. Sponsor a campus club.
3. Become an assistant coach.
4. Volunteer to substitute in classes.
5. Help with drama, band, cheerleading.
6. Take change at lunchtime.
7. Chaperon school activities.
8. Join the PTA.
9. Help decorate for school parties and functions.
10. Get involved in peer counseling programs: drug and alcohol abuse, teen pregnancy.

Every youth worker is in a small or large way an evangelist. Young people are making decisions to follow Christ and become connected to the church The fields are ripe for harvest. No doubt we will need different styles of outreach to reach the particular kids in our area, but I am convinced that they will be open to the gospel if we can just get their attention.

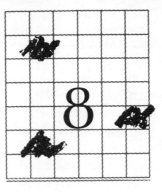

GETTING KIDS
EXCITED ABOUT
MISSION AND SERVICE

S ome years ago my wife and I took a trip with eight high school
students. We all piled in a van and traveled 1500 miles to
counsel at a camp, hold Bible studies, and do a service project. It
was a three-week drama of loving service, tension, rowdiness, and
sainthood all mixed into one experience. Today all eight of those
students are in some form of Christian service. I believe they chose
to be in service as adults because they had a chance to have their
hearts break with what breaks the heart of God when they were in
the impressionable years of adolescence. Getting young people
involved in mission and service is not an option for Christian
growth and maturity; it is a necessity.

The True Call

The Indian philosopher Mahatma Gandhi chided Christians
when he said, "In my judgment the Christian faith does not lend
itself to much preaching or talking. It is best propagated by living it
and applying it. When will you Christians really crown Jesus Christ
as Prince of Peace and proclaim Him through your deeds as the

champion of the poor and oppressed?"[1] One does not need to be a Bible scholar to observe throughout the Gospels Christ's strong challenge to us to become servants with a heart for mission. Christ's call is a call to serve. Parables of Jesus like the one found in Matthew 25:31-45 suggest that when we meet the needs of the hurting world (sick people, orphans, prisoners), we are meeting the deepest desire of Jesus Himself. At the end of the Gospel of Matthew Jesus challenged believers to "go and make disciples of all nations, baptizing them in the name of the Father and of the Son and of the Holy Spirit, and teaching them to obey everything I have commanded you. And surely I am with you always, to the very end of the age" (Matthew 28:19,20).

I firmly believe we are not giving our young people a true understanding of what it means to be a follower of Jesus Christ if we do not help them understand that the call of Christ means a lifestyle of servanthood and a heart for mission.

Getting a Global Vision

As our young people grow in their Christian faith, they will develop a global vision. Most American adolescents are not aware that we are in a relationship with our less fortunate brothers and sisters in other parts of the world. As youth workers we must educate our students to the fact that it is partly our responsibility as American Christians to meet the needs of the less fortunate. After all, it was Jesus who said, "From everyone who has been given much, much will be demanded; and from the one who has been entrusted with much, much more will be asked" (Luke 12:48).

One of our goals as youth workers is to let the students see beyond American Christianity. After a mission trip to a Mexican orphanage one of my students exclaimed to her parents, "We aren't middle class; we're rich!" True spiritual growth involves a desire to make a difference in the world.

Beyond Split-Level Theology

I believe that one of the grave sins of the church in years past was to separate the ministries of evangelism and social action.

Nelson Bell, the great Christian statesman and missionary doctor to China, put it best when he said, "If you separate evangelism and social action, you only have half a gospel."[2]

In past generations, the theologically conservative church became uneasy with the liberals' desire for social action, so they backed away completely from social action and social justice. On the other hand, the liberal church became so caught up in not wanting to look like fundamentalists that they walked away from the core of the gospel, evangelism. *Young people today must come to terms with the fact that social action and evangelism are inseparable.* Dietrich Bonhoeffer was once quoted as saying, "To allow the hungry man to remain hungry would be blasphemy against God and one's neighbor, for what is nearest to God is precisely the need of man's neighbor. It is the love of Christ which belongs as much to the hungry man as to myself. If the hungry man does not attain to faith, then the fault falls on those who refused him bread. To provide the hungry man with bread is to prepare the way for the coming of grace."[3]

Creating Awareness

For many students the idea of mission and service brings a mental picture of men and women in pith helmets and khaki clothes walking through the jungle of Africa preaching to naked natives. Creating awareness is the first step toward helping students understand the need for mission. We must create curiosity, desire, and interest. The way *not* to create an interested awareness is to bring in a boring missionary speaker or a slide show that is less than motivational. Today's adolescent needs to hear from an exciting and challenging speaker. Always screen your speakers. Show your students one of the many exciting films on mission today. You may want to have a debate on the ethics of smuggling Bibles into Communist countries. Sometimes the best way to create awareness is to study the missionary methods of the apostle Paul. These are all ways of creating a greater interest, desire, and awareness in mission.

One Step at a Time

One of the common mistakes that youth workers make is to go on a two-week trip immediately after one mission presentation.

Actually, for long-term results it is better to first sensitize the students to the needs of the world. Not very far from home are incredible needs with easy access for a youth group to experience mission firsthand. A quick trip to a rest home, convalescent hospital, or cancer ward at a children's hospital will help students become immediately aware of the health needs in their area. A trip to the inner city, a rescue mission, or a soup kitchen will remind your young people of the desperate hunger of people in their own county. By sensitizing the students to the need, you are preparing them to have their hearts broken with what breaks the heart of God.

Dirty Hands and Open Eyes

After the students have been sensitized to the needs, I think it is best for them to develop their own ministry options and possibilities. Knowing Christ comes best from experiencing the work of Christ firsthand. You can tell people all about mission and service, but until they actually experience it for themselves, they are only spectators. In order for students to experience mission and service firsthand, we must create awareness, sensitize them to the need, help them develop significant options for ministry, and then prepare them for leadership.

Show them a film on world hunger and allow them to come up with the option of having the youth group sponsor a child in a Third World country. When you've visited a rest home, read the Scripture in Matthew 25 where Christians are challenged to take care of the needy. Let them come up with ideas. Students need a hands-on experience in order to come up with genuine and realistic ideas for mission and service. As your students develop options for actual ministry, this is the time to prepare them for a life-changing experience.

Preparing Leadership

Student leadership preparation and training is an important and sometimes overlooked aspect of youth mission work. We need to prepare our young people in every way possible for this significant experience in their life. If they are going to lay bricks, give them a basic course in bricklaying before you have them do the work. If they will be running a vacation Bible school, rehearse their stories, crafts, and games beforehand. Good preparation is teaching the young people all you possibly can before the project begins. One year before building a brick wall in Mexico, we practiced on the backyard of our pastor. We received needed experience and he received a new wall with cheap labor!

Preparing your students spiritually is as important as preparing them for their tasks. If they are going to work among the poor, then before you go read Bible passages on ministry to the poor. Make sure that your group has spent time together praying and giving their mission project to God. Do everything you can to develop group unity before you go on the trip. They will be more effective ministers if the group is somewhat unified before you go on the trip. I often recommend an overnight retreat with a number of group-building experiences before a mission trip actually begins.

Because a mission and service project can be one of the most significant faith experiences in the lives of young people, we must take the preparation seriously. The more prepared the students are for their experience, the greater will be the impact during the actual ministry.

A Game Plan for Mission Ministry

Teach on mission and service regularly. Give your students the biblical base for the call to mission.

Start small. Mission experiences are so significant that usually small is better. Especially if you are new at leading mission trips, keep the venture small and manageable.

Get your key staff and church leadership behind you. You may need help during the mission trip. You will be much better off if the key leadership in the church is already behind you.

Make sure you have adequate finances for the trip. If your mission trip takes you to unfamiliar territory, especially cross-cultural and foreign mission trips, make sure you have adequate financial resources. The group may unexpectedly need to spend the night in a hotel, transportation costs may change, or a host of other problems might occur.

Build a tradition. Find a mission experience that may be continued. The kids will look forward to building a relationship and a history based on a certain mission experience.

Encourage adult participation. You will need a better adult ratio than on most youth group outings. Actually, the more adults the smoother the trip will run, and practically speaking, they make great youth-group public relations people when they return from the trip.

Debrief each day's experience. Many of the students are experiencing life on a new level. Each day is a brand-new experience, with adventures they have never before experienced. You will need a regular time to review the day. When you return from your mission experience, be sure to take the time to debrief the entire experience.

Provide opportunities for the students to share their experiences. A major factor in digesting their mission experience is sharing their story when they return home. If at all possible, allow time in the worship service to have the students share. Many of your church's groups and Bible studies would welcome a youth missions program, and the need to share their experienced faith is essential for the kids' spiritual growth.

Ideas

There are literally hundreds of mission and service ideas for youth groups. In the resource section of this book (Chapter 27) are some excellent resources for most types of mission opportunities.

This section is designed to give you a broad base of ideas. (Look to other resources for the actual hands-on program ideas.)

1. Mission to the elderly
   a. Rest home, convalescent hospital.
   b. Shut-in ministry: Have students visit shut-ins with the pastor.
   c. Adopt a grandparent: Many "grandparents" are living away from their relatives and would welcome the company and attention.

2. Mission to the sick
   a. Visit the "unvisited" in hospitals.
   b. Send cards, flowers, gifts, or books to the sick from your church.
   c. Run errands, fix food, clean house, catch up on chores, baby-sit for those who are ill or hospitalized.

3. Mission to prisons
   a. Visit juvenile halls.
   b. Provide worship services for prisoners.
   c. Establish a letter-writing ministry to lonely prisoners.
   d. Set up athletic teams to play against prison teams.

4. Mission to the hungry
   a. Every youth group should sponsor a child through a relief organization.
   b. Provide help at a local soup kitchen or rescue mission.
   c. Participate in a "planned famine."

5. Mission to the neighborhood
   a. Offer a free baby-sitting service in the local shopping mall.
   b. Provide a summer vacation Bible school.
   c. Rake leaves and shovel snow at the homes of senior citizens.
   d. Provide a job employment bank for teenagers in the community.

6. Mission to the inner city
   a. Provide a recreation league.
   b. Provide a summer vacation Bible school in conjunction with an inner-city church.
   c. Provide a monthly service at a rescue mission.
   d. Provide a special ministry to latchkey kids.

7. Ministry and mission projects
   a. Indian reservations.
   b. Construction of orphanage, camps, homes, churches.
   c. Disaster and relief work.
   d. Work camps.

8. Short-term mission work
   Connect with an established mission organization doing mission work in another country.

This list of mission experiences is not meant to be an exhaustive list. Rather, it is a list to get your mind thinking about possibilities other than the ones you may currently be acquainted with in your ministry. If you are new to youth ministry, connect with an established program for your first few experiences.

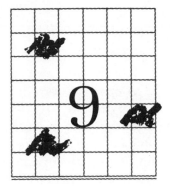

CAMPS AND
RETREATS

I t was Christian educator John Westerhoff who said, "If we really wanted to be effective in Christian education, we would eliminate Sunday schools and use the money that we spent on them for camps and retreats. If you could get everyone in your church away for two weekend retreats a year, you would have more and better Christian education than a whole year's worth of one-hour Sunday school classes."[1]

The value of retreat experiences is almost unsurpassable in Christian education experiences. A retreat has a sense of excitement and even the element of curiosity. It is a new environment away from the hassles and everyday responsibilities of home. Most of the time the atmosphere is open, fun, and much more casual than in other types of Christian education.

One of the most positive factors of a retreat is that it is inherently relational. Camps and retreats are times to focus on building relationships, strengthening friendships, and meeting new acquaintances. The element of building a stronger sense of community and the wonderful feeling of belonging come out of this relational aspect of camping. Getting away from home and church provides the opportunity to simply have more time together. There is time to develop relationships and time to focus on spiritual and personal growth.

I'm not sure if it's the expectation level, the time, or the fact that retreats are often spiritually challenging, but *students are more spiritually sensitive and open on retreats.* Campus Crusade for Christ says that 75 percent of their 10,000-plus personnel made a first-time commitment to Jesus Christ at a camp or retreat. Numerous times in my ministry I've had students tell me, "I was waiting for this camp to give my life to Jesus." Camps and retreats seem to be the place young people allow God to speak to them and challenge them to be all He desires them to be. We've all seen young people make a decision to get out of a lousy boyfriend/girlfriend relationship or decide to make a deeper commitment while at camp.

Another great value of camps and retreats is that *they build lifelong memories.* A 27-year-old man came up to me recently at a restaurant and said, "In 1977 (ten years prior) we went on a weeklong houseboat trip together. It was the greatest week of my entire life. Seldom does a day go by without me thinking about that significant week. Until recently I've strayed from God, but the memory of that single week on the houseboat with our church group has drawn me back to God." To be honest, I had almost forgotten the trip and barely recognized the man. Yet that one-week trip had created a lifelong memory for him. One of the positive results of creating memories is that a camp or retreat experience often builds a tradition. Students begin to look forward to their yearly trip to the mountains, orphanage, ski trip, or whatever tradition is set before them. Never overlook the power of creating healthy lifelong memories and traditions.

Camp and Retreat Guidelines

Set goals for your camps and retreats. A retreat can be an extremely valuable experience, yet many times because of lack of proper planning or established goals for the retreat, it doesn't meet up to the quality standards it could. Each leader should have in his or her hands clear-cut goals and a *definite statement of the purpose of the outing.*

If the camp is an evangelistic camp, let the leaders know this fact and then discuss how you plan to carry out the task of accomplishing this goal. If the camp is for the purpose of developing a stronger community within the group, it will happen better with established goals.

Prepare a flow chart. I call the flow chart my "cheat sheet" for any event. The flow chart is an organizational tool to help you plan the event, carry out the responsibilities, and keep accountability of jobs in order to make it easier to carry out your goals. (See sample chart on page 98.) The purpose of the flow chart is to let nothing slip by you. Once you've created a flow chart, you won't have to reinvent the responsibilities for the next retreat—only adapt some of the tasks.

Using a flow chart will assist you in your preparation and delegation. When people have clear-cut responsibilities spelled out on paper, they will generally follow through better than with unexpressed expectations. When you put together a flow chart for each event, place realistic dates for completion of the task. This will give other people a better understanding of their responsibilities and will let you get a better feel for the overall picture.

Provide publicity. When it comes to camp publicity or any type of publicity, *honor your students with excellence.* You are probably not a graphic artist, but most likely there is someone in your church who can make your fliers attractive. Usually a little more time and money makes a drastic difference in fliers and brochures. An attractive flier describing the upcoming camping experience is an excellent source for outreach and definitely will catch the eye of uncertain parents.

Check the facilities. I'll never forget a few years ago when I chose a lake for our water-ski trip. We were going to camp for two nights in the public campgrounds. We figured we would be right at the beach and transportation wouldn't be a problem. We didn't think we would need big canopies for shade, because I thought there would be covered facilities. Two days before we left for our trip, with all the information already in the hands of the students and their parents, I decided to call a friend of mine who lived near the lake to ask a couple of questions. I found that the campground facilities were four miles from the lake. There were no showers or changing rooms—only a few outhouses. I learned that I needed a special license to launch the boats on this lake, and that there were no fire pits for our evening times of singing around the campfire. Needless to say, I was in a panic. We ended up going to another lake with only mediocre facilities. Obviously the retreat would have run much more smoothly if only I had checked out the facility ahead of time.

Be aware of insurance liabilities. If parents knew the gambles the church often takes when it comes to insurance, they would shudder and not allow their children to attend the events. Many youth workers think someone else in the church has taken care of the insurance for camps and retreats. Before you ever go on a retreat, become extremely familiar with the entire insurance package of your church. Does your insurance cover snow accidents or winter sports? Does your church insurance cover other people's cars? What is the camp's insurance policy? Much of the time churches are inadequately covered when it comes to youth group outings. Don't make the mistake of a church in my area who had an epileptic girl drown in a water accident. They had no insurance. They didn't even know the young girl was prone to having epileptic seizures until after the fact.

Provide adequate leadership. Your camp will only be as successful as the quality of its leadership. Prepare your leaders for the camp. Let your people know what you expect from them before they go on the trip. I challenge all my leaders to have a significant conversation with each student for whom they are responsible on the retreat. I want the leaders to know the rules and regulations, and of course they should be aware of the purpose and goals of the camp. If the camp is geared with a special theme, then the leaders should have materials in front of them to help them become better acquainted with the topic of the weekend.

I've also found camps and retreats to be a successful method of recruiting future leaders. For some reason the open atmosphere of a retreat gives adults the confidence they need to work with the students. When adults enjoy a significant camp experience of kids developing relationships, they become much more prone to join the youth staff. A retreat may also show adults that youth ministry is not their calling.

Evaluate and debrief. You've made a major mistake if you do not take the time to evaluate the camp and debrief the experience with your leaders and even with your students. I believe that at the end of almost every retreat or camp the students should have the opportunity to evaluate their experience. (See sample evaluation form on page 101.) This will help you see the good aspects of the camp and what areas could be improved. It will also give the kids an opportunity to sit quietly for a moment and reflect upon what actually did happen to them at the camp.

A time of evaluation and debriefing with your leaders helps them to digest the experience, to decide what ministry-action steps are needed, and to help plan for the next event. After a camp or retreat we usually feel too exhausted to spend much time in evaluation, but it will save hours of preparation for the next experience and it will give the leaders a better understanding of follow-up. A suggestion: Have a special dinner when you get home from the event or else have a thank you party with a time of evaluation soon after the event.

Make It Memorable

Although each camp or retreat experience is different, here are a few suggestions to help make any such event a memorable experience.

Program retreats for 17 hours a day. In other words, be over-prepared. It is much easier to cut the program than to have the kids bored because they have nothing to do. Print out the schedule for the time at camp, but don't let the students ever see the schedule. The element of surprise will create an exciting atmosphere. Good preparation always means having a "Plan B" in case the snow melts or the boat breaks down. If the film breaks or the speaker doesn't show up, then a "Plan B" prepared beforehand is a necessity.

Don't be predictable, and be as flexible as you possibly can. I've heard of camps where they serve breakfast at the dinner hour and lunch for breakfast. I've been in situations where we had planned to play capture the flag, but the kids wanted to have a square dance. Sometimes it's better to go with the flow.

When you are at a retreat or camp, try to plan your time with a *balance* of mental, physical, social, and spiritual. A well-balanced program will often give the students a better time and a better understanding of their Christian faith.

Go easy on the rules. Even though there are certain rules that must be shared, try to do it in a creative manner. We've had weekly camps in which the only three rules were taken from Scripture: "Love the Lord your God with all your heart and with all your soul and with all your mind.... Love your neighbor as yourself" (Matthew 22:37,39); "Do to others what you would have them do to you" (Matthew 7:12); and "Do everything without complaining or arguing" (Philippians 2:14).

Ideas

Sometimes we get stuck with the same ideas year after year. In case your creativity needs a boost, I've listed over 50 ideas for camps and retreats. With a little planning and some creativity, you can create a memory and a ministry that will be remembered for a lifetime.

SPECIALIZED RETREATS

- Welcome to high school retreat (freshman/with student leadership)
- Adult staff—orientation and planning
- Student leaders' retreat
- Evangelism
- Parent/teen weekend
- Scripture
- Thematic—self-image, discipleship, lordship of Christ, etc.
- Activity-centered
- Family
- Silent solitude

CARAVANS AND TOURS

- Bike, canoe, hike—all on the same tour
- Ministry—vacation Bible school, youth groups, etc.

96

- Choir tour
- Drama tour
- Motor home tour

- Campgrounds
- Mystery tour

OUTDOOR ADVENTURE

- Sailing
- Rock climbing
- Backpacking
- Bicycle
- Cross-country skiing
- Downhill skiing—outreach
- 5k/10k/marathon experience

- Sky diving
- River rafting
- Snow camping
- Canoeing
- Houseboat trip
- Surfing
- Motorcycle trip

MISSION-ORIENTED IDEAS

- Planned famine, compassion project
- Refugee camping (World Concern)
- Inner-city ministry
- Visit an orphanage
- Visit an Indian reservation

- Voice of Calvary
- Vacation Bible school
- Day camp for children
- Work camps
- Help work at a traditional camp

GENERAL IDEAS

- Established camps—denominational and nondenominational
- Hotels/motels (fancy hotels give great rates on weekends or at holiday times)
- Lock-ins at the church
- Plan a one-day discipleship conference in connection with other churches
- Campground—tents, campers

- Use a nearby church facility
- Sports camping
- "Youth week"—nightly youth rally at church with events during the day
- Handicap camp—help with the blind, hard-of-hearing, etc.
- Sex education weekend
- Girls-only weekend
- Guys-only weekend

SAMPLE CAMPING FLOW CHART

GOALS and OBJECTIVES
—To be determined at May staff meeting

FOOD   Lisa/Caleen (person in charge)
—Meals

FRI.	Dinner	Snack
SAT.	Breakfast	Lunch
	Dinner	Snack
SUN.	Breakfast	Lunch

—See Daryl (nutritionist)
—Buy for approximately 100 (this number is slightly flexible)
—Have menu planned by June 13
—Buy food on or before June 22
—Box food by meals
—You are responsible for all cooking equipment (ice chests, ice, mixing bowls, utensils, water jugs, etc.) except wood, grill for fire, and a shaded area for food

TRANSPORTATION   Doug (person in charge)
—For approximately 100 (this number is slightly flexible)
—Surf racks needed
—Have all transportation finalized by June 13
—Transportation also for all gear, luggage, and equipment

PROGRAM   Katie (person in charge)
—Timing
—Rules by Tues., June 19

EQUIPMENT· Mike/Doug (person in charge)
—Surfboards
—Wood & large grill

—Balls (football, 3 volleyballs, Wiffle ball, 3 smashball sets, Frisbee)
—2 volleyball nets
—First aid supplies
—Extra tarps (for sleeping)
—Shaded area for food
—Arrange by June 13
—Collect by June 21

BUDGET   Katie (person in charge)
   —To be completed by June 13
      • Transportation   • Fees
      • Supplies   • Food
      • Income   • Scholarships

MONEY/REGISTRATION   Katie (person in charge)
   —Permission slips
   —Cash advance for trip
   —Registration due June 17
   —Camp liaison
   —Keep track of all finances
   —Make records when home

SPEAKING & QUIET TIMES   Jim (person in charge)
   —Theme by June 13
   —2 quiet times (sheets printed beforehand/tie into your talks)

SEMINARS   Katie (person in charge)
   —Give seminars twice
   —Who is talking on what by June 6
   —Meet with each kid to help prepare
   —All set by June 22

PROMO/CALLING   Daryl/Caleen (person in charge)
   —Flier made by May 29
   —Flier mailed by May 29 by Donna

—Initial calls (by area) yes-no-maybe, May 30-June 13
(call everyone on the mailing list)
—Finalize commitments June 13-June 17

STAFFING   Lisa (person in charge)
—All volunteers contacted by June 13

MUSIC   Lisa (person in charge)
—Contacted by June 13

PHOTOGRAPHS   Carl (person in charge)
—Contacted by June 13
—Film bought beforehand (4 rolls of 36 slides)
—Film developed after
—Slide show made by July 1

GAMES   Katie/Daryl/Leadership Kids (person in charge)
—Choose and plan games
—Trophies
—Run games on trip

GREAT ADVENTURE EVALUATION

1. How would you rate your overall experience this weekend?

   Awesome 10 9 8 7 6 5 4 3 2 1 Rotten

2. What things did you like best about the weekend?

   1.

   2.

   3.

3. What did you like least and/or what changes or additions can you suggest to make next year different?

   1.

   2.

   3.

4. What will you remember most about camp? (Most fun, funniest thing, serious stuff, etc.)

   1.

   2.

   3.

5. What things helped you develop new and deeper relationships and feel accepted this weekend?

   1.

   2.

6. What made you feel uncomfortable or unaccepted by others this weekend?

   1.

   2.

7. What things challenged, encouraged, or helped you the most in your relationship to God? (BE SPECIFIC.)

   1.

   2.

   3.

8. How well do you feel you got to know your counselor(s)?

9. ☐ If you would like to talk with one of the leaders, please check here.

   NAME (optional, unless you want to meet with a leader):

   _____

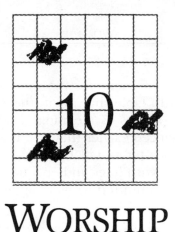

WORSHIP

One of the most spiritually moving and worshipful weekends of my life happened accidentally in the state of Texas. I was asked to speak at a convention for Episcopal high school students in San Antonio. The day before the convention I was to speak to a group of Southern Baptists in Dallas. The day after the convention I was to speak at an Assembly of God church. Our office had chuckled at the fact of me speaking to such a variety of Christian denominations. The Baptist retreat was extremely uplifting. It was like attending a football pep rally for Jesus. The kids were excited about their faith, and their enthusiasm was evident. After my talk, a pastor got up and gave an invitation. At least 100 students came forward to give their lives to Christ. I sat on the platform and could not help but have tears streaming down my face. It was a moving experience.

From there I hopped on a plane to San Antonio, just in time to catch the opening liturgy before I would speak that night. Not coming from an Episcopalian background, I was captivated by the beauty of the liturgy and the special reverence demonstrated for the same God who brought those Southern Baptist youth to the front of that auditorium. Communion that night was explained in the most beautiful and simple way. As the students came forward to take the bread and the cup, I sensed God's presence in a new and fresh way. These students looked and acted like their Baptist brothers and sisters, yet their worship was so different. As they approached the Lord's table that night, their sincerity and love relationship with God was as meaningful and powerful as the Baptists had experienced earlier that day. It was similar, yet different. The next night after my talk there was a time of affirmation to greet one another with hugs and encouraging words. What a delight to see kids committed to worship and to live for Jesus Christ!

The next day I left my Episcopal friends to enter the worshipful experience of a charismatic Assembly of God church. As the people raised their hands in praise to the Father and sang one chorus after another of adoration and thanks to God, I couldn't help but think back to the rest of my weekend. This was different, yet similar. I came home a blessed man for having been with God's people and having encountered such different styles of worship for the same living, transcendent God.

Even the word "worship" brings strong feelings and vastly different responses. Unfortunately, young people are not very enthused when it comes to worship. Many view worship as something the adults put up with, and few take an active interest in the worship service. I view this as a tragedy. *One of the main goals of a good youth ministry program should be to develop an understanding of and enthusiasm for worship.* When the groundwork has been laid effectively and the students have developed the skills to worship God, then young people can have a regular and meaningful worship experience even in the confines of a more traditional church.

Active Response to God

Søren Kierkegaard is said to have chided Christians who asked about a worship service, "How was it?" His reply was that we should say, "How did I do?" Worship is not being a spectator at a religious show; worship is an active response to God's love and redemption. The main reason young people get so little out of worship is because they put very little into it. Involvement in the worship experience is the key to enjoying it.

When we view worship as an *active response* we can understand that we are actually participating in the celebration through our own worship as well as in corporate worship, which includes praise, music, prayer, confession, forgiveness, thanksgiving, sharing of gifts, Scripture reading, proclamation, and communion. When kids say the worship service is boring, we shouldn't apologize because it didn't meet their need. We must first help them understand for themselves whether in fact it really wasn't relevant or whether they simply came with low expectations (which were then met). Since worship is an active response, we must help the young people understand why and how they can and should participate.

A Reason to Worship

Worship is a stimulated response to the unconditional love that God has shown to humankind (Romans 5:8). We must help adolescents (and adults) see that Christians are to love God out of a response for what He has done for us, and not merely out of responsibility. Worship moves from an inward response to an outward response. Genuine worship begins in the heart before it can be truth expressed from the lips.

During adolescence, as discussed in previous chapters, there is a great degree of self-absorption and self centeredness. Worship helps people focus on something (Someone) greater than self. Worship is a time to actively sit with God and listen to His call. It is a time to put our priorities in order. It is a place to reflect on our journey with God. In worship we know that God will speak. It becomes a matter of teaching our kids how to listen to God's personal and corporate word through the many aspects of the worship service.

Worship fulfills another major need of adolescents: The worshiping community gives them a corporate identity. Worship provides a sense of home in the church. It grants meaning through collective association with people and the elements of tradition. All forms of worship, whether highly traditional or free-form, have ritual and tradition. The ritual and tradition make an important environment for the individual involved.

Attitude Check

Given the reality of the need for worship, what can youth workers do to cultivate a healthy attitude of worship?

1. *Help young people understand the characteristics and nature of God.* You may want to have a series on the attributes of God. As you look at His qualities of unconditional and sacrificial love, patience, steadfastness, and creation, to name only a few, you become very much aware that God is worthy to be worshiped. Far too often young people view God as the great killjoy in the sky, a God of works and not of grace. No wonder they are not excited about worship!

2. *Take the lead as a worshiper.* If you are a person with enthusiasm for worship, your excitement will rub off. I've noticed that in youth groups where worship is a priority in the ministry it's much easier for the entire group to get excited about worship. If you personally do not participate in worship, then don't expect your group to be excited about it.

3. *Let kids participate in worship.* When we allow students to lead, plan, and implement worship experiences, it will be more meaningful to them. Hopefully your church will allow the young people to actually participate in the worship service through the reading of Scripture, preaching, ushering, providing special music, or however they can be of service. There will also be times when the youth worker will need to develop worship experiences outside the traditional Sunday morning service. This is where you can usually be more creative and even find a middle ground for the "language" of worship that has meaning for them.

4. *Let kids come as they are.* One of the points we must remind our young people is that they are always welcome to worship God. One of the personally exciting elements for me, which came out of the "Jesus Movement" in the early seventies, was that people begin to realize that God does not have a "dress code" for worship.

Music: Vehicle for Worship

Music plays an extremely important part of worship (as well as youth ministry in general). Music is by far the most widely recognizable tool in worship. The Scripture tells us to "speak to one another with psalms, hymns and spiritual songs. Sing and make music in your heart to the Lord" (Ephesians 5:19). The musical ministry of a youth group can give the program the needed and added boost of a special worship experience. The world of music is vitally important to young people. This makes it one of the easiest vehicles to translate their faith into worship.

Maggie was an Australian exchange student at Princeton High School in Princeton, New Jersey. While I was in seminary, Cathy and I were doing a Young Life Club at a different high school from Maggie's. Because there was no club at her school, she found us and asked if she could come. We would pick her up for each club meeting and then take her home. During our weekly rides we asked Maggie how she had become such an enthusiastic Christian. Her life radiantly displayed her love for Christ, and her knowledge of Scripture was better than that of most of our friends in the pastorate. She pulled out her Young Life Song Book and said, "I love to sing, and I became a Christian when I started listening to the words of the songs I was singing in my Young Life Club in Australia." "How did you get so well-versed in the Scriptures?" I asked her. "I sing the words," she happily replied. Maggie loved to sing the contemporary Christian songs filled with Psalms and other Scriptures. We have a generation of young people who have moved away from Bible memorization but when motivated will learn Scripture the same way the Hebrews did—through song.

As you look at your youth program, look for ways to incorporate music into the program. If you are unable to play the guitar or piano, then take a class. If you have absolutely no musical skill, then one of the first recruits into the program should be a music leader. Ideally you will be able to identify some musically gifted or interested students or sponsors from within your church. Even if you must initially solicit help from the outside to train others in your group, make it a high priority nevertheless.

Other practical ideas are to start with simple, fun, enjoyable songs. The atmosphere of worship is celebrative, which need not mean somber. As much as possible, sing songs the kids know or which are easy to learn. Put the words to the songs in front of the kids. Keep the instruments simple at first, relying mostly on the piano or guitar. Encourage the musically talented students to write their own songs. Keep the music moving and enjoyable.

A Little Creativity Goes a Long Way

With what I've written so far, some of you might think of my worship preference as traditional. Actually, although I sometimes enjoy a traditional style of worship, my preference is with the more progressive style of worship. I'm afraid that many students have placed worship into a very small box. Since they've never been exposed to the more creative styles of worship, they are unaware of possibilities that may make their worship of the living God a more vital and positive experience.

One of the people often overlooked by the church is the artistic, innovative person. Creative worship styles tend to relate well to this type of person. By using a more varied approach to worship, you will see that some of the possibilities that you personally might not choose can be highly meaningful to someone else. In fact, the beauty of worshiping God is that He is bigger than our particular style or preference of worship. I've listed below a number of different styles of creative worship, along with a few ideas to implement each style.

CREATIVE WORSHIP

1. *Learning About Worship*
   A. Tour the sanctuary, and discuss each aspect of the building and worship service.
   B. Visit other churches with different styles of worship.
   C. Plan an innovative worship service for the entire church.

2. *The Arts*
   A. Drama is a marvelous form of expression. You may

want to develop short dramatic presentations around the theme of the service.

B. Interpretive dance can be a means of praise and worship. When an interpretive dance is done to a beautiful Christian song, new insights can come from observing the movements of the dancer.

3. *Prayer*

A. Pray through each letter of the alphabet concerning the attributes of God's nature that begin with that specific letter. For example, using the letter P: We praise You for Your Power. We thank You for Your Patience.

B. Write prayers as a letter to God.

C. One-word prayers. Give an opening sentence and let the students fill in the sentences with their own one-word ending. For example: We thank You for.... We ask You for.... We praise You because....

4. *Singing*

A. Do as the hymnwriters of the past: Put biblical or Christian words to certain popular songs.

B. Paraphrase older traditional hymns into contemporary language.

5. *Retreats*

A. Have a weekend retreat where from sunup to sundown the kids must be silent. This is truly an awesome spiritual experience for many of them. You can guide them through this experience by giving them tools to make their time of silence more beneficial. Special Bible chapters, song sheets, workbooks, and devotionals can all be beneficial.

B. Plan a retreat where the kids are responsible for the entire worship program. You can give them guidance, but it is their responsibility to put the worship together and lead it.

6. *Personal/Private Worship*
   A. Provide devotional books and workbooks for youth throughout the year.[1]
   B. "Journaling" is an excellent method of private worship. Many people express themelves better by writing than verbally.

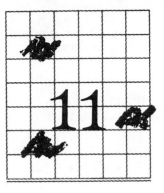

DEVELOPING STUDENT
LEADERSHIP

A s I look back over the past in my youth ministry, I realize that I've helped produce apathetic kids! No, I didn't have a "Plan for Apathy in the Church." In fact, my goal was to get kids excited about Christ and the church. But as I rethink my philosophy of youth ministry, I recognize a number of misconceptions I've had about how to get kids excited about their faith and involved in leadership.

Misconception number one: Youth groups should be entertaining. We live in a society that demands entertainment, so in youth ministry we sometimes believe that to have a "successful program" we must keep the kids amused. *Wrong.* If our young people are to grow in their faith, our first priority must be for them to experience the work of Christ firsthand.

We can never just talk about missions, for example, and expect our high schoolers to understand. They need to *do* missions. Experiential learning is always the best learning. If we must choose between entertaining students with a great speaker on missions or having them *experience* ministry by visiting a rest home or doing some other hands-on ministry, then for the sake of their spiritual growth we must choose the experience every time.

I've had to ask myself honestly, "Am I creating *spectators* of the kingdom or *servants* in the kingdom?" This is not to say that a youth group should be boring—heaven forbid! But when kids are

111

involved in and experience the kingdom firsthand, they'll tend to be much less apathetic and much more excited about their faith.

Misconception number two: Adult leadership should always take on the major responsibilities. Adults are usually more dependable than kids, but students need to have responsibilities that genuinely matter. Though a youth ministry with complete adult leadership might run more smoothly, the kids will sit back and expect to be served rather than to serve. Once high schoolers become spectators to a youth program at church, they'll quickly grow apathetic.

I remember how one of our students, Brian, came to most of our activities, yet never seemed to fit in with the rest of the group. He had told me that at his previous church he was active and enthused about the program, but he was certainly not that way with us. Finally one day I called his previous youth director and asked him about Brian. He gave me a great insight when he told me that Brian was a computer wizard and had put together a computer program for his former church.

The next Sunday at church I took Brian aside and told him I heard he was talented with computers, and that our youth group needed a person in charge of the computer program we planned to start. His face lit up and he began to explain his excitement for computers and his involvement in his previous church. Immediately Brian's enthusiasm about the youth group grew; he now felt needed. As Brian became involved, his apathy faded.

Misconception number three: Bigger is better. Whenever I'm with a group of fellow youth workers I'm always asked, "How many kids do you have in your group?" The question implies that the biggest group is the most successful. Even many church boards measure the success of the youth worker by the numbers that he or she attracts.

The other day I challenged a group of youth workers to look instead at the *percentage* of members in a church. Which is more impressive, 100 kids in a 2500-member church or 15 kids in a 150-member church? From that perspective, many huge youth groups would be considered failures.

Even when we do have a big group, bigger is not better. No youth worker can develop a large youth group with integrity unless it is broken into smaller units. It's impossible for students to feel cared for in a personal manner in a large group unless they're somehow connected to a smaller group within it. If we desire to work in the structure of a large youth group, then we must constantly be breaking down that structure into more personal units to keep the kids from becoming apathetic, overwhelmed, or simply neglected.

The bottom line of ministry is not "How many kids do I have coming to my youth group?" but "Where will my kids be five to ten years from now? Are our programs preparing them to be the Christian leaders of the future?"

Misconception number four: Students are not ready for service in the church. The call to Christ is the call to serve. Most high school students are ready to go farther and dig deeper in their Christian life; they just need a challenge. A young person on one of the leadership boards of the church, for example, can be a great source of new ideas, enthusiasm, and a different perspective.

Veteran youth pastor Ridge Burns took a group of teenagers who were mostly apathetic about their faith and set spiritual fires in their hearts by allowing them to create what he calls "Sidewalk Sunday School." His youth group took on the responsibility of having a ministry to a group of latchkey kids in a poverty-stricken housing development a few miles from their church. Every weekday the youth group was at the development. They played games, made crafts, and told Bible stories. As the kids got to know the people they became a miniature social welfare agency, helping people with shopping, electric bills, and many other important ways. The kids ended up renting one of the apartments as their headquarters and paid for the entire ministry out of their own pockets and with fund-raisers. Needless to say, the incredible renewed positive spiritual life of the kids came out of their excitement from being vessels of ministry used by their Lord.

Students need to see that they're not merely the church of tomorrow; rather, their gifts, abilities, and services are needed *today*. We must do everything we can to assimilate our kids into the life of the church. I can see now that my own youth ministry in the past has been far too isolated from the "big church." Our job will never be finished with young people until they become excited about the mission of the entire church, and not just the youth group.

Positive Peer Ministry

The best way to overcome these misconceptions and to rid our groups of apathy is through *student involvement*—what some people call *peer ministry*. We must constantly be asking questions such as "How can the high schoolers in my group feel ownership of this program?" "What areas of our ministry can best be done by students?" "Are the kids in my group getting trained and enabled to do significant kingdom ministry?"

Peer ministry is more than an antidote to apathy; it's also the most effective style of ministry. Students can best be served by other students, primarily because of a credibility factor which is not as strong when adults minister. And positive peer pressure is just as powerful in a student's life as negative peer pressure.

A perfect illustration of this was our youth group's recent winter retreat. Tony Campolo was speaking, and he was his usual dynamic self. But when we went through the student evaluations of the weekend, most of them said the most significant spiritual experience for them was not Tony's dynamic speaking but the seminars led by their peers. Though the seminar presentations were mediocre at best, the credibility of the peer speakers was important. We got a number of comments like "Lisa's seminar was terrific because she's going through the same problems I am."

The cure for apathy is *involvement*. The road to involvement is often slow and even painful, but it's worth the price. When students feel cared for, have meaningful responsibilities, and begin to use their gifts of service in the church and the community, then they're likely to remain in the church permanently. Enthusiastic servanthood will become for them a permanent lifestyle.

Developing a Peer Ministry Program

In some churches the emergence of a peer ministry program

represents a fear to the students. If they have not been accustomed to taking leadership and ownership, some will be nervous about their new role. Other youth groups will jump at the chance too quickly with almost too much enthusiasm. Here are some principles to consider when developing a peer ministry program.

1. *Students are already ministers.* The Greek word *doulos* (which means "bondservant") is the same word as "minister." All Christians are ministers. One of our goals is to help young people create a lifestyle of servanthood. I'll never forget a time when I couldn't attend a morning Bible study. At the last minute I called Wayne, a high school senior, and asked him to lead the Bible study. He wanted to cancel it instead. His philosophy was "no youth pastor, no Bible study." His comment was, "We need a minister present." I told him, "*You* are a minister." I finally convinced him to lead it. He fumbled through the Bible study his first time, but I never returned to that early-morning group because Wayne was capable of leading the group. In fact, the group grew in my absence. Young people are called to be ministers not merely for the future but for *today*. Ministry to students is best done by other students.

2. *We're in the equipping business.* The best youth ministry happens when you give the students ownership. The only way for their faith to grow is to let them lead under a supervising eye. Some youth workers have made the mistake of believing that ownership means handing over the leadership reins with no supervision. That's a wrong assumption. Your job is to equip and train your students for ministry. The only way to do that is to give them responsibilities that matter and to help them carry out those tasks.

This is also where I believe the theology of spiritual gifts comes into our ministry. The more liberal church tends to forget that spiritual gifts appear in the Bible, and the more conservative church places an emphasis on only a few of the gifts, depending on which theological slant it holds. The New Testament reveals that the purpose of spiritual gifts is to *equip Christians for the ministry* (Ephesians 4:11,12). In order to equip our youth for leadership, we will want to help them discover their spiritual gifts and help them find, at a young age, where their gifts and abilities fit into the kingdom of God.[1]

3. *Students need a specific ministry.* The high school or junior high campus is probably the greatest place for your students to have a specific ministry. They need a contact point, and the campus is where friendship evangelism can take place, as well as other service ministries. In a very interesting study put out by the Institute of American Church Growth we can see how important a role friendship evangelism plays in the life of the church. This study was on "Why people become Christians and join the church."[2]

Walk in	2-3%
Program	3-4%
Pastor	3-5%
Special need	2-3%
Visitation	1%
Sunday school	3-5%
Crusade	.001%
Friend/Relative	70-90%

Sometimes we give our students too general a task. Instead, it is wise to give *specific ministries and challenges.* For example, you may ask them to befriend one lonely person at school or volunteer to do work at a local children's hospital. As your young people develop specific ministries they will grow in their desire to serve.

4. *Let them lead now.* Most kids don't want to assume leadership in the church because they want to wait until they've become more mature in their faith. When I approached one high school student about going on a mission trip he told me, "I can't go; I don't even know all the books of the Bible."

Paul's promise to the Philippians is important; he was confident "that he who began a good work in you will carry it on to completion until the day of Christ Jesus" (Philippians 1:6). Church growth experts tell us that the most effective evangelists are new Christians.

5. *Kids have something to offer.* Recently I watched a news special on the rise of teenage murders. The news reporter said, "The kids put a lot of blame on TV and on drugs. But I think those are just excuses. I believe the major thing is that these kids just

don't have any stake in our society. From infancy on, they are told that they are not worth very much." Christian kids need to know that they are significant and that they can offer an alternative to what the world has to offer.

Your kids need to know beyond a shadow of a doubt that they do matter. They need to know that even in this impersonal world of media and technology their life counts and they can make a difference in the world. Developing a peer ministry is a shining example that the youth really do have a stake in society, in the church, and in eternity.

Building a Student Leadership Core

There are a number of models of student leadership within the church. There's no one perfect model; any model that gets peers ministering to peers is effective. I've used a number of models in my ministry, and some have been more effective than others. The student-leadership core format shown below is the model that has been most helpful for me.

The student leaders are asked to commit to a six-month program with a strong degree of accountability. Since I had watched many of my students exhibit extremely high degrees of accountability in school athletics, choir, drama, and science projects, my thinking evolved into focusing on a student leadership with accountability also. In the large youth group I was involved in, at one time we had 38 high school student leaders. However, as we increased accountability we realized that the extra time pressure on the adults would allow for only 12 students in leadership at any one time.

STUDENT LEADERSHIP CORE

Goals
1. Develop a maturing, foundational faith.
2. Teach leadership/ministry skills so the student leaders can multiply their faith.
3. Serve the high school group.

4. Represent the high school group, giving evaluation and input.
5. Serve the entire church body.

Job Description/Commitment
1. A six-month commitment.
2. They will attend a leadership meeting every other week. (They can miss only three meetings.)
3. At these meetings they will turn in an "accountability sheet" which will include the following items:
    a. Lead a growthbook with another student (one-on-one).
    b. Make five contact calls within two weeks.
    c. Work toward developing a daily quiet time.
    d. List prayer requests.
4. The adult staff person who is their supervisor will meet with them every two weeks.
5. They must be prepared for the meetings, with their home-work done.
6. Within the six-month period they will teach an area Bible study (either alone or with someone else).
7. They will help to plan and will participate in trips. Feb. to July: Mexicali, Camp Surf, and Worktrek. Aug. to Jan.: Freshman Ski Trip, Great Adventure, and an orphanage/mission-oriented trip.
8. They will be committed to attend Sunday school, church, and their individual area study.
9. At the beginning of the six-month commitment period, the leadership and their staff person will select areas of responsibility from the upcoming retreats and activities.
10. At the beginning they will be issued a notebook which will include:
    a. Blank accountability sheets.
    b. A calendar listing the youth events to help in planning ahead.
    c. A planning section for lists and notes.
    d. A section for notes on training and homework.
11. To begin the six-month commitment, there will be a full-day kickoff of training and relationship-building.

12. To end the six-month commitment, there will be an over-night retreat involving evaluation, fun, and final training.
13. At the end of this six-month period, each student will have the opportunity to reapply and go through the process again.

Selection/Process

1. Announce the new program in Sunday school two weeks in a row; invite anyone interested to an upcoming informational meeting. (Staff should be encouraging students whom they feel are ready for this type of challenge.)
2. At the informational meeting, explain the job description and heavy commitment level, and set up interviews for those interested.
3. Interviews will be completed within a two-week period (lasting 20 minutes each).
4. Student will bring to the interview a list of personal activities in which he or she is already involved, such as football, piano, and other outside activities.
5. Student being interviewed will also bring one letter of reference from a teacher, coach, boss, or youth advisor.
6. Qualities important to this position include:
    a. Servant attitude.
    b. Time availability.
    c. Established faith (ability to express a personal faith as well as live it).
    d. Personal priorities (list them).
7. Once the student is selected, the staff member should call and write the parents of each new leader to explain the program.
8. Number: Choose 12 students.

    Class breakdown: Seniors, if qualified, have first priority. Strong focus on juniors in order to develop future leadership.

    Sample breakdown: 12 total (2 freshmen, 2 sophomores, 4 juniors, 4 seniors).

Staff ownership

1. One or two staff persons will be in charge. This is a major time commitment and must be treated with equal weight as an "area."
2. This staff person will hold the leadership core accountable.
3. The staff person will filter the leadership into the various area responsibilities (growthbooks, teaching, etc.).

Training Curriculum:

1. The adult staff person will plan the entire six-month period ahead of schedule, so that the kids know the direction and the homework. Also, they can schedule guest speakers to help teach more effectively.
2. There needs to be an overall schedule to assure that each student will be involved in a variety of ministry learning experiences (participate in growthbook, teach area study, plan a portion of a retreat, plan a portion of a special event, welcome new people, etc.).
3. Meetings will include:
   a. Going through the "Fruit of the Spirit" workbook.
   b. Taking time to actively develop leadership skills. (During the first week learn about outreach; during the next two weeks develop a welcoming plan for new people and then actually go to visit the new kids. So during some weeks the homework is "Fruit of the Spirit" and during other weeks it is actually *doing* what they were trained in.)
4. On "Fruit of the Spirit" weeks, the kids will meet in groups of four to go through the workbook. They will take turns leading the group.

Pitfalls to Avoid

There are three pitfalls to avoid in peer ministry: 1) Don't delegate more responsibility than the students can realistically handle. A good principle for peer ministry is *student-led, staff-guided*; 2) don't respond to failure by imposing guilt. The adolescent temperament is very fragile. This phrase may be helpful: *Be slow to criticize, quick to encourage*; 3) don't focus all your attention on the "superstar" kids. In every group there are those who shine with more natural ability, beauty, and brains. They can be an important part of your leadership core, but in focusing on the spiritual gifts and abilities of everyone in your group you'll find others who also belong on the leadership team. *Your job is to ignite creative leadership potential in each of your kids.*

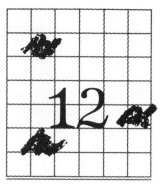

BUILDING COMMUNITY
THROUGH
SMALL GROUPS

P astor and author Bruce Larson said something very profound
about community: "The neighborhood bar is possibly the
best counterpart there is for the fellowship Christ wants to give His
church. It's an imitation, dispensing liquor instead of grace, escape
rather than reality, but it is a permissive, accepting and inclusive
fellowship. It's 'unshockable.' The bar flourishes *not* because most
people are alcoholics but because God has put into the human
heart the desire to know and be known, to love and be loved, and so
many seek a counterfeit at the price of a few beers."[1]

I wonder how many young people find the same feelings of
acceptance and community within the church as people who frequent the neighborhood bar. The strong emphasis on rugged in-
dividualism has left a deep scar on the hearts of young people who
so desperately need to belong. Many young people even compromise their faith and values in order to fill their need to belong.

Dan Yankelovich did a study of the individualistic generation of
the 1970's.[2] After very extensive research, his conclusion was that
people going through the 1970's and early 80's were in desperate
need of commitment and *community*. No longer was the American
home a place for the extended family to meet together for support.
The church had moved away from the community and fellowship

values it once centered its ministry upon. (Remember when church potlucks had real food instead of everyone bringing pizza, fast-food chicken, and store-bought potato salad?) The questions we must ask are, "Where do the kids from our generation go for community and a sense of belonging?" and "Can the church youth group be a place of community and support?"

I once asked 160 high school students in a questionnaire, "Why do you come to the youth group?" The vast majority replied that they came to the youth group because they felt loved and accepted. They were not coming to hear me speak or because our facility was so nice. The majority of students came because of a sense of community. In fact if a student doesn't feel a part of the group, then he or she will not stay very long. On all the retreats I've taken kids, never has a student asked me which biblical text I will be using for the lessons. It seems like almost every student asks, "Who is going on this retreat?" The decision to go on the retreat or stay home depends largely on who else will be attending the event.

Religious Socialization

Whether or not youth workers have ever heard the term *religious socialization*, that is precisely what we are trying to do with our kids. Religious socialization consists of the accumulated experiences that bring the students to the exact place they are in their spiritual life. Religious socialization is accomplished through family, friends, church, community, and other shared experiences. Your job is to help make this process a very positive and growing experience. The goal of youth ministry is to have community with God and community with other people (relationships). In many of the studies on death and dying the experts reveal that when on their deathbed, with all other priorities and agendas put aside, the majority of patients desire two things: a relationship with God and a relationship with loved ones. Our youth ministry must also focus on developing a vital, trusting, loving relationship with God and a healthy sense of community and support.

Youth ministry cannot be compartmentalized to meet only the

"spiritual" needs of the person. Good religious socialization in youth ministry is developing a whole-person approach. In order for a person to be growing spiritually he must be dealing with other areas of his life as well. A good youth group will have a healthy balance of physical, mental, social, emotional, and spiritual activities. In the book of Acts we see that the early Christians balanced their time together in prayer, fellowship, food, teaching/worship, and serving (Acts 2:42). For adolescents the positive peer influence and sense of community is one of the strongest elements of building a Christian self-identity and a healthy religious socialization. Some questions to ask yourself when thinking about this issue are, "Is there a true sense of community and support in the youth group?" "Are we ministering to the whole person?" "What can we do to enhance a deeper commitment to community within the youth group?"

Building Community Through Small Groups

Two common mistakes in developing community are that we either try to sidestep the importance of history-giving and affirmation in favor of straighter or deeper sharing, or else we spend all our time at the first stages of developing community and provide little opportunity for developing intimacy in a group.

I will be much more vulnerable in a group after I sense that the group knows and accepts me. For example, I sat in on a small group of high school students led by one of our volunteers. She opened the group by saying, "Why don't we go around the room and share what the Lord has been doing in our life?" She received silent stares and then all of us gazed at the spots on the carpet. Even after she shared a fabulous story of her own faith, none of us talked or had anything to say. She was asking for deeper sharing than we were ready for.

There are a number of community-building models for youth ministry. The one that has been most helpful for me to understand and work toward as a goal is Lyman Coleman's.[3] This model involves a gradual process of small-group sharing that begins on a simple, nonthreatening level and grows toward personal understanding and mutual trust. Coleman describes the process by comparing it to a baseball diamond. First base is *history-giving*. In order for a group to develop a sense of community, they must take time to share their history. Before you develop intimacy, you must get acquainted.

At second base your group needs *a sense of warmth and affirmation*. When the students feel comfortable and accepted, they will really begin to open up.

For Coleman, third base is *deeper sharing*. This is a time in the process when the other group members begin to trust each other with sharing about hurts, joys, frustrations, belief, and even doubt. To develop intimate sharing takes time.

Home plate in the process of community is *the depth of Christian community*. This is a close relationship in which people serve and respect each other. Such depth of community is the goal. It is never fully reached between everyone in your group, but nevertheless such fellowship is what our heart longs for and what keeps people living out their faith in the body of Christ.

Thinking Small

In our society the basic philosophy of ministry is "Big is better." Unfortunately, this philosophy doesn't work when developing community. One of the true blessings of the small church and small youth group is that even though the programs are usually not overwhelmingly dynamic, there is an easier atmosphere in which to develop community.

The larger group must always look for ways to break into smaller, more intimate groups. I believe that small groups and more intimate shared experiences are at the heart of building community in a youth group.

Many churches are finding that small support groups designed specifically to share and encourage have become the backbone of their ministry. Even breaking up the whole group into smaller segments during meetings often becomes more conducive to spiritual growth and community. However, leading a small group can be devastating. We've all been with kids in a small group when no one spoke or when one person monopolized the entire conversation.

Leading a small group takes a certain amount of skill that may not come easy. The small-group principles listed below will help make easier the important task of developing deeper community in the youth group.

SMALL-GROUP SURVIVAL MANUAL

1. Include everyone whenever possible.
2. At the beginning get everyone in the group to talk. (They need a victory.) Have them share a nonthreatening piece of information about themselves in the group.
3. Four in a group is best; six is okay; eight should be the maximum.
4. Be aware of new people, and include them in the conversation.
5. Remember that small groups often raise the tension level (because people can't hide).
6. Move from light to heavy discussion.
7. Ask "I feel" rather than "I know" questions.
8. The best questions do not have right or wrong answers.
9. The longer the group is together, the better they will feel about the group.
10. In a small group it's easier to share, pray, encourage, and be personal than in a larger group.
11. Do not allow one person to monopolize the conversation.
12. Write out your discussion questions.
13. Avoid any put-downs.
14. Discussion questions should be answerable.
15. Affirm people for what they are saying.
16. Allow people the right to pass and not share.
17. Create a casual and relaxed atmosphere.
18. Don't always expound on the answer yourself.
19. Call people by name.
20. Let everyone take a turn at running the group.
21. Eye contact and body language are important for the leader.

22. When you ask someone to read, make sure he is able to read out loud or else don't ask him.
23. Get your group in a comfortable atmosphere where everyone can see each other's eyes.
24. Request confidentiality in the group.

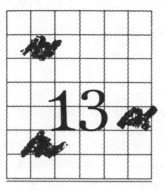

DEVELOPING
DYNAMIC
ADULT VOLUNTEERS

I will never forget being confronted by a youth worker who was observing our Sunday morning program. The morning was really a dismal attempt at programming. My talk was mediocre at best. The song leader didn't show up, and some of the students in the back actually got into a fight during my talk!

After the meeting this confident young youth worker said to me, "I don't understand how you could have a few hundred kids here this morning, while the most I've ever had is 18. I'm a better communicator than you are, and I can definitely put on a more interesting program."

I replied, "You're probably right. But did you notice all the adult volunteers sitting with the kids? I believe that God will give us only the amount of kids we can actually handle. You are the only adult youth worker at your church; it's a one-man show. How many more students can you handle by yourself? If I were you, I'd recruit adults to help you and then watch the numbers increase!"

A year later he was still having between 10 and 20 students come to his youth group because he "didn't have time to develop adult leaders." God allows us to produce more spiritual fruit when we develop a staff that cares for each other and is willing to put time into relational ministry with the students.

Perhaps the most important but overlooked aspect of youth ministry is building a dynamic youth staff. I would go so far as to say that when you are establishing a youth ministry program, your staff is more important than your youth. The writer of Proverbs reminds us that "for lack of guidance a nation falls, but many advisers make victory sure" (Proverbs 11:14). This Scripture is dealing on a national level, but the principle runs true in youth ministry as well. *The quality and quantity of any youth ministry program directly depends on the adult involvement in the program.*

Most youth workers enjoy spending time with kids but do a poor job when it comes to developing a staff. It takes time and energy to work with a staff, but the long-term results are worth it. Years ago the "Lone Ranger" mentality of youth ministry was popular, but it didn't work very well. Today any effective youth ministry is a team-oriented ministry.

Developing a Team Ministry

Bringing a group of adults together to become a team ministry is no easy task. Unfortunately, there are no simple formulas or methods that insure instant success. If you want to develop a team ministry, it will take your time, attention, and energy. Just as students need attention, so does your staff.

It is time well spent when you meet the adults *on their territory.* If Carl likes to play tennis, then play tennis with him. If John and Susan take the family to the park most Saturday mornings, offer to bring the picnic lunch one Saturday. The staff need to know that you genuinely care for them beyond the mere fact that they are the people who will drive the kids on a special outing.

You'll need a staff retreat at least once a year. Program the retreat almost as if it were for students. Take time to plan, prepare, and get acquainted, but also program intense fun times. Have a great meal together, one that is really out of the ordinary from what would be expected. Give your staff the opportunity to go to one of the many outstanding youth ministry conferences that may come to your area. The investment of money is always worth the training they will receive. Let them know they are special, and the long-term results will make it worth your effort.

One of the main problems in building a team ministry is finding the time to meet. Some staffs meet weekly; others get together every other week or every month. If you are not meeting on a regular basis, you are missing a great opportunity to develop a team ministry.

Leave room in your staff meetings for business and preparation, but also find time to include training, sharing, prayer, and fun. One of the best formats from my past experience was a weekly meeting where we ate together at 5:00 P.M. at the church for a time of fellowship. Around the table there was a time of sharing and prayer requests. From 6:00 to 7:00 we took care of planning and preparation. We were finished in two hours. Everyone has to eat anyway, and it usually takes that long to prepare, cook, and clean for a meal.

Diversity of Staff

My friend and one of my youth staff volunteers, Carl, taught me a great lesson in youth ministry. Carl was working at a bank when he volunteered to help with the youth group. My initial reaction was that it wouldn't work. Carl was brilliant but shy. The best word I can think of to describe him is *nerd*. He wore a pocket protector with what seemed like 15 pens, pencils, and other items in his pocket. He loved to wear bright green pants to church. One Sunday morning he asked me if he could give an announcement at youth group—he wanted to take the kids bowling. I replied, "Carl, our kids don't bowl; they're too sophisticated for that." But he persevered, so I let him give the announcement after all. It was a horrible display of communication. There was Carl, with his pocket full of writing utensils and wearing his bright green pants, telling the kids he would take them bowling next week. To my surprise and joy, 25 students went bowling with Carl! We even started a bowling league. Carl had a very effective ministry with us.

A diversity of staff will relate to a diversity of kids. If you have only one type of personality or interest group on staff, you will generally miss the opportunity to minister to kids who can't relate to that interest group. A good team ministry has a mixture of single adults and married couples, people interested in athletics and others who may be computer wizards. For example, I've noticed that students will relate to a grandparent on staff in a totally different manner than to a college-age student.

Training & Equipping Your Staff for Ministry

Most people in youth ministry today have a great heart but little training or knowledge. You can greatly increase the effectiveness of your staff by training and equipping them for ministry. Recently I asked the youth staff at my church, "In what areas would you like to be trained?" Here were the major answers:

> How to lead a Bible study
> Instruction on counseling adolescents
> Evangelism
> Time management
> Putting together a retreat
> Speech and communication techniques
> Sex education, drug and alcohol education
> Options for full-time ministry
> Helping build a healthy self-image
> Suicide prevention

Take time to poll your volunteers even if you have only a few, and then develop a yearlong training program to equip them for their important work in youth ministry. I have found that when volunteers are trained, the turnover rate for helpers with the youth group decreases considerably.

Much of the training in youth ministry can be done on your own. This is the method of teaching that Paul suggested to Timothy when he said, "The things you have heard me say in the presence of many witnesses entrust to reliable men who will also be qualified to teach others" (2 Timothy 2:2). In other words, keep ahead of the staff in your reading, tapes, and seminars and you will be able to teach them more than you realize. There are also a variety of effective training methods that you can employ.

Use resource people. No doubt there are men and women in your church and community who could spend an hour or two talking to your staff about their particular expertise. You can use a psychologist, nurse, doctor, school counselor, Young Life leader, college professor, other church staff members, parents, or a youth worker from another church in your area.

Go through books or tapes together. There are many outstanding books and tapes to work through as a staff. Some youth staffs will read a book together every two months and then spend an evening discussing it. The books can be on anything from youth ministry to time management, and the time spent together can be very beneficial. I like to use tapes on youth-ministry subjects and then stop the tape at certain points to discuss key thoughts.

Whatever methods of training you end up using, they will usually prove to be a positive experience of time and input for your staff. Remember, the greatest investment you can give to the lives of the kids in your youth group is to invest time in the lives of the staff.

Recruitment:
Never-Ending Exercise of Faith

I've never met a youth worker who has had enough help! Recruiting volunteers to help in youth ministry is seldom easy, and often at first it seems on the verge of impossible. Because for many of us recruiting is a difficult but necessary part of our youth ministry, we don't seem to tackle the responsibility with much enthusiasm. The answer to successful recruiting is *to have a plan and keep your eyes and ears open*.

Here are a few suggestions.

Know your needs, and list the jobs and responsibilities. In your congregation one person might imagine working with the youth group as serving punch and cookies; another thinks he could prepare an in-depth Bible study each week; another views herself as a chaperon or perhaps a counselor. When you recruit, know what kind of person you are looking for and what job you want him or her to do. For example, if you are looking for a Sunday school teacher to teach the seventh-and-eighth-grade class, then list the responsibilities, time commitments, curriculum possibilities, and accountability structure, and indicate how you will assist the teacher. When people have a better understanding of what they will be doing, they will tend to volunteer more often.

Ask the leadership body of your church or your senior pastor for a list of potential names. Sometimes the elders or your senior pastor can be your greatest help in recruitment. Most often they are in touch with potential leaders in the congregation. Ask for ten minutes in one of their meetings to have them help you brainstorm possible names. Then contact the people they suggested and say, "At our last elders' meeting your name came up as a possible person who would make a great youth sponsor." Instead of rejecting only the youth worker, they now must consider the thought that the leadership body of the church gave you their name.

Have students choose adult sponsors. One of the greatest fears of any adult asked to help with the youth group is "Can I relate? Will the kids like me?" A way of alleviating this fear is to have some of the kids choose a few names of people in the church whom they would like to have as youth sponsors. Then approach the adults by saying that the youth group chose four people to consider working with them next year, and they enthusiastically voted for you. Would you consider working with them? This is a very productive approach to recruiting.

Meet potential recruits in person. It is always more difficult to turn you down in person. Come to your appointment *totally pre-pared*, with a possible job description. If the person is unsure, ask him to think and pray about it for a week, and then you'll get back to him. If he tells you he is too busy this year but might be able to help next year, write the name down and contact the person in a little less than a year.

Be able to handle rejection. One of my good friends is an insurance sales executive. I was telling him of my feelings of

134

rejection when someone whom I ask to volunteer turns me down. His advice was brilliant: "We expect to make a sale two out of ten times. We never know who will buy, but the odds are in our favor that for every ten contacts we make, two will respond favorably to our offer. The secret is to not feel personal rejection but to expect the odds to finally work in your favor." Too many youth workers get bitter when no one is knocking down their door to volunteer their services in youth ministry. My feeling is that if you ask enough people in a thorough manner, you will get positive and long-lasting results.

Look outside your church for potential helpers. Many universities and colleges have internship programs. I've had success with students who are religious studies majors or psychology majors who would love to do an internship for school credit or simply for experience. It can be worth the cost to place an ad for help in the local college newspaper. Sometimes Christian students have moved to your area and have not gotten involved in a church. Your ad in the paper is the opportunity they need to get involved.

One time after we ran a newspaper ad the president of a local InterVarsity chapter responded and volunteered his services. We hired him that summer as an intern. Later, after he became a member of our church, we supported him through his seminary education.

Recruit a variety of personalities and individuals. This is perhaps the most important piece of advice I can give you when it comes to recruiting and staff development. Your kids need a variety of role models. They need to identify with as many different personality and interest types as possible.

Helping Your Staff Get Involved

Too many youth staffs have a few people doing all the work while other volunteers do very little. If you want to see your staff grow spiritually and stay in youth ministry, they must be involved in actual ministry with the kids. Every September at our staff retreat I issue a challenge to all the volunteers. I call it "the hour-and-a-half-a-week challenge." Here is what I ask of them:

> One-hour meeting once a week with one student
> 15 minutes of phone calls
> 15 minutes of notes

We ask our volunteers to take one hour a week with a specific person in the group. Most of the time they do a "growth booklet" Bible study with the students. Through this one hour a week a great friendship and ministry usually begins to take place. Not only is it a positive experience for the young person to have a significant adult take interest in him or her, but it also becomes vitally important to your adult leadership to be used in ministry and to affect the life of a young person in a positive manner. The growthbook study provides a time of spiritual growth and relational ministry.

Next I ask our volunteers for 15 minutes of note-writing per week. You can write three short affirming notes, address them, and mail them in 15 minutes.

The response from the kids is phenomenal, since they rarely receive a note of affirmation from an adult. I sometimes watch kids come up to our staff and offer a hug of appreciation for the thoughtfulness of a note written to them.

The other 15 minutes is reserved for phone calls. Once your leaders get over a common fear of phone calling, they will see that some of their best ministry happens on the phone.

If your staff used a model of ministry similar to the one described above, each person could realistically minister to at least seven kids a week. Your staff will feel a renewed excitement toward their youth ministry involvement. Also, the needs of your group will be reached by a staff who is willing to involve themselves in actual relational ministry.

What's Your Style of Leadership?

A number of years ago I came to a personal crossroads in my youth ministry. As our high school youth group grew, my personal time with the kids shrank. The larger and more active the group became, the less time I had available to do what I loved to do—spend time with high school students. I felt overwhelmed with administrative responsibilities and out of touch with the kids I was supposedly influencing for the kingdom of God.

Then one day during lunch with an old college friend, things came together for me. Tom sold insurance—he was such a good salesman, in fact, that his company wanted him to go into management. It was a great opportunity, but he couldn't decide what to do because the part of his job he loved most was spending time with his clients. The management job was a positive step forward in his career, but he had to ask himself, "Am I sacrificing what I enjoy and what I'm good at in order to build my career?" We came to no decision that day about his own situation, but his dilemma helped me come to some conclusions for my own career.

I had to ask myself the same type of question, translated into youth ministry terms: As the head of our youth staff, should I be in management or sales? Should I supervise our ministry by training and equipping leaders, or should I devote my time to the high schoolers themselves? For the first time in my life I realized that I was kidding myself to think that I could do both effectively in a large youth group setting.

Management or Sales?

One of the most freeing experiences for any of us in youth work is to make the choice between management or sales—and to feel okay about our choice. This doesn't mean that if we choose management we'll never talk with a student, or vice versa. It does mean, however, that we must *define our role* as a youth worker.

My own experience is a case in point. I love working in the trenches with kids. I love contact work on campus and meeting new kids for a soft drink after school. But I eventually realized that I could be *most* effective over the long haul if I shifted to managing and equipping a staff of adult and student leaders to do the work of the ministry. Certain passages of Scripture have had an important influence on my perspective:

> ... to prepare God's people for works of service, so
> that the body of Christ may be built up until we all reach
> unity in the faith and in the knowledge of the Son of God

and become mature, attaining to the whole measure of the fullness of Christ (Ephesians 4:12,13).

The things you have heard me say in the presence of many witnesses entrust to reliable men who will also be qualified to teach others (2 Timothy 2:2).

The time I have invested in leadership has been time invested in more kids' lives, with better long-term results, than I could have achieved on my own. I chose management because I wanted to remain in a large-group setting with continuing growth. If I had placed my emphasis on sales, I would have had to move to a smaller church where a "jack-of-all-trades" model was more feasible.

Learning How to Make Your Choice

As I look back on my decision-making process, I can identify a few principles that helped me work things through. If you're facing a similar decision, consider these insights gained from my experience.

1. *Realistically identify your gifts and interests.* This particular principle was difficult for me because I love working with high school students, and if I had my choice, I would take people over administration any day. Yet I could see that for the best long-term results I needed to focus on my training-and-organizing gifts. I had to see that every time I helped other adults or student leaders to be more effective ministers, they would reach more kids than my one body ever could.

2. *Be aware of your vulnerability to the Peter Principle.* The Peter Principle teaches that most people continue to climb the ladder of success until they reach their level of incompetence. In youth ministry, this happens when people who are excellent with kids (sales) become so successful that they're moved to a supervisory role (management), where they grow increasingly frustrated, incompetent, and unhappy.

I saw this happen when I worked in Young Life during my seminary days. Many of the best "kid people" had been promoted to area directors, where they were inefficient and frustrated. The key is to evaluate your gifts, talents, and desires, and then be true to your calling.

3. *Do what you do best, and hire someone else to do the other work.* This is the advice of Peter Drucker, one of America's best-known business management writers. You may or may not be able to hire someone else, but it's vitally important to find people to fill your gaps.

A good friend of mine was once at a large church with a thriving youth group. As the youth group grew, so did the administrative responsibilities. So he made a wise move. He hired an administrator so he himself could spend most of his time with the kids. My friend was smart enough to realize that administration was not his specialty. He solved the problem by finding someone who had the gift of administration, loved kids, and preferred to work behind the scenes. Their youth group is still thriving.

Management or Sales—It's Still Ministry

Whichever direction you go, whether in "sales" working directly with kids or in a "management" role where you equip others to minister to youth, take enjoyment in the knowledge that youth ministry in any role is a high calling and a high privilege. You're playing an invaluable part in the future of some of God's most special people. That's a product which any salesperson would be proud to sell and a corporation which any manager would consider a privilege to supervise!

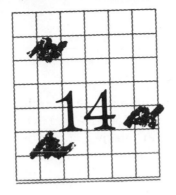

WHAT ABOUT
INTERNS?

Many churches today are using interns as a way to minister more effectively to their young people while at the same time giving these interns practical, on-the-job training. For most of my youth ministry years one of the primary focuses of my ministry has been developing and working with an intern program. I have seen God use an intern program to change the face of a church in a very positive manner.

My first impression of interns was negative. Most of the "student interns" at seminary had a very difficult time. Usually they were given the entire youth program at the church. They were responsible for all the teaching, recruitment, retreats, and whatever else they could get "dumped" on them. Often they had very little support or encouragement from the pastor. The kids were leery of building a relationship with the student intern, because for some groups they had seen four or five interns go through their program within a short timespan. Just when they were finally getting to know the intern, he or she would leave them to move on to bigger and better things.

Many student intern programs are not really intern programs at all. Some are simply a way to get a few extra credits while others become a paid "baby-sitting service." For some churches such a program is a chance to get the problem of finding youth workers off the backs of the leadership and parents.

However, an intern program done right can greatly benefit both the church and the person involved in the internship. A good working definition of an intern is a person who is assisting an experienced youth worker and learning how to properly serve the needs of youth. We must always remember that an intern is "in training."

Supervision Is the Key

The key ingredient to a successful intern program is the *supervisor*. I'm convinced that almost anyone can be fairly successful in youth ministry if he has a supervisor who is willing to invest time and energy in his life. If the supervisor looks at acquiring interns primarily as a way to decrease his work load, he may be mistaken, since the time and input are simply rearranged, with more time being placed in training for interns.

Two very important questions for a supervisor to ask before getting involved in an intern program are: "Am I willing to invest the amount of time it takes to do an internship program right?" "Am I willing to take possibly less time with the kids and put more time into the lives of the interns?" The time commitment is costly and the price is high.

Measuring Effectiveness

A good intern program has accountability built into the program. Since *training* is so important, we must find ways to hold the interns responsible for their job description. For me, one of the most effective ways of keeping my staff accountable is through a weekly staff sheet. At first most interns do not enjoy taking 20 minutes of their time to fill out such a sheet. Eventually, however, they see it as a measurement tool. They appreciate the feedback I give them on their sheet.

The staff sheet is divided into nine areas which provide an

opportunity for the intern to reflect upon and react to his or her week. I use the sheet as an opportunity for discussion and interaction.

1. *Contacts and visitation.* This section gives the intern and myself the ongoing knowledge of who he is spending time with and how much time he is putting into contact work. It is also very helpful if you have more than one intern. You might find out that your interns are spending most of their time with the same kids and that the other kids in your group are not getting much contact time.

2. *Staff contacts.* Since I believe it is very important to make sure the volunteer staff gets time spent with them, I ask my interns (paid staff) to meet with the volunteers and with each other. If the staff-contact section is left blank for a couple of weeks, I challenge the intern to put some time in that direction.

3. *One-on-one (growthbooks).* This is a particular program we do at our church in which we have a one-on-one Bible study with the kids in our group. (This is discussed in greater detail in Chapter 6.) Within the job description of each intern, I have placed his one-on-one growthbook as a strong priority for his or her ministry.

4. *Devotional life.* This might sound like an area that is none of my business as a supervisor. However, I believe that a healthy devotional life with God will make the intern a much more productive minister to the kids. In a very nonthreatening manner, this section keeps me in touch with the interns' devotional life and how I can be of ministry to them. It also challenges me to keep my own priorities straight, because they surely have the right to ask me how I'm doing as well.

5. *Prayer requests.* As supervisor I set aside time each day to pray for the interns. This section helps me to be specific when I pray. They appreciate the care, and I always try to ask about their prayer requests when I see them.

6. *Highlights of the week.* This section gives the interns a chance to evaluate what the highlights of their week were, and it gives me a

better understanding of what is going on in their lives. Many of the highlights deal with the youth ministry, but others deal with outside interests which are really good to be concerned about with them.

7. *Physical health.* Too many churches run their staff into the ground physically. I want to hold our interns accountable to keep their bodies in physical shape. I ask them at the beginning of the year to set personal physical goals and to work on these during the year. A person who is in good physical shape will be able to handle the stress of ministry much more capably. (This also helps develop a priority that could carry on for life.)

8. *Thoughts on ministry.* This is a section for the interns to write whatever they want to or else to leave it blank. Usually they use this space as a time to vent feelings and share thoughts on previous or upcoming events. Many times they will share personal struggles. This section is a *must* in order for good supervision to take place. What your staff might not tell you in person they will write on paper, which then becomes a springboard for good discussion.

9. *Hours (work-related).* I ask the interns to list their hours for each day. I don't usually use this as a means of checking up on lack of time but instead as a way of holding them accountable to take a day off (time away from the church, etc.). If I see a staff sheet with too many hours listed or no day off, I ask why. We can burn out young interns before they ever get started if we don't help them establish a discipline of rest and relaxation.

Meeting with Your Intern

Interns need to meet with their supervisor on a regular basis—if not every week, then at least every other week. This time should be set aside for support and encouragement as well as for training and input. I use our staff sheets as an opportunity for discussion. Too many intern programs fail from lack of input into the life of the intern.

Evaluation

I keep using the word "supervisor" instead of "youth minister." The reason for this is to convey the impression that interns need supervision.

They need you to observe how and what they are doing and then to critique them. Remember, critique doesn't always mean negative comments. Many "supervisors" never take the time to observe and supervise. You must be willing to sit in the middle of the kids and get the feel of how the intern is doing. Sometimes you will want to write down your observations and then debrief later with your intern.

Teaching/Training

Some supervisors think they can stop preparing for meetings when an intern comes along. Actually, an intern needs teaching and training also. *You* are the one to help them in areas such as counseling, Bible study preparation, retreat planning, and all the other aspects of youth ministry. After one of my interns took a youth ministry position on his own he soon called me up to say he had no idea of how to prepare a budget. But that was actually *my* mistake because I never worked through the area of finances in youth ministry with this intern when he was on my staff.

Shepherding

A supervisor must realize that he can greatly minister to the spiritual needs of the intern. For many interns this is the first time they have ever worked seriously in a church. They usually have the sense of awe and wonder and fear that asks, "How could God use a person like me?" You can prevent the interns from burning out. They need your transparent and caring relationship with them. I find that much of my pastoral ministry centers around my intern staff. If I can help keep them spiritually healthy, they in turn will help the students grow in their faith.

Selling Your Intern Program

If you have looked at all the commitments of a supervisor and still feel that you and your church are ready for an intern program, then you must realize that you will probably have to become a salesperson! The most important person you must sell the idea to is your senior pastor. With the senior pastor on your side, you then need to sell the elder board on the idea. In order to do this you must carefully prepare a polished presentation that is well thought out and geared toward the mind of your elders. Most elder boards think not only in spiritual terms but also in dollars and cents, so your presentation must also take finances into consideration.

Do Your Homework

Before you ever present anything to the board, put the idea on paper. Even the quality of typing can be important. Make sure you have a thorough job description written out. List the pros and cons of an intern program. This will let the board see that you have put a great amount of thought into this idea. Discuss the financial cost to the church. I believe that interns should earn a stipend because it will free them up with more time, and the small stipend will help hold them accountable. Within your presentation you will need to discuss the benefits to the intern as well as the benefit to the church. I ask the board to look at an intern ministry as an investment in the future of the Christian church. We have the privilege of training someone in youth ministry who will use his or her training to minister to our kids and then be used by our Lord in the future at our church or somewhere else. We also need to help the elders see the benefits to the church. Stress the idea of more individual attention to the youth and a greater capability of outreach.

When preparing a presentation, it is best to have your senior pastor and a board member help you work on the formal presentation. If they assist you, then most likely you will have their support.

Special Guest Stars: The Interns

Once you have the program going, the best way to keep it going is to put the intern program in front of the congregation often. Let them see the interns in the worship service. Give reports to the governing board on the progress of the program. Encourage the interns to meet and spend time with the elders and staff.

Working with interns can be a great joy, as it has been for me, or it can be an administrative nightmare. Before you take the plunge, make sure you look at all the consequences thoroughly and ask yourself, "Am I willing to watch my ministry and time commitment change?" Almost always the change is for the better.

SAMPLE STAFF SHEET

Name _____ Week of _____

1. Contacts and visitation

2. Staff contacts

3. One-on-one (growthbooks)

4. Devotional life

5. Prayer requests

6. Highlights of the week

7. Physical health

---

8. Thoughts on ministry

9. Hours (work-related)

Friday:

Saturday:

Sunday:

Monday:

Tuesday:

Wednesday:

Thursday:

SAMPLE INTERN JOB DESCRIPTION

I. *Salary and Benefits*

  A. Basic benefits
     Salary will be 500 dollars per month.

  B. Professional expenses
     1. Any out-of-pocket expenses will be reimbursed as long as they are within your approved budget. (If you have any questions, ask before you spend!)
     2. We encourage you to participate in outside educational experiences, and (depending on the budget) we want to help you out as much as possible.
     3. All work-related vehicle expense is tax deductible.
     4. You may purchase from your salary a group health insurance policy. If you do not have a health insurance policy, we strongly recommend it.

  C. Vacation and time off
     1. Paid vacation will be two weeks of a calendar year.
     2. One week paid study leave.
     3. You are required to work 80 hours a month.

II. *Job Responsibilities*

1. Assist in the high school ministry.
2. Direct an area ministry.
3. Assist in Sunday school, retreats, and special events.
4. Develop a growthbook/discipleship ministry with your area ministry.
5. Develop and help train volunteers for your area ministry.
6. Have a contact work ministry in which you are on campus two times a week.
7. Participate in all youth staff meetings (weekly and monthly).
8. Direct one evening meeting a week in your area.
9. Meet on a regular basis with the youth minister.

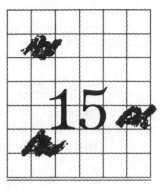

BUILDING SUPPORT WITH YOUR PASTOR, STAFF, AND CHURCH

I remember walking in the front door of our home late on a Monday evening after an explosive elders' meeting where both of my proposals were tabled. I complained to Cathy, "I feel no support from the staff or the elder board. They have no idea what great things are happening in our group. They have no vision for what can take place in our youth ministry." My philosophical (and at times blunt) wife questioned me, "Have you ever told them what's happening? Have you ever taken the time to build relationships with the adults of the church? Jim, do you communicate your desires and dreams with these leaders?"

Did she ever burst my bubble that evening! I was still angry, but her point had come across loud and clear. *If you want to build support with the leadership of the church, you must be willing to invest the time necessary to build relationships and communicate your ideas.* I was the one who lived with my youth ministry program, not they, and I had no right to expect them to join the bandwagon without proper relationships and proper communication.

Battle Stations

Too many youth workers look at their relationship with the

leadership in the church with a them-versus-me attitude. For some workers it is almost a paranoid feeling that the rest of the church is out to get the youth ministry. There are some definite action steps which youth workers can take to develop better relationships with the leadership of the church.

Take the Initiative

The youth worker is often the one who must be willing to initiate the communication and relationships. As you look at all your priorities and time commitments, I suggest that a very important part of your ministry as a whole is taking time with the leadership of the church. Make it a habit to have lunch with each elder in your church at least once a year. During the meeting share your dreams and desires, but also get to know the elder as a person. Ask him about his family and work. Ask him his dreams and desires for the church. Seek his advice in his field of expertise.

I remember a breakfast that Cathy and I had with an elder and his wife. We had a wonderful time of sharing about life. Toward the end of the breakfast he asked, "Jim, what did you want to meet about this morning?" I replied, "We have no agenda. We just wanted to get better acquainted." He smiled and said, "Oh, I was waiting for you to ask for a donation for some youth project." I was sorry he thought the only reason for the youth pastor to get together with a leader was to ask for something. When you take the initiative to meet with the leadership, you are building a foundation of relationships. The leadership will tend to be more supportive because they have a relationship with you.

I believe the same philosophy should go for the staff at your church, including the janitors and secretaries. I see nothing wrong with befriending our coworkers. Regular times together will help you understand the total needs of the church and will help them understand the unique world of youth ministry. Many youth departments have a habit of separating their ministry from the ministries of the church. There is no better witness than a group of diverse ministries striving together in unity.

I especially believe that youth workers should court their senior pastors or supervisors. A regular time together away from the confines of the church office is best. My senior pastor liked to play tennis, so I asked if we might play tennis together. This was the beginning of a stronger relationship as well as a regular time commitment to play tennis. Not only did the weekly tennis match enhance our relationship, but we were able to "talk shop" before, during, and after the match.

If you wait for the leadership of your church to develop a relationship with you, it will probably be a long, quiet wait. People in the church are basically too busy and overcommitted. They will seldom take the initiative to develop a relationship with you. Yet if you take the initiative to get on their calendar, it will be well worth your time and effort.

Unexpressed Expectations

Norm graduated from college and went directly into youth ministry. He had been discipled by one of the leaders in his InterVarsity group at the university for three years. Norm was a gifted youth worker. Although he had never talked about it with the senior pastor, when he applied for the job he expected that they would meet regularly to discuss his job as well as to share their personal lives, as in his discipling experience. It never happened; the pastor was overcommitted. He liked Norm and even enjoyed the time they spent at staff meetings together with the rest of the church staff. The pastor's philosophy of ministry was to hire someone who could do the job and didn't need his input.

The only time he contacted Norm was if there was a problem. Norm was deeply hurt and angry at the pastor for the apparent lack of interest in him and the youth ministry. Yet the pastor never knew that Norm was so frustrated until the day Norm resigned.

Youth workers often rallied to Norm's support because of the insensitive ministry style of the senior pastor, but Norm was as much to blame as the pastor. Norm's expectations were never expressed. Before he ever took the job, he should have had in writing his and the pastor's expectations for supervision. Even after the fact, Norm could have communicated his feelings much more clearly.

Conflict on church staffs, as in any working environment, is normal. Yet in the church we tend to believe that it is unchristian to have a difference of opinion, so we tend to repress our conflict until anger takes over our logical thought process.

Unexpressed expectations are one of the major hindrances in church work. If you want to save a great deal of future misunderstanding, learn to express your thoughts and expectations. Even though the church is the bride of Christ, expectations should be in writing. This saves many hurt feelings in the future.

Get a Job Description

Not long ago I heard that one of this country's finest youth workers had been fired. A slip of morality? A theological difference? Underqualified for the job?

The answer to all the above questions is a resounding "No!" Dave (not his real name) is a veteran youth worker in a growing church in suburban San Francisco. He had been employed by the church for five years. And he's no slouch—a week *after* he was told to activate his resumé, he took almost 200 high schoolers to winter camp. At a training session a year before this incident I had spoken to over 70 adult leaders who were involved in his youth ministry.

When I heard that Dave had been fired, I was stunned. Needless to say, Dave, his wife, and their two children were also stunned. They had absolutely no idea that their job would be terminated. The day before the elder board's six-month review of staff, the senior pastor told Dave that he was excited about their team ministry and that he looked forward to a long-term ministerial relationship together. A day later, armed with the full support of the elder in charge of youth ministry, the senior pastor told Dave that he needed to find a new job because the elders had fired him.

Here are the facts I could discern: Neither the pastor nor any elder had interviewed the students, adult volunteers, two paid interns, or Dave himself. Furthermore, the firing was a complete surprise. Finally, no one ever conducted a review of his work—unless you counted casual pastoral discussions of the church's youth ministry as evaluative reviews.

The church, of course, was up in arms over the fiasco, and even called in denominational representatives to examine what appeared to be blatant irresponsibility of the elders and the senior pastor. Yet this is not an isolated case. I had heard of two other such firings in the same year. What can you do to prevent this travesty from happening to you?

Get Regular Evaluations

First, ask for a performance review every 90 days. A monthly review is common in many businesses, yet most churches conduct no reviews at all. If you take the initiative to sit down with your staff supervisor and an elder every three months (assuming they aren't taking the initiative themselves), you'll be able to better determine what they expect from you. You'll also open up communication lines. Don't expect it to just happen; you'll probably have to set up the performance reviews yourself, months in advance.

Furthermore, ask for your performance review in writing. If there's ever a question about your ministerial performance, you'll have hard evidence of whatever criticism and compliments you've received. As ugly as it seems, church employees are often fired because of hearsay and uninformed hunches. Even if this sounds too formal for your tastes, guard yourself by putting it in writing.

Preventive Defusing

Invite your superiors—senior pastor, immediate supervisor, the entire elder board—to youth events. Since elder boards and pastors often react prematurely and without deliberation on a seeming problem in the youth department, let them see the youth ministry firsthand. In fact, have them participate in some of the group's events in order for them to get a feel for your ministry.

After an elder and his wife spoke to our group about Christian marriage, he was almost ecstatic in his report back to the board about how wonderful the youth group was. Actually, I thought the evening was mediocre at best, but I sure appreciated the compliment.

You can keep church leadership informed by adding them to the youth-group mailing list. Don't assume they know what's going on with the kids; they're busy people with their own priorities. If they get a copy of whatever publicity the kids get, you'll undoubtedly hear interested comments from them about your events.

Ask your superiors to articulate their expectations. Dave's case was definitely a case of unexpressed expectations. Look again at your own job description. Church leaders can forget exactly what you were hired to do, and some pastors conveniently forget that they hired you for youth work and not a host of other jobs. If you don't know your superiors' specific expectations, then you're gambling because you may not be spending your days (and nights) how they expect you to. If you don't have a job description, stop what you're doing and get one immediately.

Take Your Role As a Servant Seriously

One of the challenges among youth ministry professionals is how to realistically cope with the prospect that our status may never be viewed with the respect that we feel our calling merits. David White points out five important principles to keep in mind when building a stronger relationship with other leaders in the church.[1]

1. Focus on the true source of worth for Christians: our relationship with God.
2. Seek ways to serve the staff of the church.
3. Express your support of the pastor explicitly.
4. Take a positive attitude toward accountability.
5. Periodically plan activities which would exhibit an attitude of servanthood by the youth program toward the rest of the church.

The famous comic Rodney Dangerfield's cry "I get no respect!" is also the cry of youth workers. However, perhaps it's time for the youth worker to take a long look at his or her role as a servant. Youth workers who willingly serve the leadership of the church are taking on the philosophy of Jesus and will in the long run have a more productive ministry.

Before You Take the Job

A few years out of seminary, my old seminary support group got together for a weekend retreat. We were spread out all across the country in churches of various denominations and sizes. The common thread was that we were all somehow connected to youth ministry, and we all worked in the church. We spent the majority of the weekend complaining and griping about our senior pastors, the leadership board, and the politics of the church. A couple of the men were extremely disillusioned with church work and were contemplating major career changes. Only a few years earlier we were in school with idealistic thoughts that we would change the world, never giving a thought to the types of conflicts we were now facing in the church.

No one had helped us prepare for the trauma which sometimes takes place within the politics of the church. Listed below is a checklist of items to discuss before you ever take a youth ministry job at a church.

Job Description

1. What will my job description and expectations be?
2. Who is my supervisor?
3. What are the hours expected? (Note days off, nights out, etc.)
4. What is the financial package?
5. Are there other pastoral responsibilities?
6. Will I receive continuing-education time and finances?
7. What is the vacation policy?
8. What are the insurance benefits?
9. What is the personnel review process?
10. What is the overall budget? What is the youth budget?

For Discussion

1. Be aware of personality differences on the staff.
2. Discuss philosophical and theological differences *before* you take the job.
3. Ask to meet with all the staff members, including secretaries and janitors.
4. Meet with the students; ask questions.
5. Attend a worship service.
6. Ask about the leadership's dreams and visions.
7. What would the leadership imagine a healthy youth group looking like?
8. What is the history of the youth ministry? Of the church?

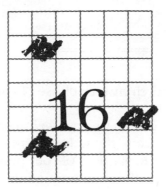

COPING WITH FINANCES

A t the first church in which I interned for youth ministry, the senior pastor asked me for a budget for the year for the youth group. He informed me that the previous year's budget had been 400 dollars. I had been at the church three months and didn't even know I had a budget! I came to the meeting the next week with no plan and suggested that the leadership increase the budget by 10 percent (40 dollars). They immediately okayed my request. The music minister was next; he handed out his plan. It was a three-page summary of what he expected to accomplish, including plans for a special Easter event that he had already put together in September. He asked for a 300 percent increase, and with the same reaction given to my request they granted him his entire budget request! The next day I made an appointment to sit with one of the elders and learn how to prepare a budget. Throughout the years I've usually had to learn the hard way, and I've come to realize that dealing with finances is a larger part of youth ministry than I had ever imagined.

No one ever told me that if I went into the ministry I would spend so much time dealing with money. There have definitely been days in my youth ministry when I felt like a money changer in the temple of the Lord. Between budget proposals, costs of supplies and curriculum, camp fees, facility rentals, and my own financial pressures from choosing a ministry career, there are times when I feel as if business and finance courses would have been more helpful than the church history classes I had to take in order to graduate from seminary.

Even within the church we have well-meaning Christians who call money anything from "the seductive mistress" to "the blessing of God's prosperity." Regardless of your personal view of money, the fact remains that if you choose to be involved with youth ministry, you will need to learn how to cope with finances.

Did Someone Say Budget?

Paul Borthwick has raised four excellent questions to look at as you prepare a youth ministry budget.[1]

1. *What is the budget history of the church?* It is important to see past budgets as well as find out who makes the final decisions. I usually ask the decision-makers to help me write out my budget.

2. *How much am I willing to plan ahead?* When you plan ahead you will have a much better idea of your financial need. The people making the financial decisions in your church are very accustomed to making financial decisions in their own work two or three years ahead of time.

3. *Are there alternative means of financing?* The church should not be stuck paying for everything. Most youth events can be paid for by the students themselves and/or their parents. Plan on giving scholarships for other events, and the more low-cost or no-cost activities the better. Borthwick makes a good point when he says, "Good budget planning does not require that we make the students pay for everything, but students must be allowed to 'own' their own program by being involved financially."[2]

4. *Does the budget represent actual need?* One of the mistakes that youth workers make is that they move from one extreme to the other. They either budget much lower than their real need or else propose a budget that looks like they took lessons from a government bureaucrat. We can never forget that the budget represents stewardship of God's money. We are ultimately accountable to God for the way we spend *His* money. A budget must be prepared with integrity.

When dealing with budgets, I believe we must learn to prepare them in much the same way as the elders and leadership of our church prepare their own budgets at their work. This means that the budget should be well researched and documented. The extra time you take to make sure the budget package is typed attractively will make a difference. People are much easier on the purse strings if the person requesting funds has done his homework.

On the following pages is a budget from a large youth ministry where I was youth pastor. It will give you an idea of what categories to budget as you look at your program. A suggestion I would make is to acquire the youth ministry budgets of several churches of your particular size in various denominations. This will give you a way to compare your budget. It can also be helpful to show your senior pastor and leadership other budgets if yours is unusually small. Remember that each church does its budget a little differently; the budget below is merely one example.

SAMPLE YOUTH DEPARTMENT BUDGET

Printing	Junior high	$ 1,000.00
	High school	1,000.00
	College	1,000.00
		3,000.00
Postage & shipping	Junior high	800.00
	High school	1,000.00
	College	800.00
		2,600.00
Staff leadership, curriculum, subscriptions	Junior high	800.00
	High school	1,250.00
	College	600.00
		2,650.00
Facility rental	Junior high	500.00
	High school	750.00
	College	400.00
		1,650.00

Travel	Junior high	600.00
	High school	600.00
	College	600.00
		1,800.00
Conferences (staff leadership)	Junior high	800.00
	High school	1,200.00
	College	800.00
		2,800.00
Other	Junior high	500.00
	High school	500.00
	College	500.00
		1,500.00
Supplies & materials	Junior high	2,200.00
	High school	3,800.00
	College	2,200.00
		8,200.00
Meals & entertainment	Junior high	1,000.00
	High school	1,000.00
	College	1,000.00
		3,000.00
Outreach & evangelism	Junior high	1,500.00
	High school	3,000.00
	College	1,500.00
		6,000.00
Camps & scholarships	Junior high	1,000.00
	High school	2,000.00
	College	1,000.00
		4,000.00
Mission	Junior high	
	High school	8,500.00
	College	

162

Transportation	Junior high	1,000.00
	High school	1,000.00
	College	1,000.00
		3,000.00
	Subtotal	$48,700.00

Salaries (The youth pastor's salary is normally included in a general administrative budget. Other youth workers' salaries are part of this youth department budget. Due to the many variables that affect salary ranges, dollar amounts are not given in this sample budget.)

Junior high pastor	$ _____	Senior high intern	$ _____
High school pastor	$ _____	Senior high intern	$ _____
College-age pastor	$ _____	Senior high intern	$ _____
College-age intern	$ _____	Senior high intern	$ _____
Junior high intern	$ _____	Senior high intern	$ _____
Junior high intern	$ _____		

Total Youth Ministries Budget .... =========

Fund-Raising: The Universal Youth Event

A few years ago I was asked to address a denomination's youth worker convention. After my speech to the group they asked if I would do a workshop on fund-raising. I agreed to it, expecting only a few people to attend the workshop. When I finished my general session, the person in charge told me I would be doing my workshop "here in the ballroom."

"Why?" I asked. She replied, "You'll have the biggest workshop." As I looked at the printed agenda all the other workshops looked more interesting and important than mine. I opened my talk on fund-raising really intrigued by the number of people present in the room. I asked, "Why are you all here?" One man in the back yelled, "Fund-raising is one of the main events of our ministry." Everyone nodded in agreement.

Most youth groups must raise funds, and most youth workers have a strong dislike for fund-raising. "It comes with the territory" and "It's a necessary evil" are replies I hear when talking about fund-raising.

Have a Plan

One of the adult sponsors reminds you, "It's getting close to Valentine's Day, and we *always* have our winter fund-raiser." This is your first year on the job, and you've never heard of the winter fund-raiser. But you go ahead and make the arrangements because you won't want to break tradition and because your senior pastor also reminded you of the need for the annual winter fund-raiser.

Unfortunately, this is the case for too many youth groups in the country. There is no plan; it's just tradition. One youth worker for a large church told me he had a very large budget; the only problem was that he had to raise it all through fund-raisers. I asked him if any other department in the church had the same budget arrangement, and he quietly shook his head no. The only reason to do a fund-raiser is if there is a specific plan for which you need funds and there is no better way to get the necessary funding.

Have a Purpose

Most fund-raisers are self-centered and self-propagating. What are we teaching our kids when we ask them to raise funds for *their* annual Valentine's Day party? Many youth ministries are moving away from raising money for self and toward raising money for worthy mission projects. Not only are they raising money for others but even their fund-raising event serves a purpose. One youth group in Illinois raises thousands of dollars a year for the needy of their community by having the City of Chicago hire them to pick up trash in certain sections of the city every two months. They in turn donate the money to important shelters for the homeless in the city. The kids in my group put together a 10K Run for Hungry Children that has become a yearly community tradition. All the money raised goes to meet the needs of hungry children in the world. I've seen that as we raise funds with a selfless purpose the kids become more motivated.

Have Sponsors Involved

If people in your church are willing to sponsor your students on a mission trip, then make sure the sponsors get an update before you leave on the trip and while you are on the trip, as well as a report after the trip. This keeps them involved with you and lets them see that their money was spent on a very worthwhile project. Here's a method to accomplish this goal.

1. The week you receive a donation, have one of the students write a thank-you note to the church family.
2. The week before you leave on the trip, write a page update yourself and a list of prayer requests.
3. Reserve one night on your trip for the students to write postcards to all the sponsors. Every sponsor should receive at least one postcard.
4. After the trip the sponsors should be invited for a celebration meal and program. This will give the young people an opportunity to share their special experiences and to give the sponsors another word of thanks. Incidentally, these sponsors will be the prime candidates for next year's fundraiser.

What About Our Own Finances?

I am definitely not a financial planner. In fact, Cathy handles our checkbook at home because she does a better job at it than I do. However, there are a few principles we've chosen to live by that I would like to pass on to you.

1. *Develop a budget.* No one chooses youth ministry as a career because of the exceptionally high salary that he or she receives. So write out a budget and live within the budget. One of the greatest areas of stress in ministry centers around money or lack of it. A well-put-together budget will help you make wise decisions about your finances.

2. *Prevent anger and bitterness.* Mike came to me filled with rage because he just realized that three months after taking his intern position he was making less than the minimum wage. It was

a bad financial situation, but Mike knew what he was getting into before he took the position. He was paid for 15 hours a week, but he seldom worked under 40 hours. The extra time was his choice. As his supervisor, I continually challenged him to put less time in at the church. Mike's bitterness and resentment got in the way of his ministry.

If you are married, make sure your spouse understands exactly what the financial situation is, and do not take the position if you believe that either one of you will be bitter about it in the future.

3. *Don't be afraid to talk about money in the church.* For some reason many of us believe that because the church is a Christian institution we should not bring up our financial needs there. As a result we don't allow the church to give us the financial support we need and deserve. I've learned that if I don't bring up the subject, usually no one else in the church will look out for my financial needs.

My friend Judy candidated at a Presbyterian church in Denver. After two visits and a really good feeling about her new potential position, she was offered the job. She called the church back and said, "I have some good news and some bad news. The good news is that I feel God wants me to be at Central Presbyterian Church." They asked hesitantly, "What's the bad news?" She replied, "I don't feel that God is calling me to the salary you offered." They renegotiated the salary, and Judy moved to Denver.

4. *Have the church pay for legitimate expenses.* I shared an idea with my senior pastor that Cathy and I wanted to start having five kids every other week come over to our home for dinner. He thought it was a great ministry idea. He clearly saw it as a ministry of my job. I then asked for the funds to pay for those "ministry meals." It took him a lot longer to agree to this request. The church organization you work for is responsible for your legitimate expenses. Make sure that you get prior approval before spending the money or else you may be disappointed.

5. *Seek a wise tax consultant.* You will want to find a person knowledgeable in church work to help you with your taxes. Many youth workers have found out much too late about the tax benefits

of working in the church. There are specific benefits and tax credits that you may receive from your work with young people.

6. *Make your own giving a priority.* How you handle your finances is a role model to the people you work with in the church. This may sound overly simplistic, but most of the people I know who make Christian giving a high priority in their lives have a much better handle on their finances than other people do. How you handle your finances and your financial stewardship plays an important role in how you carry out your Christian commitment as a whole.

LIGHTING
THE CREATIVE SPARK

PRINCIPLES FOR STRATEGIC PROGRAMMING

I have been in too many seminars where the "successful" youth minister comes in to share his or her new programming technique to bring hundreds of kids to my youth group. I usually try the technique and then watch it flop. Maybe I didn't take good enough notes—what ingredient did I miss in this technique?

We always seem to be looking for the quick fix—some technique or program that will give us the perfect youth group. If you read this chapter looking for some such program, you will be disappointed. Programs that I used in one church have failed miserably in my next youth group. My focus in this chapter is on *principles for strategic programming*. Our natural tendency is to put the cart before the horse when it comes to programming.

Goals for Programming

Most youth ministries have very few goals for programming. The average youth worker plans programs anywhere from three days to one hour before the youth group meeting, with little attention given to content. This style of programming produces few measurable results. Unfortunately, such "maintenance-oriented" youth ministry has no continuity, and the programs are often inconsistent and repetitive.

Develop a goal-centered strategy. Mike Yaconelli told a group of youth workers studying at our National Institute of Youth Ministry, "One of the common characteristics in youth work is no continuity of program. I find too many youth groups with no plan, no sense of direction. They have no long-term or short-term goals. There is no method of evaluation and concern for the whole."[1]

When I arrived at my new church in 1980 we had six ninth-graders attending a high school Bible study. I met with two of the students, my wife, a volunteer, and an elder from our congregation to make plans for our youth group. We spent the first hour brainstorming content topics that we hoped these ninth-graders would learn through their entire high school years. We asked the question "What do we want them to know when they graduate from high school?" We came up with ideas and subjects that I would have never thought about myself, ranging from love/sex/dating to doctrine. Many of the topics were repetitive, but in brainstorming anything goes. When we finished we began to take these topics and put them into our four-year plan. Many of the important topics were repeated each year. None of the topics went for longer than six weeks.

I can't tell you that after this one evening we followed our four-year outline perfectly. However, those students received a broader topic presentation than my previous youth group because we had taken the time to list those content needs which we thought to be important.

A number of positive results happened because of this one evening of planning. We planned our content far enough in advance to give us the time to do research on good programs for a certain topic. For example, if Katie knew in September that she would be responsible for "Missions Month" in March, she could put together a higher-quality program. In September we asked a psychologist in our church to speak on sexuality in May. He would have been unavailable had we waited until April before asking him.

Planning content in advance helps you see the long-term plan. You don't have to worry about giving the kids too much too quickly. When you plan in advance you give the parents a better view of what you will be teaching, and even the students will begin to look forward to certain upcoming series. Should you decide to leave your church, the next person has a much better idea of what the kids have already learned and the direction you were planning to take them. Even if the new person chooses to change the program, he will have a better handle on what has already taken place.

Make events creative. This same idea of planning applies for youth group events. If you plan events a year in advance you will have the opportunity to plan better events with a broader base of help. There is no reason why the February roller skating party can't have a date on the calendar in September. If the party is planned at the last minute you have to take most of the responsibility, but given enough time most of the preparation can be done by students or adults who normally do not get as involved. I'm not saying that every element of each event must be planned out in detail months ahead of time; my suggestion is to have a date and someone in charge of the event far enough in advance to give ample time to do high-quality planning. Someone once told me, "When you fail to plan, you plan to fail." Planning in advance frees you to be more involved in the relational aspect of the event than in the logistical aspect.

Create a positive atmosphere. Programs rise and fall around the aspect of atmosphere. Most youth group meetings take place in sterile church rooms, with uncomfortable chairs lined in a row to give the feel of school.

When you are planning a program, take into consideration the size of the room, the seating arrangements, and the location of the meeting. If the room is too large, the seats are not comfortable, or the location of the room is next to the choir-rehearsal room, then you already have three strikes against you.

The mood of the program should be upbeat and lively. It's best to create an easygoing atmosphere which is very friendly. In order to have successful programs with adolescents you will need to be spontaneous and extremely flexible.

A very important principle in youth ministry programming is that *it is always better to go too short than too long.* My preference is to keep the kids asking for more rather than asking, "When is this going to end?" The attention span of the average teenager is

173

approximately ten minutes. This means that we need to keep the pace moving, change experiences regularly, and keep the meeting short.

I believe that the most important part of the youth group meeting is often the interaction that takes place after the program is over. Whenever possible, serve refreshments to keep the kids available for discussion and interaction. If you stop the meeting a little early, this will provide a greater amount of time for interaction before the parents come to pick up their kids. It may be necessary to remind your adult volunteers that the program includes not only the meeting itself but also the interaction time before and after the meeting. This is where the best ministry takes place.

The important transition from junior high to senior high is one of the most important yet frustrating parts of any youth ministry program. When the day comes each year in which the graduating junior highers move into the high school group, I experience two very different emotions. My first reaction is excitement. I look forward to new faces, extra energy, fresh enthusiasm, and a new group to laugh at my old jokes.

My other emotion is more subtle, yet always very present. It is almost a feeling of despair. I ask myself every year how many of these new high schoolers will slip through the cracks of our group and never make the transition. In my years of youth ministry I can think of what seems hundreds of kids who were excited about their faith in junior high but never really became an active participant in the high school group and slipped out of the church altogether by their late high school years.

In the past couple of years I've tried to implement some ideas to help make the transition from junior high to senior high a little easier.

Here are a few ideas that might help.

Have a few junior high sponsors "graduate" with the group. This fall Heidi, one of our women junior high youth sponsors, graduated to the high school group. We've noticed that many of the junior high girls have commented how great it is to have a sponsor they have known from their junior high days. Heidi will be the consistency which some of the kids need. The difficult task of the high school youth worker is to make sure he is filtering high-quality sponsors back to the junior high group as well.

Build a tradition of a positive freshman leadership summer experience. Every summer just before school is to begin our adult leadership team and our student leadership core plan a weekend water ski trip for the new freshman. We keep the price extremely low so that money isn't an excuse. We plan a year in advance so parents won't make vacation plans. We let the student leaders put on the program, and the entire weekend is to give the freshman the opportunity to get to know the leadership in our group. We place a big emphasis on building relationships and a small emphasis on program.

Develop an "adopt-a-freshman" ministry in your high school youth group. Your leadership kids can take responsibility for one or more of the incoming freshmen. Their job is to make the newcomer feel welcome and needed. The older student leaders should be responsible for making a weekly contact (by telephone or at school), finding a ride if needed, sitting by the freshman at meetings, and generally helping the freshman feel socialized into the mainstream of the youth group. We have a senior in our group who has made it her ministry to provide transportation to a whole group of freshman girls not only to church functions but to school events and weekend outings as well. She has become a big sister and a positive role model for her little group of "adopted freshmen."

Include high school leaders on a few of the key junior high retreats and outings. This summer one of our high school interns, Bart, attended a couple of junior high events. After his first outing with the group he told me the kids were asking questions about the high school group and looking forward to the next time they could see him. You might want to have some of your high school adult leaders speak at one of the junior high retreats. This gives the high school ministry good exposure and can sometimes help the junior high leadership to concentrate on relational ministry rather than on program. I'm aware of one church where the senior high student leaders and adults cook and serve the meals on the junior high winter retreat. They also turn it into a mini-leadership-retreat for the high school group.

The same church has the high school youth minister teach the eighth-grade Sunday school class the summer before these kids make the transition to the high school department.

Get freshmen involved immediately. I don't mean to oversimplify this point, but I believe that *kids who stay in the church are involved, and kids who leave the church in high school leave because they find something else to do.* I've had high school youth leaders tell me they don't let their kids get involved in leadership or much of anything until they are sophomores. I think that is a tragedy. The younger the kids become involved and socialized into the group, the better the foundation for keeping them in the fellowship and serving the Lord.

High school youth workers need to realize the importance of the transition from junior high to senior high for the people coming into their group. We need to be aware of all the "new experiences" coming into the freshman life.

Some of these experiences come in the form of a first job or even a more serious look at boyfriend/girlfriend relationships. The young high schooler is also dealing with changes in his mental, psychological, and spiritual development.

The reason I remain in high school ministry is because with all these new experiences high schoolers are making major decisions that will affect the rest of their lives. Your part in their decisions and in their transition to high school makes you a very important person in their life.

Content Topics

These content topics were done at a brainstorming session with adults and students. The list is not exhaustive, but it provides representative ideas for you to expand upon.

Sex
Fasting
Holy Spirit
Disciples
Temptation
Guilt
Worry/depression
Temper
Tongue
Satan
Fruit of the Spirit
Doubt
Prayer
Worship
Sin
Introduction to the
New Testament
Mission
Other faiths
Parent/child rela-
tionships
Dating
Witnessing
Authority, govern-
ment
Servanthood
Prejudice
Self-acceptance
Nuclear power
Relationships
Materialism
Peer pressure
Sermon on the
Mount

Lord, make my
life count
How to study the
Bible
Books of the Bible
Lifestyle assessment
Church
Ethics
Abortion
Death and dying
Euthanasia
Divorce
Pacifism
Stewardship
Basics of the faith
Faith
Love
Obedience
Spiritual gifts
Rock music
Drugs
Spiritual battles
Revelation
Genesis
God's faithful promises
Love or infatuation
Walking in the light
Who's who in the Bible
Communication skills
Family
Life of Christ
Christian apologetics
Perseverance
Stress

Forgiveness
Walk your talk
Gossip
Community
Career
Evolution
Philosophy
End times
Body life
Heaven
Introduction to the
Old Testament
Drinking
Tough questions
Law
Commandments
Paul's missionary
   journeys

Psalms
Proverbs
Prophecy
Current events
Environmental respon-
   sibilities
Balanced lifestyle
Discipline
Christian vocations
Homosexuality
Leisure time
Body as God's temple
Preparing for college
Ministry/calling
Assurance of salvation
Cost of commitment
Worship
Fellowship
Humility

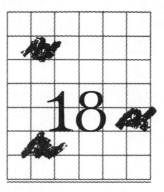

CREATIVE
TEACHING

M ost people have a dominant teaching and learning style that affects their teaching ministry in more ways than they may realize. Your style of teaching greatly determines your impact on the people you are teaching. Studies in the field of education show that there are four different learning styles which are most comfortable for people. These styles include: *innovative* (feeling), *analytic* (watching and listening), *common sense* (thinking), and *dynamic learner* (doing).[1]

Styles of Teaching

If you are going to teach, you will want to understand each of these styles and which one style you feel most comfortable with or tend to use the most.

Innovative (Feeling)

These people like to learn from specific experiences. They relate to people easily and are usually very relational. They love small groups and the opportunity to share ideas. Innovative people tend to be sensitive to feelings and to other people. They can be extremely imaginative and usually function best in social settings.

They need to feel a part of the group, and unless they are accepted among friends, their learning may be inhibited.

Analytic (Watching and Listening)

Analytic learners are listeners. They make careful observations before making a judgment. These people like to view things from different perspectives and are always looking for the deeper meaning of things. They seek facts and ask what the experts think, and their strength is in creating concepts and models.

Common Sense (Thinking)

Common-sense learners look for logical analysis of ideas. They are excited about systematic planning and act only upon an intellectual understanding of the situation. They are very practical-minded; usually they want to know how things work and if they relate to real life. They are the kids in your youth group who ask questions such as "Is this story practical?" and "How does that work?" Since I'm not a common-sense learner, I sometimes get perturbed when this style of learner asks me, "What does that illustration have to do with your point?"

Dynamic Learner (Doing)

Dynamic learners do not lead a dull life; they influence people and events through *action*. Dynamic learners have the ability to get things done and are not afraid to take a risk. You'll find that they prefer the trial-and-error method, which sometimes can come across as being pushy. Their favorite question is, "What can this become?" I once asked a dynamic learner on my staff, "What are the theological implications of the project you want to do?" His answer: "Who cares? It needs to get done!"

Which learning style tends to be your dominant style? Christian educator Marlene LeFever believes that for a brief overview you can choose one of these four statements and usually discover your dominant learning style:

1. As I was talking with my friends, I came up with some new ideas (innovative).

2. I read several experts and came up with a conclusion (analytic).
3. I experimented with something I heard about, then kept what worked and threw out what didn't work (common sense).
4. I put myself into a challenging situation and learned as I went along (dynamic).

Although all people are strong in one style, no learning style is better than any other. As far as educators can tell, each style has the same number of geniuses and the same number of people in general.

What are the implications for teaching? We tend to teach in our dominant style. If we are not careful, we will risk the chance of losing kids who are least like us in learning styles. Therefore we must vary our method of teaching. We must constantly be asking the question, "Is my teaching meeting the needs of *all* the kids in my group?"

My dominant learning and teaching style is innovative; I'm a feeling person. A few years ago I received this letter from three seniors in our group who definitely had different learning styles from mine.

Dear Jim,

We love you. We think you are doing a great job. But . . . we think you should teach on apologetics and doctrine. You never tell us what you believe in a systematic way. None of our weekly Bible studies go deep enough. How about an inductive Bible study for the more serious-minded? We hope this doesn't hurt your feelings, but many of us in the group want to study the meat of the Word. We are tired of small groups and "experiential learning." Don't get us wrong; we love the group. We just want more from it.

Love in Christ,

Dave, John & Chris

I thought I *was* giving them the "meat of the Word." In reality,

I needed to vary my teaching methods to include those young disciples. People tend to learn best in their own style.

Factors in Learning

Creativity

You can be more creative than you are right now. Creativity does not necessarily mean "wild and crazy." It means using your *imagination* to *risk* trying a learning experience that you've never tried before. Sometimes being creative takes less time than you have already been using to plan a Bible study, since you can use someone else's ideas.

Wayne Rice, one of the founders of Youth Specialties, once told me, "The essence of creativity is the ability to copy." I first laughed, then realized the profound truth of his statement. He wasn't talking about plagiarism; he was simply saying that we learn best from others who have tried things before us. My first sermon was a *copy* of structure, gestures, and even much of the content from my pastor. When I tried to learn how to play the guitar, I *copied* the way my teacher held his fingers on the strings, and I strummed exactly like he did. To be creative does not mean that we can't use other people's ideas.

Creativity requires exposure to new and innovative ideas. If you want to be a great teacher you'll need to venture out beyond your own dimension and comfort zone. You'll need to take educational classes or seminars from people you may not totally agree with. One of the most effective creative exposures for us comes in the area of brainstorming. I love getting together with other youth workers and sharing our favorite ideas. Sometimes putting a few heads together can result in a totally new creative event. If you are not willing to expose your mind to new and creative methods of teaching, you will not likely have innovative teaching times.

Creativity also requires time alone. I'm afraid that many people seldom come up with creative ideas because they never take quiet times to simply think and let their thoughts flow on creative teaching methods. All of the most creative people I know take time to be alone. I know people who walk on the beach, sit in the bathtub, hike mountains, and lounge in a park—all for the same reason: to relax and come up with fresh, creative ideas. Our fast-paced society has led us to believe that solitude is wasted time. But I believe that if you are not taking time to be alone to think, your creativity will dry up very quickly.

Freshness

There was a story circulating about a preacher who every Sunday morning had the children of the church come forward for the weekly "children's sermon." One Sunday he asked the children, "What has a gray bushy tail, stores acorns for the winter, and climbs trees?" After a long pause one of the children blurted out, "I know the answer is supposed to be Jesus, but it sounds like a squirrel to me." Sometimes we are simply too predictable in the church when it comes to Christian education!

The Teacher

By far most of the people working with kids in the church are the unsung heroes, the lay volunteers. Many times I've met with people who tremble at the thought of creative teaching. The truth is that you don't need a college major in education or need to be a great communicator in order to have an effective teaching ministry. You are the most important ingredient of effective learning. More than anything else, kids need to see that you love them and are willing to spend time with them. The relational aspect of ministry far outweighs the theoretical or technical side. The greatest secret of effective teaching is to spend time with your audience and get to know them as real people, and to allow them to get acquainted with you as well.

Experience

We learn best by experiential learning. I am grateful for Edgar Dale's "cone of experiential learning" in helping me realize how important it is to get people to experience the work of Christ rather than to simply create listening spectators. Dale's cone of experiential learning states that the average person only retains 5 to 10 percent when he or she must learn through either verbal or written teaching styles. Yet the church has continued to put Christian education's emphasis on lecture reading. Dale's thesis is that the more *involvement* there is in learning the more learning will take place. When people *experience* something they will retain over 80 percent of the content.

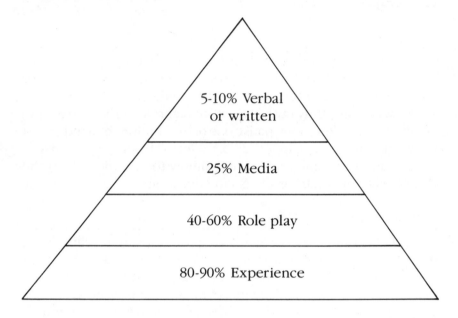

Guided Discovery

One of secular education's favorite terms is *guided discovery.* Kids learn best when their learning is self-appropriated and self-discovered. Motivation plays a big factor in discovery. We must continually evaluate our learning experiences by asking the question "Am I motivating my young people to *want* to learn?" One of the main goals of a youth worker should be to create a desire for spiritual growth and knowledge.

Simplicity

We need to stay away from learning experiences that are not clear and practical. The most effective communication style is to *keep it simple.*

In our teaching it is imperative to provide an opportunity to respond. Sometimes when I must lecture I hand out a piece of paper with these three statements:

React (I felt . . .)
Fact (I learned . . .)
Act (I will do . . .)

This gives the listener an opportunity to respond and interact with what he or she is hearing from the lecturer.

Creative Teaching Strategies

Keeping in mind the different learning styles as well as the need for a variety of teaching strategies, I've listed below a number of possible teaching strategies that work well. As you look at the various possibilities, take the risk of trying a new style in your teaching ministry.

Role-Play

Role-playing is pretending to be someone else, and in so doing you begin to understand a little more of what it is like to be that person. You can role-play stories in Scripture, and you can role-play issues in the Christian faith. This strategy helps students get into the subject in an enjoyable and nonthreatening way. The discussion after role-play is often very lively.

I've seen Bible stories come alive when role-played. We recently used the story of Mary telling Joseph that she was with child (Matthew 1:18-25). The beauty, sacredness, and humanity of the situation became so much more clear as the kids read between the lines and caused Mary and Joseph to have an argument. At first I was offended, but then I realized that Joseph *was* going to quietly divorce Mary until he was paid a visit by an angel of the Lord. The story will never be the same for any of us.

Simulation Games

A simulation game is a game or experience that is meant to bring home a point. No one ever said learning could not be fun. A simulation game tries, in one form or another, to reproduce some aspect of reality so that the students will understand the point better.

I was speaking at a youth camp where lunch became a simulation game. All the tables looked the same, but at each table was the name of a country. The kids who sat at the table for the United States had as much food as they wanted, along with their choice of desserts. The table next to them was from Ethiopia, and they were given two spoonfuls of rice. At first the group thought it was funny; then they became deeply resentful and angered. Simulation games are a good illustration of experiential learning.

The Significant Event

Despite what some Christian educators say, I firmly believe that the mountaintop experience or significant memorable event is an excellent learning experience. The campfire on the last night of camp is usually what we remember best years later. In the Old Testament the parents of our faith had significant events with God, built an altar, and continued to remember their encounter with God for the rest of their life. I believe we should periodically create significant memorable experiences. I know of a youth worker who invited a prostitute to speak to his group. She was not a "reformed prostitute" but a practicing prostitute. She was not an exceptional speaker, but her story of sexual abuse, drug addiction, and running away motivated the kids to begin a ministry to runaways and prostitutes in their city.

Case Studies

"Case study is bringing a chunk of reality into the classroom."[2] One of the best discussion starters and group learning experiences is using a case study as a teaching technique. University and graduate schools, psychology projects, and the business world all use case studies. When you study a real, live situation with a little tension in the story, this brings out excellent response and discussion.

You can purchase case studies already written or you can write your own. When you write your own case study, keep in mind that the kids should never be able to figure out who the person is (in case it is an embarrassing story). When you have finished writing a case study, write out important discussion questions and relevant Scriptures to help the students work through the case study.

The following is a case study written to help students deal with the area of conflict in the church.

The Mission Debate

There was a major debate going on in the youth group. The question was raised, "What should the church do with the 250,000-dollar gift from a multimillionaire who had recently died?" The elders of the church had already decided to enlarge the sanctuary to meet the pressing need for more room to accommodate the growing numbers attending the Sunday morning worship.

Many of the youth group members agreed. They thought the large sum of money was God's gift to the church and a sign to enlarge their building. After all, the more people who came to church, the more people would be helped. In the long run the enlarged sanctuary would have a very positive impact on the community and eventually the world.

On the other hand, an equal number of the youth group were upset that the money was not going to relieve the life-threatening hunger and shelter needs in Africa. Their reasoning was as impressive as that of the group for enlarging the sanctuary. They kept asking, "What would Jesus do with the money? Would He build a nicer sanctuary or save people's lives?" They cited Bible verses stating the Christian mandate to minister to the poor and oppressed of our world.

The debate was getting intense and the feelings in the room were getting explosive. Both sides were emotional. In fact some young people from both sides were even crying when they pleaded for their position.

Finally the youth pastor stepped in and closed the meeting for the night. Everyone wanted to know his opinion, but he didn't tell them. The next day his senior pastor, four elders, and eight parents contacted him to give him their opinion of the youth group meeting.

1. Is this a subject that should have been brought up in the youth group? Why or why not?
2. If you were the youth pastor, would you have told the group your opinion?

3. Which side would you have been on in this debate?
4. Do you think there was a right and a wrong answer on this subject?
5. What biblical guidelines can you find for handling conflicts?[3]

Inductive Bible Study

A vital part of good teaching is giving students the tools to learn for themselves. Unfortunately, most youth groups seldom give the opportunity to learn *how* to study the Bible. The inductive method is a simple tool to help students discover a greater appreciation of Bible study. The inductive Bible study shown below is a sample of what I have used with my own ministry. At the top of the sheet fill in the Scripture you want to study, and don't forget to work through the application section.

INDUCTIVE BIBLE STUDY

Scripture: _____

1. Who?
    • What persons are involved in the verse?
    • Who wrote it?
    • Who is it written to or about?
    • Who does it refer to or mention?

2. What?
    • What is taking place?
    • What words are repeated, omitted, or emphasized?
    • What actions should be taken?
    • What can I learn about God, Christ, sin, redemption, or man?

3. Where?
    • Where is it happening?
    • What places are referred to?

4. When?
    • What time of day, year, etc.?

• Look at the timing of a particular event.

5. Why?
   • Are there reasons given for actions to be taken?
   • Are there consequences mentioned?

6. How?
   • Does it state how something is to be done?
   • Does it state how something was done?

7. Application
   • So what?
   • How does this passage apply to my life?

Creative Expression

Rarely do we in the church give kids the opportunity to use their artistic expression in Christian education. Many kids need the opportunity to be creative and to express their ideas and learning through the arts. Poetry, creative dance, art, and drama are all very important ingredients for many kids to express their faith. And of course music is another important ingredient in giving kids the opportunity to express their faith. Look for opportunities to allow students in your group to express their faith creatively.

Look for kids in your group who will write poetry for your newsletter. Many girls who take creative dance at school may want to perform for the group with an interpretive dance to a Christian song. Some of the kids excited about drama can not only perform dramatic productions but may want to write their own dramas.

Storytelling

Children grow up reading and listening to stories. They love stories. Yet somewhere around junior high age, storytelling goes out of style. This is very unfortunate, because some of the best learning takes place through storytelling, illustrations, and object lessons.

The great preachers of our time are great storytellers. Jesus used parables more often than any other method we have recorded in Scripture. One of the secrets of good teaching is collecting as many good story resources as possible. Always be on the lookout for good stories, illustrations from life, and object lessons. People tend to remember the story long after they have forgotten other sections of a message.

Field Trips

On-site learning can be one of the greatest learning experiences. I recently asked a group of youth workers if they had ever been on a field trip when in elementary school. Most had been on some type of field trip. As they shared their experiences, I also asked them what else they remembered learning that year in school. Most could remember small details of the field trip but couldn't remember major details of the school year.

On-site learning can be something as simple as a field trip to a hospital, rescue mission, or a cemetery. You can be creative and visit the tallest building in your city or the largest mountain in your area. When you are at the top looking down, read the temptations of Jesus described in Matthew 4. Let the kids feel the temptation when Satan said to Jesus, "All this [that you can see] I will give you if you will bow down and worship me." Your role in a field trip is to create a memorable learning experience. One of the most memorable field trip experiences for me was visiting a funeral home as a high school student. It was scary, but it helped me talk to my leader about my fear of death.

Media

A very influential person in my life once said, "When you preach, have the Bible in one hand and the newspaper in the other." He wasn't demeaning the infallibility of the Word of God; rather, he was saying, "Keep it relevant." The use of good creative media is no longer an option in Christian education; it's a necessity. Fortunately, today there are excellent films with a powerful message to young people. The two rules to keep in mind whenever using films are: 1) Always preview the film, and 2) always have a discussion after the film. Videos have also become an excellent learning opportunity.

Music is another excellent tool for Christian education. Since students are tuned in to music, play a song. When you play the song, make sure you print the words. Discussing the lyrics is an excellent method of stimulating education.

Newspaper and magazine articles provide an opportunity for discussing current events. By bringing in a biblical base you have allowed the young people to look at their Christian life through the context of the happenings in today's world.

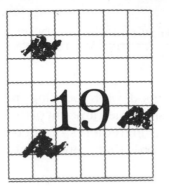

HOW TO PLAN AND DELIVER CREATIVE YOUTH TALKS

W hen I was fresh out of seminary, my first Sunday school class had four high school students—three girls and one guy. They were sitting in a room that would comfortably seat 200 people. As I stumbled through my lesson, one girl read a book while another girl sat on the lap of the only guy in the class and giggled the entire class time. Marcia was the only one actually listening to me, and after the class she told me her family was moving next week! After that "speaking engagement" I seriously questioned my call to ever get in front of an audience again.

However, if we are going to work with kids we will have to speak to them. It doesn't always have to be a disastrous experience. Effective speaking to youth is 10 percent inspiration and 90 percent perspiration. That's why I'm convinced that there are not very many excellent youth speakers: Few are willing to commit the time and energy it takes to move a youth audience.

This chapter is not written to cause a false sense of guilt. I'm well aware of the horror of preparing for three talks to the same youth group each and every week. When my preaching professor in seminary challenged us to study one hour for every minute we were in the pulpit or classroom, I believed him—until I completed my first week of youth ministry at my church. In this chapter I want to cover the basics of good youth speaking and how to put together quality material in a shortened amount of time. I also want to look at the most important ingredients of effective speaking—more important than the words that come out of your mouth.

Excellence Versus Perfectionism

A good youth speaker must be committed to excellence, yet not be a perfectionist. People who work in the church and give a few talks a week along with all the other responsibilities of youth work cannot afford to give the "perfect message." There simply isn't enough time.

However, a busy schedule is not an excuse for giving boring messages. Tony Campolo says, "Poor preaching is responsible for a lot of poor presentations of the gospel and the loss of a host of opportunities to lead people into the Kingdom of God."[1]

Commitment to excellence in speaking means taking the time to honor your students with preparation. When a speaker stands before a group of people and talks for any length of time, he or she has the rare privilege of having people actually listen to what he or she has to say. If the presentation has not been well thought out or put together, then the speaker is actually robbing the listeners of precious time that they could be using for something else.

Attitude

I'm not very comfortable with the word "speaker" because it brings images in my mind of a dynamic, good-looking, powerful, motivating, and incredibly articulate person moving an audience on the sheer beauty of the presentation. We would all be looking for new jobs, including most of the fathers of our faith, if this were the job description for a good speaker. I'm more comfortable with the word "communicator" because its emphasis is less on speaking and more on the total atmosphere of getting the message across.

Studies show us that in the art of good communication and persuasion your attitude is much more important than your words.

194

We've all sat through mediocre speaker presentations but have been moved by the integrity of the person. There are times when I have sat through a sermon and been moved to tears because of the passion or enthusiasm of the speaker rather than the words. *If you want to speak to kids effectively, you'll need to live what you teach and get across the fact that you genuinely care for them.* Your attitude is the deciding factor on whether someone will listen to you or just tune you out.

Young people respond much greater to the nonverbal message than the verbal presentation. I was speaking at a major denomination's youth gathering in which the two keynote speakers had been placed back-to-back. A professor was to give a 45-minute address, then one song, then me. Needless to say, it was a pathetic way to place the speakers. The professor stood to address an overflow crowd in this great convention center. He picked up his 14 pages of nicely typed notes and *read* his entire speech. He never noticed the toilet paper rolls flying from the balcony. As he neared his conclusion, at least half of the kids were talking and many were walking around the auditorium. I'm convinced that some of the kids didn't even notice when he sat down. *Eye contact is as important as your words.*

If you're wondering what happened to me that day, I turned my 45-minute "address" into a shortened 20-minute Scripture story with one humorous point and one serious point. I'm still not sure if their ovation was for my message or for the fact that they wanted to leave the convention center for recreation time.

The nonverbal message of eye contact, a smile, a tear, or even your posture is what makes the difference between a good speaker and a mediocre speaker. Using notes is fine, but know your material well enough to seldom look at your notes. And when you speak with kids, spend as little time behind the pulpit as possible. Anything between you and your audience will get in the way of good communication.

Ethos, Pathos, and Logos

There are three Greek words that help us understand the importance of our attitude in the world of communicating to young people: *ethos, pathos,* and *logos.*

Every talk to a young person should have all three of these elements within the speech. *Ethos* is the credibility factor. The kids will be asking the question "Can I trust you?" Our word "ethics" comes from *ethos*. Are we ethical people? Do we believe what we are urging the young people to believe? Is there evidence in our life and presentation that we can be trusted?

The second element is *pathos*. This word connotes empathy. Kids are asking the question "Do you really care for me?" "Do you understand me?" In order to speak effectively to kids we must earn the right to be heard. I've noticed that in our youth group, if I've met with a person that week and he senses that I care, he will sit closer to the front. When we speak to our people they must know that we love them and that we feel with them.

The third element of attitude communication is *logos* or the Word. If the kids know we are sincere and that we care, then we can give them the truth. The proclamation of the Word is essential, but remember that people don't care how much you know until they know how much you care. Make sure that as you present the Word, you do so on a level which the young people understand. We've got to scratch where they itch. I would sum up these three words *ethos*, *pathos*, and *logos* with this simple sentence: *Always be yourself, always love your audience, and always do your homework.*

Organizing Your Message

The most important piece of advice I can give for preparing a message is to *keep it simple*. Simplicity is the key factor in a good presentation. I believe the reason we remember the words of Jesus so well is because they are simple. Jesus used short phrases. He spoke to the common person. The Sermon on the Mount is brilliant in its simplicity.

The second piece of advice is to *keep it short*. Just because the Sunday school class goes for an hour, this doesn't mean that you need to speak for the entire hour. Because of the onslaught of media in the lives of teenagers, their average attention span is somewhere around ten minutes.

The Big Idea

When you prepare a message you will need to know exactly what you want to get across to your audience. Many people give talks to young people with only a vague idea of what the theme of their message really is. Write down in as few words as possible your Big Idea. You'll want to keep it simple and straightforward. Here are two illustrations: *The call to Christ is the call to serve* and *You are what you think.* Your Big Ideas could be a little longer than these two, but you do want your audience to remember the main idea. Here is an example of a longer Big Idea: *The decisions you make today will affect you the rest of your life.*

Once you've developed your Big Idea or theme, you want to look at the body of your talk. The body will consist of an introduction to the Big Idea, main point(s) surrounding the Big Idea, application, and conclusion.

The introduction of any talk is the most important. All of your audience is not eager to listen to your every word. They are coming to the youth group with other things on their mind. Some have had a knock-down-drag-out fight with their family; others are exhausted from lack of sleep; some are coming to the meeting because of a cute potential date; still others aren't sure you have anything worthwhile to say. Your introduction should be a real attention-grabber. You will need to very quickly (in the first 30 seconds) help them make the decision to listen to what you have to say. You may give them a startling statistic, nagging question, or interesting quote or story in order to create a curiosity in them. Whatever you choose, vary your method and make it interesting. Convince them in the first 30 seconds that they need to put away the other agenda on their mind and listen to you. In your introduction you will want to introduce the Big Idea.

After the introduction you can choose to surround the Big Idea with a main point (or points). For young people, the more points you have the more confusing the message may become. Make sure that the main point explains in greater detail the Big Idea. The main point will usually include a Scripture, an illustration, and an explanation. The real job of the main body is to expound on the Big Idea. We make a mistake by drowning kids with too many points.

Every talk should have an application. This is what I like to call the "so what?" of the talk. We must give the young people an opportunity to respond. If you are talking about the fact that "the call to Christ is the call to serve," then after the talk have sign-ups for the next mission and service project. Truly effective communication brings *results.*

The Home Stretch

The conclusion of the talk is what the young people will really remember. That's why I like to end with my most powerful and moving illustration that points back to the Big Idea. Some speech teachers tell us that this is where we should give our "haymaker" illustration. A few rules to go by in the conclusion: If you say "in conclusion," mean it! We've all experienced the time when the speaker said "now in closing" and then went on for another 15 minutes. Most of the audience went home in their mind immediately after the "first conclusion." Another vital principle (often broken by pastors) is to *conclude on time*. If you have announced that the meeting is to be finished at a set time, then end at that time. Kids will get fidgety and tune you out because they had committed to a certain amount of time. They have other agendas on their mind, such as homework, parents picking them up, a date, or other things. My suggestion is to go shorter rather than longer. Have them asking for more, not looking at their watch wondering when the message will be finished.

PROGRESSION OF A TALK

Opening Illustration

The Big Idea

What is the theme of your message? (One sentence; keep it short and straightforward.)

Introduction

You will win them or lose them in the first 30 seconds. You will need an attention-grabber.

Main Point(s)

What main point(s) will support the Big Idea?
Scripture
Illustration
Explanation

Application

So what? How does this apply to my life, and what can I do about it?

Conclusion

Most powerful illustration (the haymaker) that points back to the Big Idea.

What do you want them to remember?

Where to Find Material

The challenge of always giving the kids fresh material is extremely difficult. One of the mistakes that youth workers make is not developing a good enough resource system. Listed below are a number of ideas on where to find material.

1. *Draw from your life experience.* Every day you experience events that may give meaning to a future message. Make a habit of carrying a notebook to jot down potential ideas. You'll receive illustrations and ideas from conversations, reading, people-watching, TV, newspapers, and a host of other sources.

2. *Read books written for youth.* One of the greatest sources of material is from the books of people who write to kids. They are usually outstanding youth communicators. They have spent years developing their material. Don't plagiarize, but use their insight.

3. *Read the Bible.* My goal is to read the entire Bible in a devotional manner once a year. As I read the stories in Scripture, ideas pop into my mind that I want to share with students at a future time.

4. *Listen to tapes.* If you want to be a good communicator, listen to the tapes of the best speakers you know. Not only will you be inspired, but the tapes are a source of good material. You will want to be careful to develop your own style and not imitate the speaking style of your favorite communicator. Be yourself.

5. *Talk with students.* Continually ask the students what is important to them. I like to ask, "If you were going to speak to the group, what would you want to tell them?" Ask questions. Ask about their culture, their music, their likes and dislikes.

6. *Read commentaries.* In order to get better insight into God's Word, read Bible commentaries. Many times the authors will give insights that you never saw before or an illustration that is perfect for your youth talk.

PERSONAL RELATIONSHIPS

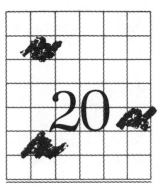

BUILDING SELF-IMAGE IN STUDENTS

Laurie, a junior in high school, summed up her feelings of low self-image in a note to me: "I don't like my looks. I don't like my actions. I don't like my church. I'm far from excited about my relationship with my boyfriend. I make more mistakes than I do successes, and I'm really not sure why God allowed all this to happen in the past two years. Life used to be so easy. Now it is so complicated and getting worse. I'm coping by experimenting with drugs and having sex with my boyfriend, but I'm still desperately unhappy. The pain runs deep."

Building a positive, healthy self-image rooted in Christ is a key to effective youth ministry. Eric Ericson said, "The primary task of the teenage years is to construct a strong sense of self-identity." The adolescent years are times of confusion, discouragement, searching, and openness to change. I strongly believe that when you help build a strong self-image rooted in Christian values, you are actually opening up the students for a deeper spiritual life and a better understanding of the God of creation. The teenage years are not easy years on self-image. The key word for this transition from childhood to adulthood is *change*. Adolescent minds are developing, and their bodies are going through tremendous change. Attitudes about parents are often in transition, and even the depth of social relationships is often in a real upheaval.

The Mirror Problem

As Scott Peck pointed out in the opening line of his bestseller *The Road Less Travelled*, "Life is difficult."[1] This is especially true for adolescents in our society today. Young people are under a great amount of stress and pressure, and there are a number of blocks to a healthy, Christ-centered self-image.

Physical Appearance

Our media-focused society places great importance on physical appearance; our world is caught up in beauty and ability. Unfortunately, much of the Christian culture has fallen into the same trap. We are a society which focuses on outer appearance rather than on inner virtue. All we have to do is ask the question "Who gets more attention in your youth group, the pretty girl or the homely one?" "Who gets more dates?" "Who is most likely to become student body president?"

Adolescents have an incredible need for their physical appearance to measure up to the cultural norm. I remember a meeting I had with a 15-year-old girl and her mother. The mother had dragged her daughter into my office because the girl had announced a month earlier that she was not coming to youth group any longer. Her mother wanted me to "straighten her daughter out and convince her to come back to church." As we sat in my office the air was tense. Finally I said, "I know this is uncomfortable for all of us. Leslie, would you like your mom to step out of the office?" She blurted out, "No! It's her fault I don't come here anymore. She won't buy Jordache jeans, and *everybody else wears Jordache*." I had never noticed that everybody else was wearing Jordache jeans, but it was the major obstacle to Leslie's attendance at youth group.

We cannot underestimate the importance of physical appearance. Leslie's problem was not primarily spiritual; she simply felt out of place because she assumed she would not be accepted if her physical appearance did not measure up to what she considered the cultural norm. (Incidently, the answer isn't to go out and buy designer jeans for everyone.) Connie is too tall, so she stays home from any social setting. Chuck has a new outbreak of pimples on his face, so he stops going to church until they go away. The other kids tease Carl about being short and skinny. He laughs and shrugs it off, but he seldom attends the youth group any longer.

Not learning to accept our physical appearance devastates our self-image. Think back to when you were an adolescent: What was one of the primary concerns of your life? When I was in seventh grade I received this poem in my yearbook:

> God created rivers,
> God created lakes,
> God created you, Jim—
> Everyone makes mistakes!

For an insecure seventh-grader that poem was anything but cute and funny. In fact I silently broke away from the kid who wrote it and stopped including him as one of my friends.

We must convey to young people the fact that God's concern is for inner beauty. He does not put prime importance on outer beauty.

The Lord gave Samuel some very sound advice about Eliab, David's brother, in 1 Samuel 16:7: "Do not consider his appearance or his height. . . . The Lord does not look at the things man looks at. Man looks at the outward appearance, but the Lord looks at the heart." We must help young people understand that beauty and happiness are not always compatible words.

Sexuality [2]

Young people with poor self-images are easily seduced sexually. You show me a sexually promiscuous person and I'll show you a person with a poor self-image. Today's young person is confused about his or her sexuality. The powerful media teaches them different values from the ones they often get from church and home.

The statistics on sex are staggering.[3] By age 19, 80 percent of males and 67 percent of females are sexually active. Half of those boys first had sexual intercourse between the ages of 11 and 13. Each year more than a million teenage girls will become pregnant, 30,000 of these under the age of 15. If present trends continue, 40 percent of today's 14-year-old teens will be pregnant at least once before age 20. The numbers bombard us. They stretch us to the edge of reality. What's happening to our kids today? In a recent survey, 47 percent of the boys and 65 percent of the girls 15 to 16 years old admitted they said yes to sex when they really didn't want to. Among the reasons: "I didn't want to hurt his feelings." "I didn't know how to say no." "I was afraid he would stop liking me." "I felt pressure to do it because all my friends were doing it."

The pressure to perform sexually is enormous, and not just from other teenagers. The media inundates young people with the message that sex is everything. The average TV-viewing American student is hit with actual or implied sexual occurrences approximately 9230 times a year. And 88 percent of all sex portrayed on TV is sex outside of marriage.

The number one reason that teenagers say they have sex is because there is an intense desire for love and acceptance. The often-heard cry is "I want to be loved." Young people with low self-images consider sex a necessary ingredient for being accepted and loved. Another reason for teenagers having sex is simply cultural confusion. In 1969 students were asked, "Is it wrong for a man and woman to have sexual relations before marriage?" The result: 68 percent said yes, 29 percent said no. In 1985 the same question was asked, but this time 36 percent said yes while over 60 percent said no.[4]

The culture is changing so rapidly that the church must stand up for biblical values and morals. Students need help in forming their own moral codes. In the name of value-neutral education, many parents have set their children adrift to make up their own mind on important matters, without the proper tools and insight to help them make the right decision. I believe that as we help students develop a proper self-image we will help them say no to the unhealthy sexually promiscuous attitudes permeating our society today.

Materialism

In one of the recent youth group meetings, the kids sat around my living room and shared what they wanted to do and be when they grew up. One tenth-grader said, "I want to be rich." I asked him, "What do you want to do to become rich?" He replied, "I don't care. I just want lots of money." Another ninth-grader in that same meeting said he wanted to be a wealthy entrepreneur.

Far too many young people are believing the slogan on the bumper sticker which reads "The person with the most toys wins."

We must help our young people understand that success is not spelled m-o-n-e-y. The Bible warns us that materialism is perhaps the most dangerous religion known to humankind. "No one can serve two masters. Either he will hate the one and love the other, or he will be devoted to one and despise the other. You cannot serve both God and Money" (Matthew 6:24).

Somehow we must convey to young people that money does not necessarily bring them the happiness, fulfillment, or acceptance which they so desperately seek in their lives. We must teach them the scriptural principle "Where your treasure is, there your heart will be also" (Matthew 6:21). Students with poor self-images will constantly seek flashy items in order to impress their friends, at the expense of deeper and more meaningful qualities of life. Materialism is an enemy of our faith and self-image, but there are few youth group meetings on the subject, mostly because materialism has pervaded the church in America in such a major way.

Peer Pressure

The intense desire to belong, to be liked, and to be accepted is running at full force in the teenage years. Students will tell you that there is no greater desire than the need to be included and accepted by a peer group. This powerful force is what causes a 15-year-old Christian girl to "accidentally" get pregnant or the 16-year-old boy to drink, drive, and crash. They want so badly to be loved and accepted that they make decisions against their basic values in order to feel included.

Several years ago some psychologists designed an interesting experiment to study peer pressure. Seven teenagers sat in a room and were shown cards that looked like the following:

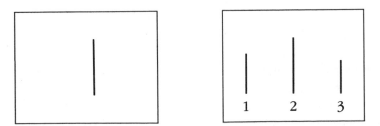

The teenagers were asked, "Which line in the box on the right is the same length as the line in the box on the left?" The answer of course is number 2, but before the experiment began, six of the seven teenagers were told to answer "number 1." How would you feel if you had been the one person in the room who didn't know the secret? Number 2 is clearly the right answer, but if everyone else said "number 1," would you go along with the crowd?

Almost 75 percent of the people tested did just that. When asked about it later, most admitted that they had used excuses to talk themselves into going along with the group. "Maybe I don't understand the instructions," some thought. Others decided that something must be wrong with their eyesight. Those who resisted the peer pressure and said what they thought felt a lot of discomfort and didn't like being different.[5]

No one wants to be different. From the "flower children" of the sixties to the punk rocker of the eighties, we still see a strong desire by teenagers to be accepted by a peer group even in the midst of their desire to be different.

However, there are positive as well as negative factors in peer pressure. In the above experiment, if only one person in the room went against the group opinion, it was much easier for the other students to say what they really thought. Having someone to agree with you can really help you resist peer pressure. The church should help young people deal with the potential negative influences of peer pressure.

David Elkind keenly notes, "It is important to remember at this point that peer pressure has no power in and of itself. The peer group is powerful only because there are teenagers with a patch-work self, particularly of the conforming variety, who lack the inner strengths that would weigh against conforming."[6]

His point is important for youth ministry. Negative peer pressure can be overcome when teenagers have positive influences in their lives. The church can provide positive relationships, affirmation, teaching, and ministry in the life of young people to help them prevent negative peer pressure.

Important points to communicate to young people are: 1) Everyone you spend time with has an influence on you; 2) choose your friends wisely; 3) remember your uniqueness—you are special in God's eyes; 4) seek first the kingdom of God; 5) God loves you unconditionally .

Self-Image

One of the most destructive factors in the self-image of adolescents is the negative view they have of themselves. Most young people play the comparison game—comparing their life, looks, personality, and brains with someone else—and they always lose. They also focus on the "I-wish game," saying, "I wish I looked like a movie star" or "I wish I could play football like an NFL all-star." Kids need to understand that they always lose with these kinds of games. There's always someone more talented, prettier, and smarter.

One of the responsibilities of a good youth worker is to help students understand the power of what sociologists call *the self-fulfilling prophecy: You become what you believe yourself to be.* If you believe you are a failure, you will become a failure. If you believe, as many adolescents do, that you are ugly, you'll become ugly. If you believe you can't do it, you won't be able to accomplish the task. *But the opposite is also true.* If you believe you can accomplish something, you'll probably be able to. If you believe you have inner beauty, you will radiate from the inside out, and you will have a beautiful appearance.[7] One of the outstanding youth workers of our day recently told me he went into the ministry because his youth worker kept telling him that he would make a great youth pastor.

We must be careful not to strengthen a young person's inadequate feelings about themselves by teasing students or giving them negative nicknames. The old children's poem "Sticks and stones may break my bones, but words will never hurt me" is *wrong*. People become what their nicknames remind them to become. The self-fulfilling prophecy is extremely powerful in the lives of adolescents. Studies show that children who grow up in an environment full of put-downs, negative nicknames, and criticism often become critical adults with a poor self-image.

God-Image

How students view God plays an extremely important part in their self-image. We must help kids see that God is not the great cosmic killjoy when it comes to life. The good news for adolescents is that in Jesus Christ they can find a personal source of identity and freedom.

Students suffer from two major misconceptions of God that really play havoc on their self-image. The first misconception is that the God of the Bible is a God of works. Students have a difficult time accepting the concept of grace. In the words of Robert Capon, young people are "like ill-taught piano students; they play their songs, but they never really hear them because their main concern is not to make music but to avoid some flub that will get them in Dutch."[8] Students fall short of their expectations and even walk away from God at times because they can't meet up to their misconception of His expectations.

The other misconception is that the God of the Bible is slow to forgive. We must help young people see that forgiveness is for the asking, and that "God demonstrates his own love for us in this: While we were still sinners, Christ died for us" (Romans 5:8). Through Christ's atoning death and resurrection we find forgiveness and freedom. That message is what young people need to hear over and over again.

Healthy Self-Image

Achieving a healthy, Christ-centered self-image is definitely a challenge to young people, although not an insurmountable task. Youth workers can have a significant impact in the lives of young people and can make tremendous progress with the self-image deliverance. Listed below are seven very practical but useful steps you can use to help young people in their struggle of self-acceptance.

1. *Build positive relationships.* Young people need to be constantly reminded that they become like the people they spend time with on a regular basis. I challenge my students to spend time with positive, energetic people. Enthusiasm rubs off on everyone.

One of the major goals of any youth group should be to provide a supportive community of fellowship. Most youth group activities should be planned around the idea of building community. Frankly, the first and foremost reason that kids come to youth group is to make friends, and this is a perfectly acceptable reason. Although most students have a genuine desire to grow in their faith, friendship is usually first on their list. Deepened Christian friendships lead toward the strong desire to grow in their faith.

The element of socialization is important to the youth group. Socialization is the aspect of incorporating (socializing) the church to become an important part of a young person's life. It becomes his or her place for friendships, learning, worship, fun, etc. When a young person feels socialized into the fellowship, the result will be long-term participation and usually a positive change in lifestyle.

Another factor of positive relationships in dealing with peer pressure is the adult role model. With school classrooms getting larger and larger and with parents getting busier and busier, many young people have few relationships with significant adults. Young people today are losing the benefit of a mentor and hero. A positive relationship with an adult who truly cares can make all the difference in a young person's life.

2. *Help students gain an "attitude focus."* Young people are idealistic and extremely hard on themselves. Many of the aspects of life that students want to change will simply never change. *Let your students know that many of their circumstances will never change, but their attitude can change, and that this makes all the difference in the world.* I love the prayer of Saint Francis of Assisi. "God grant me the serenity to accept what I cannot change, courage to change what I can, and wisdom to know the difference."

3. *Check the physical warning signs.* I'm convinced that at the core of many young people's self-image problem are poor eating and sleeping habits. (For example, more than 50 percent of American high school students are overweight.) The youth group should be a place where kids can get input on proper nutrition, rest, exercise, and other aspects of the body. God made the body, mind, and spirit to work together. Ineffective use or function of body, mind, or spirit can reduce self-image in a major way.

Another suggestion to students is to get a regular physical checkup. Often students act a certain way because of a physiological problem and not a spiritual one.

4. *Give your kids success experiences.* Many young people with a poor self-image need a few successes to build up their confidence. Sometimes it is something as easy as setting up a tennis tournament so Bill can show off his ability or asking Janet to use her artistic talent to make a poster. Find ways to help kids experience success. You may need to become a math tutor or to delegate the planning of the youth group party to someone who can plan a great evening and who needs the affirmation.

5. *Help your kids practice thankfulness.* Happy people are thankful people. I'm challenged with what the Bible says in Thessalonians: "Give thanks in all circumstances, for this is God's will for you in Christ Jesus" (1 Thessalonians 5:18). Recently a twelfth-grade girl came to me with an extremely negative attitude about life. For the first half-hour of our conversation she grumbled and complained her way through every topic she brought up. Although I'm not suggesting that this is always a good counseling technique, I stopped her and asked if there was anything in her life she was thankful about. After a long pause she said, "My cat." I told her I was going to introduce her to what I call "thank therapy." I asked her to take a piece of paper and a pencil and write at least 20 reasons why she could be thankful. I'm not saying she received a miraculous cure from her bad attitude. However, she practiced thank therapy and walked out of my office a much happier person, focusing on reasons why she was thankful. Sometimes kids need a reminder to focus on all the reasons in the world why they can be thankful instead of focusing on their problems.

6. *Let your kids know that counseling can be a positive option.* Cathy and I were recently speaking to a large group of single adults on the subject of proper self-image. Cathy shared with the group that for her life, involvement in a counseling relationship was extremely helpful for her own self-image. We were an infertile couple for eight years. After numerous operations and years of frustrating doctor's visits, Cathy sought counseling to help her through our hurt and pain of infertility. After she told the story we were amazed at the number of people who came and asked questions about counseling. We were also surprised at the number of people who said, "I'm so happy to hear that a pastor's wife needed counseling too!" When you look at the stress-filled situations in

which young people find themselves today, you must look at counseling as an important option for help.

7. *Get your kids outside themselves.* Kids with a low self-image are extremely self-absorbed. There is so much going on inside their own lives that they have little desire to reach outside themselves. Yet when students are challenged to serve and become other-centered as opposed to self-centered, they will see their self-image rise. Find every opportunity to get your students involved in mission and service.[9] One of the greatest benefits of this kind of involvement is that they begin to feel like they are doing something positive with their life. Everyone needs to be needed, and I believe that everyone has deep within him or her a desire to be used by God in some special way.

The Spiritual Factor

This may seem like an oversimplified viewpoint, but I believe that building a proper self-image in students is a spiritual matter. When young people understand the true essence of grace and the depths of God's love, they are free to build a healthy self-image that is rooted in the life of Jesus Christ their Lord. We need to constantly remind our young people that *God's ways are different from our ways.* The spiritual factor of self-image is rooted in four simple yet profound statements based on Scripture.

God loves us unconditionally. In order to have a healthy self-image, young people must understand the fact that God loves them not for what they do but rather for who they are. God's love knows no limits. God's love is the ultimate sacrificial love. The concept of unconditional love is vitally important in a student's self-image and spiritual life and yet it is difficult for students to understand a love with no strings attached.

We are created in God's image. The apostle Paul gives us such insight when he says, "For we are God's workmanship, created in Christ Jesus to do good works" (Ephesians 2:10). The Greek word translated workmanship can also be translated poetry. We must remind our students that they are God's workmanship and poetry. They are totally unique. There is no one quite like them in all the world. They are gifted and different than anyone else because they are created by God from a different and unique mold. Remind your young people that they are special.

We are children of God. Give your students the opportunity to understand the fact that once they become Christians they are children of God with all the rights and privileges of any other child of God. They are children of the Father and heir to the throne of God. God takes care of His children. He loves them and wants the best for them. Sociologist Tony Campolo loves to tell his audiences that if God has a wallet, then Tony's picture is in it, and furthermore God is proud of that picture. The interesting fact about this principle is that when people understand they are children of God, they are then liberated to love. They are set free from a poor self-image. They are released from being so self-absorbed and can now make a difference in the world. They are free to love as God loves. "Yet to all who received him, to those who believed in his name, he gave the right to become children of God" (John 1:12).

We are forgiven by God. Young people are walking away from the church because they don't really believe they can be forgiven. When we tell students they can be a new creation in Christ, they don't understand the concept; it is too foreign to our modern way of thinking. People are in mental institutions today, completely broken down mentally, physically, and spiritually, because they have never understood or experienced the simplicity of God's forgiveness. It is essential for a proper self-image to help students comprehend the fact that confessed sin is forever forgiven. In the words of our God, "[I] will remember their sins no more" (Jeremiah 31:34). Through forgiveness comes freedom.

Setting a person free to be all that God desires him to be is found in these four simple yet often-overlooked spiritual factors relating to our faith. Jesus was right: "You will know the truth, and the truth will set you free" (John 8:32).

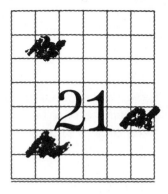

COUNSELING
YOUTH

F resh out of seminary and on my first day at the job, I was putting all my theology books on the shelf when someone knocked on my door. There stood a mother, father, and their 16-year-old daughter. This was no welcoming committee; they were intensely serious. "Can we talk?" was their opening remark even before introductions. I said "Sure" and moved some boxes out of the way.

"Wendy has cancer. The doctors give her six months to live." They cried, and I cried. In fact, even as I write about this event, I cry. Wendy died four months later. Until that very hour, I never realized how much pastoral counseling goes on in youth ministry. Planning youth programs and giving Bible studies I was prepared for, but the ever-present counseling needs in youth ministry caught me totally by surprise.

"No one ever told me I would spend so much time counseling teenagers in my youth ministry," is an often-heard cry. A large part of youth work is counseling. Some youth workers feel comfortable with counseling; most feel terrified.

As a youth worker you are a counselor. You are perhaps not trained in counseling and feel inadequate to counsel, but nevertheless at times your mere position in the church will cause your students, their parents, and even the community at large to look to you for counseling.

This chapter is by no means meant to be a comprehensive book on counseling teenagers; it is meant to be an overview in one of the most important yet often-overlooked subjects.

Common Characteristics of the Adolescent Years

David Elkind has called adolescence the "unplaced years." In his excellent book *All Grown Up and No Place to Go*, he contends that our society today has very little place for teenagers. Children have a position in life. They have a place in the family and society. Adults have their place, but the teenager is in an ambiguous position with little responsibility and no important place in the American home. Adolescence is a relatively new position in life. Even 50 years ago the transition from childhood to adulthood was much quicker and more well-defined.

In order to counsel and work effectively with this generation of young people, we must become aware of the thread of common characteristics which they are dealing with during their transition years.

Because of the many transitions in the life of a teenager, you will find them *self-absorbed* and *self-conscious*. They are looking inward, and often they don't like what they see. What appears to be an incredibly self-centered attitude is typically a lack of confidence combined with intense feelings of confusion.

Today's teenagers are often filled with *anxiety*. They worry about their physical looks, their relationships, and their future. It is a time of uncertainty. As teenagers, they know that life is moving rapidly toward adulthood with its greater responsibility, but they may not be sure they are looking forward to this marker in life called adulthood.

Another common characteristic is *experimentation with new behavior.* I was shocked to hear that Dave and Jay, two of the stronger leaders in our youth group, got drunk on Saturday night and then led their Sunday school groups the next day. Eventually I asked Jay about their little escapade, and his answer was insightful: "Dave and I were talking at dinner together; we both admitted we had never been drunk. The more we talked about what it might be like, the more we convinced ourselves to try it. So we tried it." With the added freedom as adolescents, mixed with curiosity and mystery, comes experimentation with new behavior. Your role as a counselor is to turn the experience into a learning situation without being shocked. The fact is that most teenagers will at one time or another compromise their beliefs and values. They need understanding, accountability, and guidance in order to help them make good decisions the next time around.

With the onslaught of puberty also comes the rise in emotions. Adolescent counselors must realize that teenagers will tend to be very emotional. Moodiness seems to come with the territory. Some of the strongest feelings are anger, depression, guilt, failure, and passion. We must take these common characteristics seriously, yet we must balance the roller coaster of emotions with logical thinking and consistency.

Listening: The Language of Love

You have most likely heard this statement from a young person: "No one ever listens to me." The most important counseling technique does not need to be done by a professional. Students will know you are taking them seriously and will open up their life to you if they know you will listen to them. Listening is the real language of love.

I am convinced that kids do not always need to immediately hear the "right answer" as much as they need an atmosphere of openness in which they genuinely feel that you are actively listening.

H. Stephen Glenn in his excellent course *Developing Capable Young People* has listed various roadblocks to effective listening. As you reflect on your own listening ability, these roadblocks may help you evaluate your listening skills. Glenn's valid concern is that we adults show power and give "you" messages. He calls these adultisms. Following are examples of what he means.

	Examples:
1. Adultisms	"You should know better by now."
2. Showing power • ordering • threatening • commanding • directing	"You'd better change your attitude or you'll never pass in school."
3. "You" messages or showing superiority • moralizing • preaching • lecturing • advising • diagnosing	"If you'd dress neater, you'd have more friends." "You must work harder or you'll never be successful."
4. Attacking • interrogating • criticizing • blaming • shaming	"It's your own fault."
5. Avoiding/playing down • nonspecific praise • false reassurance • sympathy • humor or sarcasm[1]	"Don't worry about it." "I'm sure it'll look better in the morning."

Effective Listening Qualities

A good listener is actively involved in the conversation. It takes work to develop the important qualities of listening to young people. One of the special people in my life lives in a little town in Oklahoma. She will never have the "up-front" ability to be famous. Some would say she dresses out of date. In fact, she really doesn't keep up much with the latest teen music idols or fads. Yet when I recently asked one of the kids in her youth group how he liked the group, he replied with so much enthusiasm that I was taken back a little. He said, "Sydney is the greatest youth leader in the world. She listens to all of us. She's available, she's not judgmental, and we know she cares." I've probably never known of more young people year after year who want to go into full-time youth ministry or the mission field than from Sydney's group. It's not her up-front skills but rather her quiet, gentle listening ear. It's her attitude that really says to the kids, "I care about you."

Effective listening qualities are 1) a genuine desire to listen to young people, 2) a willingness to accept their feelings and emotions whether they are right or wrong, 3) a desire to not always need to be right, 4) a nonjudgmental attitude, 5) eye contact and little fidgeting, 6) showing appreciation to the young person that you feel honored to have him choose to share his story with you, and 7) a willingness to not only listen but keep in touch and be supportive.

Problem-Solving

By effective listening I do not mean that we never help students work through their problems. In my own pastoral counseling ministry I have a five-point process of problem-solving that has been helpful to me.

1. *Find the real problem.* If we jump into problem-solving too quickly in the discussion, we may miss the real problem. It is important to be direct and ask the student what he or she considers the problem to be. Sometimes you'll need to ask, "What's on your mind?" or else the student may never get to the point. A young man made an appointment with me this year, and we had a wonderful time of fellowship. As I was getting up to leave for my next appointment, he dropped the bombshell on me that his father had just

been diagnosed as having cancer and was about to die. Now I was in a time bind. I could easily have said earlier in the conversation, "Is there anything in particular that brings you here today?"

2. *List alternative solutions.* Once you have assisted in clarifying the problem, you can help the young person look at various alternatives to the solution. "The problem is that my parents and I fight over use of the car." Possible solutions might include: 1) a meeting with you, the student, and the parents to discuss the specific problem; 2) a discussion with the student about what makes his parents irritated, and developing a plan to alleviate the problem; 3) purchasing a used car; and the list could go on.

3. *Select a plan of action.* If one of the alternatives seems to be the best idea, then work on the problem by using that plan. Sometimes it's very helpful to role-play or rehearse the plan. At this stage of the process youth workers often make a mistake by thinking that their counseling job is now over. The process is only half-finished.

4. *Establish and enforce accountability.* Most action plans with teenagers are not as beneficial as they could be unless there is some method of accountability. I don't believe the youth worker should be a dictator, but accountability is very helpful in problem-solving. You might say, "Since you really want to quit smoking, let me challenge you to stop for a week. Call me if you get the urge. If I'm unavailable, I'll get back to you as soon as I can. Next week let's compare notes after the youth group meeting to see how you're doing." Then make sure you follow through on your promise to hold the person accountable. I believe that it is more damaging not to follow through on your promise of accountability than it is to not set it up in the first place.

5. *Set up an evaluation procedure.* As part of the problem-solving accountability structure, put together some method of evaluation. We all need to see small chunks of success along the way. Don't look for perfection, but rather find a method that will encourage attainment of the students' goals. A regular phone call, checkup meetings, and journaling are all simple methods of evaluating. Of course, the more complex the problem the stronger the

evaluation process will need to be. If a young person is chemically addicted to drugs, then the evaluation procedure must be more in line with that particular problem.

Referrals

Some youth workers need to be constantly reminded that they are not professional counselors. Seldom should youth workers be involved in long-term counseling therapy, personality reconstruction, or issues that they have very little knowledge about.

A good referral system is one of the most important aspects of youth ministry. I believe that it is extremely important to have personal relationships with a few counselors in your area. By doing this you will be able to become more knowledgeable in your referrals, and you will have a professional who can offer you advice on different counseling issues. I make it a habit to have lunch with a professional counselor at least once a month. I use that time to ask questions, seek advice, and develop a relationship. I've never had a counselor turn me down, because they all need a network of referrals.

One of the most common questions I receive is "Yes, I need a referral system, but where do I begin?" Usually you can get information from your pastor, other youth workers, or members of your church. If you still haven't found anyone, you can consider universities or organizations that deal with crises, or you can look in the telephone directory.

I recommend that you keep a file of resources for referral, perhaps cross-referenced by the type of problem or expertise area. Many youth workers put together a resource directory of institutions, ministries, and organizations in their community which have some type of resource or service to provide for people in need. The resource directory could have sections on Sexual Abuse, Suicide, Family Problems, Drug and Alcohol Rehabilitation, Legal Advice, Medical Problems, and so forth.

As you begin the process of seeking referrals, don't be shy. Ask the hard questions, and don't settle for superficial or glib answers. As an entree, indicate that you are trying to find good referral resources and would like to know more about this person's approach and practice. Most professionals will be pleased to respond to such requests. (Any who are not should probably be avoided for referrals.)

Referral Checklist

William Miller has put together an excellent format for pastors to ask questions of professional counselors.

1. *Clients.* What kinds of clients do you like to work with? With whom do you work best? Are there particular problems or age groups with whom you have special expertise?

2. *Training.* What degrees do you hold, and from where? What special training have you had for dealing with the kinds of clients and for problems you work with?

3. *Approach.* What is your general approach to therapy? What do you do with clients? (A favorite answer here is "eclectic," which is very noninformative. It may mean that the person has no particular system for formulating and uses a ragtag collection of techniques or poorly specified methods. On the other hand, it may mean that the person is skilled in a range of alternative interventions and chooses an approach based on reasonable and valid criteria.)

4. *Evidence.* An interesting question to ask, particularly when a specific client or problem area is being discussed: What scientific evidence is there for the effectiveness of what you do? What proof is there that this approach actually helps? The individual may cite specific research or may dodge by referring vaguely to "many studies" or "my years of professional experience."

5. *Length of treatment.* How long do you usually see a client? What is the average number of sessions? (The answer ought to be different depending on the presenting problem. Some problems are relatively easy to treat while others require a somewhat longer course of treatment.)

6. *Fees.* How are fees determined? Is there a sliding scale? Is the person eligible for insurance payments? Does the person accept public assistance clients, whose fees are paid (usually on a more minimal scale) by the state or federal government? Is payment in advance, on monthly billing, or on time payments?

7. *Credentials.* Is this person certified or licensed in his or her field? By whom? If not, why not? If the person is currently working toward credentials under the supervision of another professional, clarify the extent of supervision and find out more about the supervisor.

8. *Group.* Is the individual part of a professional group, such as a group practice? What other professionals does he or she work with regularly?

9. *Religious views.* Here we refer not to a personal statement of faith, but rather to the professional's general views on religion and its relationship to mental health and treatment. How, in the person's opinion, is religion involved in the processes of health and treatment? How comfortable does the person seem in talking about religious issues? How forthright are the answers?

10. *Collaboration.* How willing is the professional to collaborate with you? What about progress reports, consultations, and joint sessions as called for?

11. *Recommendations.* Finally, it can be very interesting to ask each professional to recommend other professionals in the same field or related fields with whom he or she has had good experience in making referrals.[2]

Confidentiality

People are giving you an incredible vote of confidence when they confide in you. If you choose to break their confidence, you have not only hurt your credibility with them but news will travel

quickly to the rest of the youth group and church. You will immediately lose respect and the opportunity for more counseling from
your people. Many of the worst offenders of breaking confidence
are pastoral staffs, who in the disguise of sharing prayer requests
tell stories about people in their congregation and violate their
trust. A woman told me recently that she left her church because
her pastor had shared her marriage problems as a staff prayer
request.

The only time it is reasonable to break a confidentiality is when
a life-threatening situation is at hand, and even then you should tell
the person who you are counseling what you are going to do ahead
of time. Fourteen years ago I told a pastoral colleague a personal
problem I was having. Two days later I got a call from a mutual
friend wanting to help with my problem. This pastoral colleague is
still a friend, but that was the last time I ever trusted him with
personal problems which I did not want broadcast. An effective
counseling ministry is based on trust. Breaking a confidence may
destroy your credibility.

You Will Counsel

Dave Rice, adolescent psychologist and expert in youth ministry, says that there are primarily three tasks of adolescence: 1) to
develop an identity, 2) to establish relationships, and 3) to make
life decisions.[3] With these important tasks in mind, youth workers
have the great opportunity to help young people find meaning in
life and establish positive, Christian goals that will set a foundation
for their entire adulthood. You *are* a counselor, even though most
of your counseling won't take place in the environment of the
office. Your counseling will take place in the mall, on the way to
camp, or after a volleyball game, and in this way you will help your
young people make decisions that will last a lifetime.

WORKING WITH YOUR KIDS' FAMILIES

I never thought I would publicly say this, but I actually miss one of the rowdiest and most hyper students I have ever worked with, Danny. Danny could not sit still; he interrupted almost every lesson I ever gave while he was in the group. His foot was tapping at all times; he talked loud, and he talked fast. He was a bundle of energy. His family did not attend our church, so I reluctantly became his personal chauffeur after meetings. It never failed that as the youth group was dispersing to head for home, Danny would come bouncing up to me and ask me for a ride home. He couldn't even sit still in my car. He fidgeted and talked during the entire ride to his house.

One evening after attending a seminar on family ministry, I decided that it was time to meet Danny's parents. As much as I don't like visiting families (since I'm basically shy), it seems that every time I do, good things come from it. When we rolled up to Danny's house that night, I asked Danny if I could meet his parents. He said sure and ran (Danny never walked) inside, leaving me at the door. Finally his mother came to the door and invited me in. She was a beautiful woman with true Southern hospitality. For some reason I couldn't put Danny's hyperactivity together with his mother's slow, calm spirit. His mother then called for her husband, Dan, to come out of the back room to meet the minister. Literally bouncing out of the back room came Dan, pumping my hand and talking even louder and faster than Danny. I couldn't help but smile and think *"So that's why Danny acts the way he does."*

Sometimes we in youth ministry forget that kids have parents and that they are part of a *family system.* Their actions, socialization process, and faith are all intertwined with their family. No one is an isolated island. Our family heredity and environment play the most significant factor in who we are and who we are becoming. Because of this truth, youth workers are involved in family ministry whether it is in their job description or not. Youth workers can no longer afford to compartmentalize their ministry to work only with kids. The family plays too much of an important role in the spiritual, mental, emotional, and physical development of young people.

As discussed in previous chapters, the American family is caught in transition. The nuclear family is now a minority in the United States. Today when parents say to their kids, "when I was your age," their children snicker and say "another place, another time." Parents are no longer secure about their parenting ability. They are often paralyzed with fear, and because of this fear they quit parenting all together. Instead of digging in and preparing for this new world of adolescence, they give up and let the young people guide themselves. You don't need to look very far in your group to see exactly what I'm writing about.

Our Task: Support

No matter what the family situation is like, you can never take the place of the parent. Don't even try. *Your task is to support and strengthen the existing family unit.* A few years ago in preparation for a Youth Specialties seminar on "The Family and Youth Ministry," veteran youth worker Rich Van Pelt polled a number of successful youth ministries across the country. He asked this question: "What are you doing as a youth worker to help families succeed?" The overwhelming response was "I believe it ought to be happening, but I just haven't gotten around to doing it! It's one of those items on my 'to-do list' that I never seem to get around to doing."

In order to meet the goal of strengthening and supporting the family, you'll need to see your ministry to parents and families in light of these three objectives: 1) Communicate clearly to parents; 2) challenge kids to make their family a priority; 3) provide resources and opportunities for family ministry.

Communicate Clearly to Parents

One of the main complaints that parents have about youth workers in the church is that the parents perceive the youth worker as doing a poor job of communicating with them. Youth workers can't assume that their students are passing on important information to their parents. I've been asked numerous times, "Why didn't you tell me the money was due yesterday?" I would reply, "I sent a letter to your daughter and reminded the entire group every time we were together for the last month." However, the parent would say, "Well, I'm sorry, I never heard about it."

It's important to keep the parents informed about your events. It is also important to let the parents know who you are and what your role is. As a parent myself, I don't blame them for being suspicious of who is spending time with their kids. I also don't blame them for wanting to know your role in their child's life. It's very important that you let them know that you are there to support them and not compete with them.

I suggest that in the first year of your ministry at a church you should attempt to meet with every family in the youth group. This way they know you, and they will undoubtedly feel more comfortable about the "mystery person" at church that their son or daughter talks about. Most youth workers are much younger than the parents of the kids in their group. However, this should not stop the youth worker from developing meaningful relationships with the parents.

Holding a parents' informational meeting at least twice a year is a necessity for good communication with the parents. A regular mailing to the parents covering upcoming events, topics to be covered in the forthcoming weeks, and any other important youth group happenings will alleviate many of the complaints about a lack of communication. If you have attempted to visit the family, have held parents' informational nights, and have sent regular mailings to the parents, but they still complain, then most likely they are the problem and not you.

Family Is a Priority

It's no secret that many students have strong confrontations with their parents as they develop their independence. Yet when it comes to resolving these conflicts, too many kids expect their parents to do most of the work. My ministry has made a shift toward challenging students to take more responsibility for helping to resolve difficult family situations. There is no reason why young people can't begin to view family conflict from both sides of the fence.

A few weeks ago one of the guys in my group was complaining about his parents' irritability. I innocently asked if his parents were under much stress at home or work (or financially). He replied, "Have you talked with them? My dad has moved out; my mom lost her job, and we might lose our house." I asked, "Don't you think that could be causing their irritability?" We then went on to talk about how he could help be a solution to their turmoil rather than another problem.

There are five important things which high schoolers need to understand about their parents in order to take more responsibility in working through conflicts. These ideas are for "normal" families; they do *not* apply to families with intense or complex problems.

Parents have problems too. We should ask the kids in our groups to walk in their parents' shoes and look at some of the pressures and struggles which their parents are facing. Kids can be very self-absorbed. They need to be reminded that there are other people in their family besides themselves.

Our high school Sunday school class once invited a panel of parents to participate in a series on "Getting Along With Your Parents." We chose a divorced mother, two sets of married parents, and my wife for the panel. We asked them to share with the group some of the problems and struggles they faced as parents. What a response! The parents shared deep feelings about loneliness, insecurity at work, financial pressures, relational struggles, and problems communicating with their kids. It was an eye-opening experience for our kids to hear that parents have many of the same problems that they have.

Communication is a key. Most parents do want to communicate with their children. They simply do not know how to, and their children are not much help. A typical conversation between a parent and a high schooler would go something like this: "How was school today?" "Okay." "What did you learn?" "Nothing." We must challenge our youth to initiate communication and conversation. We can give them the tools to help them discuss their feelings rather than merely the curt facts.

Steve Dickie, the junior high pastor at my previous church, developed an excellent resource for helping our junior highers and their parents communicate about what the kids were learning in the youth group. Each week after the meeting he would put out "Parents' Information Sheets" for each parent to pick up and use as a tool for family discussion during the week.

Spend time together. With our hurried lifestyles today, some parents and teenagers cross paths at only a few meals each week. Why not encourage our young people to take the initiative to ask Mom to do something she likes to do, or to ask Dad to go to a ball game? Often the best communication takes place in a neutral environment like a lunch date or shopping at the mall.

Some of the best times with my dad during my adolescent years were when we would work in the yard together or when I would go with him to his office and "help." This usually gave us some quality time alone and a meal together with his full attention.

Let's challenge our high schoolers to initiate a "date each month" with each parent. We can brainstorm creative dates with parents at a group meeting. Here are a few ideas from our youth group:

- Play tennis
- Go to a play
- Eat out for three dollars
- Volunteer at a local hospital together
- Read a book together
- Take a class together at a community college (photography, crafts, computers)

God gave us our parents. "You created my inmost being; you knit me together in my mother's womb. I praise you because I am fearfully and wonderfully made; your works are wonderful, I know that full well. My frame was not hidden from you when I was made

229

in the secret place. When I was woven together in the depths of the earth, your eyes saw my unformed body. All the days ordained for me were written in your book before one of them came to be" (Psalm 139:13-16).

God had an intricate part in bringing parents and children together. However, kids in truly difficult family situations may think that this verse is a cruel joke. Yet most will understand the fact that no parent is perfect. Even in difficult situations, God can be a part of their relationships. A very mature junior in high school recently said to me, "I've finally accepted the fact that even though my father is an alcoholic, he loves me—and God has used me to help other kids who have alcoholic parents."

Honor and obey. Exodus 20:12, Colossians 3:20, and Ephesians 6:1 tell us that honor and obedience are well-pleasing to God. Students need to be reminded that God's desire is for them to honor and obey their parents. I am not talking about blind obedience; I am simply saying that high schoolers should be challenged with this scriptural mandate.

Gently reminding our youth that they can be instruments of God (and can at times lead the way in building a more positive environment at home) is an important ingredient of high school ministry. Parents have problems too, and some of the most influential healers in a parent's life can be his or her own children.

Your Number One Job

Since most youth workers are not looking for more things to do in a day, making time for family ministry becomes a matter of how high a priority it is within your ministry. One of my biggest struggles in ministry is not having enough time to do all that *should* be done. When it comes to family ministry, you'll need to realize that you will never be able to do all you want to do. However, this should not keep you from providing excellent resources and opportunities for family ministry.

Listed below are ten ideas to assist you in the ministry and care of parents and families.

1. *Parents' information meeting.* Hold a meeting at least twice a year to communicate the direction of the youth ministry with the parents. Keep the meeting informative, enjoyable, positive, and relational.

2. *Parents' advisory board.* Have a small get-together in the casual setting of a home to brainstorm ideas with parents. This can also become a support group for the youth ministry.

3. *Parents' update.* Provide a regular mailer (my goal was six times a year) to the parents communicating upcoming events, topics to be covered, and additional resources for parenting skills.

4. *Visit in the home.* You can learn a lot about a family from being in their home and observing how they relate to each other. If you've been in their home, they will feel more comfortable about coming to you with their problems.

5. *Mothers' tea.* Have a regular meeting with the mothers to discuss the youth group. Talk about their kids and pray for the group. This can become a support group for the mothers.

6. *Dads' breakfast.* Provide a regular time for the fathers, using an agenda similar to that of the mothers' tea.

7. *Family camps.* The youth ministry can sponsor a camp which is geared to dealing with family relationships. Have the students serve their families during this time together.

8. *Family resources.* Many churches are now providing re-source centers for parents. In the resource center you can provide a place for checking out good books, tapes, and videos to assist parents of teenagers.

9. *Parent/teen meetings.* Good family interaction and minis-try can be enhanced through intergenerational programs which give the parents and their teenagers the opportunity to interact and discuss important topics.

10. *Parents' seminars.* Periodically throughout the year you can provide opportunities for parents to receive tools to help them become more effective parents. Topics can include substance abuse, sex, communication, and self-image.

How About Your Own Family?

After a recent talk on youth workers and family ministry one worker asked, "Working with families is well and good, but how can I add that to my high school ministry when my own family relationships are in shambles?"

Most people I know who are in ministry are so overcommitted and overstressed that relationships with their own families are mediocre at best. This section is about ministry and marriage. Even if you are single, read on—you can prevent much of the heartache that some of your married peers are experiencing.

We can become so emotionally spent that we have little time or attention to spend building our marriages, despite the fact that our greatest ministry is our own marriages. Before I came to South Coast Community Church in 1980, I told the board of elders that if they wanted me to come they had to understand that I believed one of my primary witnesses to the young people was a healthy marriage. This meant I was willing to work only three nights a week. (Most youth workers spend at least five nights a week out of the house.)

I also asked for budgeted meal money in order to have kids into our home for dinner. We liked bringing in five at a time and spending the evening together. The elders agreed. So having discussed it beforehand, it was easier for them to handle when I couldn't attend every evening function.

If you're not giving time and energy to your spouse, then I question your witness to your group. A healthy marriage is a strong model for your kids that will give them a sense of security.

Dealing with Fatigue

What undermines the building of a youth worker's marriage is overcommitment and fatigue. I don't think the heavy turnover and burnout of youth workers is due to lack of education or low finances as much as it is fatigue. Overcommitment and fatigue will always cause tension in your family. Why we youth ministers think we have to take on a job description that's bigger than life I don't know. In order to nourish our ministries and our marriages, we probably need to cut back and do less.

When I graduated, a wise man warned me of postseminary reality. "Jim," he said, "if the Devil can't make you bad, he'll make you busy." That warning sticks with me still.

Then what's the answer? *Rest*. Even God rested one day of the week. If you are not, as a couple, taking at least a 24-hour period at a different pace once each week, then your marriage and ministry may be in jeopardy. Without rest we tend to spend all our energy on our students and church, leaving us with nothing for our families except burnout. I've used every excuse in the book, and then some, for my glazed eyes and exhausted spirit. "It'll get better after this one retreat," I've said. Yet after 12 years the excuses sound flimsier and flimsier.

Building Your Relationship

If rest goes a long way in keeping fatigue away from yourself, what can you do for the two of you—your marriage—to keep your relationship strong?

Date Night

Plan a weekly date together. You've got to *continue* courting your spouse throughout your life, and a weekly looked-forward-to date helps inhibit the creeping peril of a stale marriage. We can always find time for weekly Bible studies or one-on-one discipleship encounters, so why not a two-hour date with our spouse?

Pacing

Youth ministry has a tendency to move so fast from one event to another that we take little time to reflect or debrief. Cathy and I are learning what we call pacing. Even though I feel drawn to the office after a big event, we try to take the next day off. If we know I'm going to be out of town for a few days, we try to make the week before my departure less hectic than usual.

Positive Modeling

During a recent seminar which I taught on ministry and marriage, I was surprised by the intensity—even anger—of most of the youth workers' opinions about the poor role modeling they receive from their workaholic senior pastors. Face it—role models for a strong, happy marriage may be uncommon among your pastoral staff. If that's true for you, find an older couple who really works at making their marriage and family a very important aspect of their lives.

Using the Phone

Youth workers usually work long hours and consequently find it difficult to communicate with their spouses. The ad's right—the phone is the next best thing to being there. Use it daily to call and communicate. When I'm away from home, Cathy and our children get a phone call every day.

Growing Spiritually Together

I wish I had an easy answer for growing together spiritually. There are no magic formulas. However, let me suggest three helpful ideas on growing spiritually as a couple.

Solos. A solo is a spouse's regular time away from the routine hassles of life in order to have an extended period of devotion, reflection, and quiet time with God. Once a month I watch our kids in the morning and Cathy takes her solo. We try to have a meal together soon after a solo (or sabbath) in order to share with each other any thoughts from the solo.

Support group. With the hectic pace of life that a youth minister lives, I cannot understand how couples can grow spiritually without the help of a support group. We both have our separate, weekly support group meetings as well as our twice-a-month couples' support group. These help us keep our perspective, and our individual support groups especially help us vent feelings and receive encouragement from someone besides our spouses. If you don't have a support group, find or create one.

Overnighters. One night away from the routine hassles really helps Cathy and me, as a couple, gain clearer perspective on things. Our overnighters tend to be the best spiritual growth times. They can be programmed with reading and prayer, or you can have a more spontaneous time together. If you have children, it's even more important to have periodic overnighters. You can sometimes trade baby-sitting with another couple in your church who also need overnighters.

Keep the Fires Burning

One of the tragedies of the eighties is the trouble that so many ministry marriages have grown into, and the culprit is often an emotionally drained minister, so emptied by his work that he cannot pay proper attention to his family. I think what Gail Mac-Donald wrote in *High Call, High Privilege* relates perfectly to this problem. "Untended fires," she wrote, "soon become nothing but a pile of ashes." If you're concerned about ministering to families in your church, you can't afford to neglect your own hearth.

SAMPLE SUMMARY

Junior High Ministries

Topic

Seeing things from your parents' point of view.

Introduction

As we continued our look at the theme of moms, dads, and other endangered species, we focused on what it means to see life from our parents' point of view. We accomplished this task by focusing on understanding our parents' needs, and then taking very real and practical steps toward meeting them.

Content

1. We must understand that parents have physical, emotional, social, and mental needs that need to be met (just like we do).

2. We must take action on meeting those needs. (We discussed some practical steps.)
   a. Ask your parents' forgiveness if you have been a cause of conflict.

---

b. Begin to cooperate with them.

c. Tell them you love them.

d. Avoid raising your voice with them...anytime.

e. Thank them for all the things they have done for you.

f. Prove to them, through obedience, that you are responsible.

Family Discussion Questions

1. List your basic needs. Share them with each other.

2. Parents, share with your junior highers the answer to these questions:
   When do you feel lonely?
   How do you feel about your job?
   How do you feel about yourself?

3. Junior highers, ask your parents how they would like you to understand them better.

4. Read Philippians 2:3. How could this apply to parents and their junior highers understanding each other?

5. Make out a list of practical things you can do to see life from each other's point of view.

Recommended Reading

Try these great resources on parenting junior highers. A detailed bibliography is available from the junior high office.

1. *Parents and Teenagers,* by Jay Kesler.

2. *When a Junior Higher Invades Your Home,* by Cliff Schimmels.

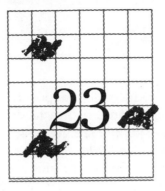

How to Teach on Sex and Sexuality

I was told of a 16-year-old boy who heard that kids have a sexually influenced thought on the average of every 20 seconds. His response was, "What am I supposed to think about the other 19 seconds?" Your kids have sex on their minds. In fact, many of your kids not only have sex on their minds but are already in over their heads with sexual experiences. It's time we asked two important questions: Why should the church teach sexuality? What is "Christian" sexual education?

Perhaps no other issue in the church is more misunderstood than sexuality. The debate about whether we should teach sexuality in church will rage until our young people are old and gray. Yet with all the debate, we still can't change the fact that a major issue—if not *the* major issue—in all of our young people's lives is their sexuality.

Why Discuss Sexuality?

Why should the church teach sexuality? First of all, I believe that people who question sex education programs because they fear that information itself can be dangerous are simply mistaken. Studies have shown that the more sexual education a young person has, the less he or she is apt to be sexually promiscuous. This reason alone is enough to convince me that positive sexual education in the church can prevent future heartache.

Second, our young people are growing up in a culture where sex is the dominant issue. Television, movies, radio, and even advertising billboards keep sex prominent in the mind of our nation. Like it or not, we can't ignore the subject.

Third, sex is mysterious to young people. The mystery and wonder of sexuality helps keep sex on their minds. Why is it that whenever the youth group has a series on sexuality, attendance increases? Kids want information. They want answers, and Christian kids truly desire to know what God has to say about sex.

Fourth, kids today are receiving mixed messages about their sexuality. The majority of young people receive a "DON'T DO IT" message from their parents, with little or no accompanying explanation (that is, if their parents say anything about it at all). From the church, kids often hear "DON'T DO IT BECAUSE IT'S SINFUL!" but again with little elaboration. Many public school systems teach only "HOW TO DO IT" (technique) without discussing sexual values and morals. Still another message that kids get is from their peers: "I DO IT ALL THE TIME." (In fact, though, it doesn't happen with the regularity that kids brag about.)

Kids want someone to be open and honest with them. They sincerely want to know the truth about their sexuality, and I believe they're frustrated because no one seems to be giving them straight answers.

A fifth reason why the church should engage in sexual education is that parents often do not fulfill their proper role in this area. A professor at Wheaton College told me that when he polled his students about their own sex education, he found that only 20 percent had ever had any kind of sex education at home. Many parents have a great deal of trouble talking about sex with their kids. Let's face it—many parents (and youth workers) didn't handle their sexuality well as teenagers, so they don't know how to approach sexual issues with their children.

The church must not (and cannot) take the place of parents in sexual education, but the church can help parents and their young people deal with the topic together.

Finally, the church should be involved in sex education because far too many adolescents have a difficult time integrating their sexuality with their relationship to God. Many young people believe that God is the great killjoy when it comes to sex. They forget that God created sex (Genesis 2:18-25) and that He sees His creation as very good (Genesis 1:25,31). Since we want our young people to understand that God cares about all aspects of their lives, it is imperative that the church teach about sexuality from a Christian perspective.

What Is Christian Sex Ed?

What is distinctive about the Christian approach to teaching sexuality? Actually, there is no "Christian method" to sexual education. There isn't a single Christian technique available to teach about sexuality within the church. There are elements, however, of a Christian-oriented sexual education program that we must consider.

Many education programs seem to focus only on the techniques of sex or the biological factors involved. These are important, but the major emphasis should be on the individual. God cares about individuals. Positive Christian sexual education is person-centered—it deals thoroughly with feelings, thoughts, questions, and attitudes. A person-centered program allows plenty of room for discussion. Issues are raised that might cause tension and even open debate.

Christian sexual education is also relationship-centered. Christian adolescents usually become legalistic when it comes to the question "How far is too far?" They don't want to go against God's words, but they want to know exactly how far they can go without committing a sin.

People miss the boat when sexual education is approached with that kind of attitude. Christian sexual education focuses on the concept of a "radical respect" for the other person in a romantic relationship. Although most sexual educators don't use the beautiful passage in Philippians 2 in their programs, they surely could. Paul's teaching in verses 3 and 4 capsulizes the principle of radical respect: "Do nothing out of selfish ambition or vain conceit, but in humility consider others better than yourselves. Each of you should look not only to your own interests, but also to the interests of others." The relationship-centered focus continually looks at the other person's long-term spiritual and emotional well-being. This focus helps make sense of the Christian standard of restraint and control in premarital sexual behavior.

Finally, Christian sexual education emphasizes the spiritual dimension of sexuality. Many non-Christians affirm the spiritual dimension of sexuality. For them it is undefinable, and even for Christians there is an element of the sexual and spiritual that is beyond definition. Christian sexual education, however, helps young people understand that God is intricately involved with their sexuality. Creation, procreation, and love relationships have spiritual aspects to them because they are part of God's awesome, creative, loving plan.

Christian sexual education teaches what the Bible has to say about sex, but it doesn't spend all of its time in the "thou shalt nots." Adolescents are ready to discuss the Song of Solomon and how this R-rated book explores married love. It's time to discover what the Bible says about homosexuality, venereal disease, lust, and any other related subjects.

Positive Christian sexual education also explores what the Bible doesn't mention about sexuality. Since statistics tell us that the majority of kids (both male and female) are engaged regularly in masturbation, it's time to talk about it. Petting, peer pressure, and pornography are only a few of the issues the Bible doesn't address directly, yet they are important for Christian young people to discuss.

Value-Rich Sex Ed

In a world where much of the teaching that young people get is value-neutral, the church can provide moral and value-rich sexual education. It's important to let kids know that everybody isn't "doing it," and that it is better not to "do it."

We can help kids set the right standards. Many sexual decisions are made in the midst of an intense emotional environment that is beyond a kid's ability to handle. We can provide a less stressful environment that will provide kids with the moral and spiritual underpinnings necessary to properly understand, process, and accept the Christian standards we teach.

With sexual promiscuity on the rise, the church is one of the greatest places to help kids deal with anger and receive forgiveness. In youth groups across America there are many bleeding hearts that have been broken by negative sexual experiences. In Christ we can offer forgiveness, hope, and a strategy for living out a healthy, constructive sexual life. The church rather than the street can and should be the place where our kids can find advice, healing, comfort, and people willing to talk about the mystery of their sexuality.

Practical Ideas for a Christian Sex Education Program

1. *Include the parents.* Keep the parents informed about what you will be teaching. This will set their minds at ease and will challenge them to talk about the subject with their children at home. Invite the parents to special sex education meetings just for them. At other times have a mixed group of parents and youth. This will help stimulate discussion outside the classroom (where, incidentally, the best learning and dialogue can take place). Respect the students' privacy. Not all classes should include parents. It seems that when parents are in the same room, kids are not free to express their opinions or ask important questions.

2. *Meet with the health education/sex education teachers in your local schools.* Many times youth workers feel like they are in opposition to the public school teacher who teaches about sex. This is not always true. I believe that most of the sex education teachers really do care about the kids, and although they might be teaching from a value-neutral viewpoint, they are giving the students helpful information.

When I first met Mr. Dunn, the sex education teacher in our local high school, I expected to meet someone who was trying to convince the students to have sexual intercourse. I was mistaken.

He invited me to sit in on his classes. They were excellent; I learned a few things! After looking at his curriculum I restructured our church's sex education program, realizing that I didn't need to repeat some of the positive aspects of the public school systems. Instead, I then could put more of my time and attention on presenting the positive Christian perspective.

3. *Use films.* There are many excellent films on sexuality. You can pick them up at your local library, Christian film distributors, and videotape rental outlets. Films can be a great springboard for discussion. I'm finding that secular movies can be shown on a video at home as an excellent discussion and learning experience.

4. *Use books.* Today there are a number of excellent books on the subject of sex and related subjects. You can read books together that will bring on good discussion.

5. *Bring in an expert.* If you feel uncomfortable teaching in the area of sexuality, find someone in your congregation (doctor, nurse, psychologist, or homemaker) who feels comfortable dealing with these issues. Your church could bring in experts from the community, or a group of churches or a denomination might have a one-day seminar. As you use your imagination, great ideas will come your way.

6. *Avoid simplistic answers.* No matter what some of us were taught, sexuality is not black and white. In fact sexuality is much more than sexual intercourse. Encourage questions and disagreement, and remember that we must help kids make decisions about their sexuality on their own. If I make the decisions for them, then they really never made a decision.

7. *Talk about all the issues.* Remember that knowledge can't hurt the kids; it doesn't lead to promiscuity. Kids really appreciate an open and honest approach that deals with all aspects of their sexuality. I would suggest a good sexuality course dealing with many of these issues:

1. Guidelines of overcoming sexual temptation
2. How far is too far?
3. Why wait?
4. Sexual intercourse
5. How the culture influences our thinking about sex
6. Basic male/female sexual differences
7. How do you know if you're in love?
8. Conception and pregnancy
9. Unconditional love
10. Sexual abuse
11. Homosexuality
12. Venereal disease
13. Birth control
14. Options for pregnant couples (individuals)
15. Peer pressure
16. Dating
17. Drugs and drinking
18. Parties
19. Guilt and forgiveness
20. Pornography
21. Lust
22. AIDS

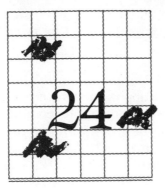

WORKING WITH KIDS FROM BROKEN HOMES

A few years ago I was away from my youth group for ten days. While I was gone, three couples who were parents of teen agers in my group split up. This experience of divorce within the church moved me to get as much information as I could about working with kids from divorced homes. No one likes divorce, and few if any divorces are easy, but we have to face the facts. There is one divorce every 27 seconds, and many of these are within the church. We as youth workers are seeing our ministries becoming filled with kids who are dealing with the trauma of a parental split. We must learn how to work effectively with these walking wounded.

Statistics help us see the pain of divorce. About 92 percent of the children live with Mom by either consent or default. Of those who are 11 to 16 years old, 16 percent see Dad one time a week, while 84 percent see Dad less than once a week. In fact, 45 percent of the kids of divorce do not see Dad more than twice a year. The average length of a first marriage is seven years. A second marriage lasts four to five years.

Awareness in the church is not enough; it takes understanding and at times a special ministry to deal with broken homes.

Everyone Loses

Every divorce involves loss. There is not only personal loss, but the more pragmatic loss of living standard. When a family splits into two households at approximately the same amount of income per month, there can be a drastic 50 percent reduction in income, since many fathers pay little or no alimony or child support. This is the one loss that kids may feel first.

A second loss is directly related to this loss of income, and that is loss of neighborhood. Many divorced households must move to cheaper housing. This can result not only in the loss of the familiar surroundings of a teenager's previous home but also the loss of their school or even of their church.

Young people also feel the loss of emotional support, since Mom and Dad are usually less able to give such support after a divorce. The teens feel loneliness, lack of understanding, lack of love, and often guilt. This became painfully real to me when Robert, a junior in high school, broke down and cried in my office over his parents' divorce. He had overheard them saying, "We would never have gotten into this mess if it hadn't been for Robert!" Robert found out that 16 years earlier his parents had conceived him out of wedlock. He was the result—their reason for marriage.

Other kids simply blame themselves. I've heard statements such as, "My sister and I argued too much, and finally my parents couldn't stand it anymore, so they broke up." Christian teenagers with non-Christian parents can especially browbeat themselves. "If only I'd talked to my parents about God more!"

Even the loss of church comes into play for many students. A few years ago we had a new girl from our community begin attending our church and youth group. She was wonderful. Not only did she have a servant's heart and know more Scripture than I did, but she brought friends to the group. About two months after Cindy arrived, it dawned on me that she had lived her whole life in our community. This said to me that there was undoubtedly another youth worker in the area who was depressed about losing her. I asked her about her church background, and sure enough she said she had been brought up at another church in our community. She didn't give me much information, but she did tell me that her father was an elder at that church.

That afternoon I called the church's youth worker and told him how much I had enjoyed Cindy's presence in our group, but I wondered if I could help her return to his church. He agreed that Cindy was a young, dynamic Christian with a vibrant, radiant faith. But his answer shocked me: "She can't come back right now."

"Why?" I asked with extreme curiosity. He replied, "Oh, hasn't she told you? Her father and mother are going through a messy divorce, and he is still active here. Her mother refuses to allow her to attend our church." For Cindy, even the loss of her own church was a direct result of her parents' divorce.

Each divorce consists of "minidivorces" and loss. For a teenager, the difficult decisions of who to live with or where to go on holidays is sometimes too difficult to cope with. The emotions and reactions of a child of divorce are complicated and changing. It's time that we in the church begin to understand the reactions and results of children of divorced families.

The Children of Divorce

There are numerous reactions to a divorce. In fact usually even in the same family the reactions will vary, sometimes in a major way. Youth workers need to be aware of common reactions to divorce in order to provide a better support base and help ease the pain. I will list briefly a few of the more common reactions to divorce. In your mind, see if you can't identify students in your group with the various behaviors discussed.

Pseudomature

This reaction to the divorce is to excel in growth and mature quickly. Pseudomature kids want to prove that they can do it on their own and take care of themselves. You'll often see this type of person marry early or quit school and get a job. He or she has had an abbreviated adolescence at best.

Childish

This behavior is the opposite of the pseudomature adolescent, yet you may find the two opposing reactions in the same family. This teenager is very immature. He gets stuck and won't go forward in progress and maturity. He wants to be taken care of and will make life difficult for anyone who doesn't baby him along. Mike's parents divorced when he was ten. He had been an excellent reader before the divorce, but at age 16 Mike was still reading at a ten-year-old level.

Spouse Replacement

A major reaction of many young people is to try to take the place of the ex-spouse. Their goal in life becomes to make Mom or Dad happy. Parents often play into this reaction because they like the attention. Such parents make the mistake of using their children as a replacement for the spouse.

Tom was a 14-year-old, 200-pound football player who slept in the same bed with his mother because she got so lonely at night. This was definitely not a healthy situation for his mom or for Tom. When I confronted their behavior, they both innocently said, "You have misunderstood; we aren't having sex." Neither could see any problem with Tom sharing a room with his mother.

Ping-Pong

Most adolescents from a divorce feel torn between Mom and Dad. They feel a responsibility and guilt to be good to both parents. The torn teenager feels a great deal of tension and stress during the holiday madness of the divorced family. I call them the "parent hoppers," trying to make everybody happy and to smooth out any problems between Mom and Dad. This person eventually becomes extremely discouraged and unhappy. The torn teenager often becomes the "jealous teenager." This is the person who begins to sabotage Mom and Dad's new relationships. He may tell lies or fail to give phone messages from the "new persons" in his parents' lives.

Money-Wise

One of the major problems in the vast majority of divorces is money. Finances are on the minds of everyone involved in the divorce. The money-wise teenager will work to help out because he desperately wants to continue living at the same standard. You'll find that this person is consumed with money problems. Parents (usually fathers) make the mistake of enticing their kids with money. Mom is barely making ends meet, the home is for sale, and they are moving to an apartment. Dad has not sent "the check" for three months, and one day Frank comes home with a new convertible: "It's an early birthday present." The frustration and confusion levels heighten.

Ostracized

Many young people want to feel "normal" immediately after the divorce. Dad has moved out of the house and the shouting has stopped, so now let's get on with life. *Immediate normality is not the case for everyone.* Psychologists tell us that it takes at least three years to feel somewhat normal, to have the custody settled, and to have the new roles in place. Often the parents are so emotionally distraught that much of the emotional support from parent to child is not available.

Children of divorce are looking for role models. They want significant adult relationships and a peer group to feel identified with. This is where the church can be a life-support system to children of divorce. Adults can come alongside, not to take their parents' places, but to provide role models during the transition time of divorce. The youth group can be the positive peer group which the young person needs to keep his or her life from falling apart. The misidentified teenager will search for role models and a peer group, and the church is the best option. However, if this is not available, he will keep looking until he finds an identifiable group. Unfortunately, many teens choose drugs, alcohol, promiscuous sex, and the "party life" instead of the church. Often the fault falls on a church which did not take time to care, listen, and respond.

Oversexed Teenager

I read a story recently by a young woman who had lived a very sexually promiscuous lifestyle as a teenager. It was simply titled "In Search of My Daddy's Love." Need I say more? Oversexed/under-loved teenagers desperately search for attachment. They want to feel loved and accepted. You'll even find teenagers who start their own families in order to get out of their situation. Often the result of an early marriage is the continuing story of another broken marriage and children from one more divorced home.

Karen never missed a youth group meeting. She was the first to arrive and the last to leave. The adult staff affectionately nick-named her "the clinger." She always had her arm around me or one of the other adult male sponsors. It was very uncomfortable, but we really didn't know, how to handle her "clinging actions." One afternoon at our adult staff meeting we decided to confront her, and I was elected to do so.

249

The next evening after youth group I invited her into my office and told her how much I appreciated her, yet the clinging was getting out of hand. She began to weep. She said, "I didn't mean for it to be sexual." My first reaction was to say, "Of course it isn't sexual," but I didn't say anything. I let her regain her composure, and then she kept talking. In the next 45 minutes she unfolded a story of her father leaving when she was six years old. He called the next year on her birthday and never called her again. Eleven times in her life men and much older teenage boys had sexual intercourse with her. Yet she wasn't looking for sex; she was screaming for male attention and had been sexually abused by self-centered men who took advantage of her desire to "search for her daddy's love."

Emotional Fallout

Not only do children of divorce react to the divorce in many different ways, but there are a number of common results of a divorce that youth workers must be aware of if they are to have an impact-filled ministry with these students.

Loneliness

Since Mom and Dad usually can't give much emotionally for the first few years after a divorce (even though they often try), many teenagers become increasingly lonely. You find them withdrawing from friends, relatives, and even school or church activities. There is a distance and detachment in which they often put up defense mechanisms. They've been hurt, and they don't want to get close again.

Sometimes their loneliness comes in the form of depression. Most kids from a broken home will feel depressed at times. They are hurt, angry, confused, and even embarrassed. Watch for dropping grades, a personality change, or even addiction to television.

Guilt

A common thread in all adolescents is guilt. Yet for many young people there are especially intense feelings of guilt that go along with a divorce. *Many young people blame their own misbehavior on the failure of their parents' marriage.* They believe that they have failed in some way. One of the very important things a youth worker can do is to allow their students to talk about this guilt. Help them see that they did not cause the divorce. Challenge the young people to talk with their parents about their feelings of guilt. Unless a parent is not mentally healthy, he or she will ease the guilt feelings by not placing blame on the children. Above all, let the young people know that their feelings of guilt are normal and can be dealt with in a positive manner.

Inability to Trust

Four out of five students are not prepared for the divorce of their parents. Many students will tell you that the separation came as a complete surprise. They feel let down, and don't be surprised to hear that in their mind *God* let them down. There is a lack of trust in parents, other relationships, and even God. As the defense mechanisms go up, there is an overwhelming feeling of not wanting to get hurt again.

You may find some students with a lack of understanding love. Their emotions have been wiped out, yet they are making major decisions based on their damaged emotions. "It is not uncommon for the child of a broken home to become hard and callous, seemingly unable to give or receive love. Time usually eases the hurt and heals these emotions. Kids can make silly mistakes when they have shut off their emotions. They can reject anyone who reaches out to them. They can pretend that everything is okay."[1] Their inability to love or trust can be overcome when significant others stick with them even if at first they reject all friendships.

Misfit Self-Image

David Elkind writes about the "imaginary audience" in his book *All Grown Up and No Place to Go*. He claims that teenagers view themselves as "on stage." Their vivid imagination produces feelings of uncertainty about how other people view them now that their family is divorced. Kids from divorced homes view themselves as being watched. Some of these students will become very sensitive at church, school, and family gatherings. Studies show that kids from broken homes are less optimistic and seek psychological help more often. In a sense they are different, but different isn't always bad or negative.

Anger

Anger can be a major emotion in divorce. Some anger can be very healthy, but extreme anger directed at self or family members can be destructive and cause disturbing behavior. Low self-image is a very common result of anger over the divorce. You may see such kids act out their behavior in your youth group through withdrawal or disruption or even by being belligerent to the adults in the group.

The anger may cause a real lack of direction. For many teen-agers of divorce, hopelessness pervades their life. Their motivation and drive slows to a crawl. There is simply too much going on inside, and their direction in life shuts down for a while.

Poverty

Financial loss is one of the major results of divorce. Of all families who get a divorce, 35 percent will move from above the poverty level to below the poverty level in one year. Parents usually try to maintain the same lifestyle with less money. The added stress and extra hours of working usually do more damage than lowering the lifestyle.

Youth workers must be aware of the added financial strain which church camps and retreats play on many single-family households. If at all possible, develop a fund where kids can work off camp scholarships for church-related events. Try to keep the costs down to insure the opportunity for everyone to attend your event.

Easing the Pain

The stark realities of divorce are not easy to handle. The reactions and results, however, are very real. Yet the good news is that you as a youth worker can give hope to teenagers of divorce. You can shine some light on an otherwise-bleak situation.

Provide an accepting community. Stability is a real need for kids of divorce. Life is going crazy in every direction for the person experiencing a separating family. The consistent support of you and the church youth group can be the one aspect of this teen's life that is not falling apart.

Unfortunately, some adolescents from divorced homes feel like lonely, abandoned, second-class citizens within the church as well. To combat this, develop a peer ministry in which teens learn to care for each other in any kind of crisis.

Try to provide "adoptive partner" relationships for each teen of divorce, in which one youth sponsor really takes that kid under his or her wing. Don't be afraid to refer a teen for pastoral or psychological counseling if you sense he needs it.

To create an empathic atmosphere in the congregation at large, some churches have sponsored divorce recovery workshops, led by adults and students who have "been through it."

Let them talk. More than anything, kids going through divorce need to talk about it. And at times they certainly can't do that at home because everyone else is also feeling the same hurt, anger, pain, and chaos.

You, however, can provide a sounding board. Whenever it's possible and appropriate, give the teen a chance to talk about his or her feelings. And make sure you keep current on what those feelings are. A teen's feelings, rarely a docile mare under normal circumstances, can turn into a plunging bronco during the stress of divorce. One day Jennifer tells me she is thrilled that her father has finally left the house. The next day she asks me to pray for her father's return. A week later she learns that her father is having an affair, and she never wants to see him again.

Talk about forgiveness and grace. After a disrupted family situation, family members usually experience an inability to trust. They may find it hard to accept the love that you and your caring community are offering. Be consistent in surrounding them with unconditional love, forgiveness, and grace. The gospel needs to be continually placed in front of them as their source of hope and strength. Eventually it will seep through.

253

Don't let a conservative theological stance on divorce (which I hope you have) get in the way of ministering to hurting people. God may not love divorce, but He certainly loves the victims of divorce, especially the children.

Help kids see the long view. Adolescents generally have trouble seeing the future, and kids of divorce get especially stuck in the here-and-now. Help them to see that even though life will be different, it will continue to go on.

Model good marriages. Teens of divorce need to know married couples who are living out their love for each other and their commitment to make the marriage work. It's part of your ministry to provide those models, even if it is not a perfect model.

Cathy and I have considered a major part of our ministry in recent years as being a role model of a married couple who aren't perfect but do love each other. At times we've cut back on our own Bible study involvement in order to free up our time to have students in our home. On a regular basis we invite students to our home for dinner. We all prepare the dinner, eat together, do the dishes, and then play games or sit and talk. We have found this unstructured time together to be one of our most valuable ministry opportunities as the students get better acquainted with us as a couple.

A little preventive maintenance is also a great idea. Provide programs in your youth group on building a positive marriage. At least 95 percent of your students will choose to get married at one time in their life, and few of them will have had much positive Christian input on how to make their marriage work.

Encourage the parents. Even though you as a youth worker may be younger than the parents involved, don't hesitate to express your caring for them. Perhaps you can be a reminder to them that the Christian community still loves them.

You can often be the catalyst to help the parents seek counseling. Even if I don't know the family, I try to make it a habit to visit whichever parent is still at home. It gives me a better understanding of how to help his or her teenager, and almost always the parent wants to talk. It has even been good for helping the nonchurch parent make the decision to become a part of the church.

As you deal with teens of divorce, remember that *you can make a difference*. Your presence, encouragement, and listening ear will help more than almost any kind of therapy. I asked a recently divorced mother of two teenagers in our church how she was doing. Her reply sums up this chapter: "It has been the most difficult experience in my life. I'm still a little numb. However, I've never experienced more love, encouragement, and acceptance than from this church. I would never choose to go through this, but it has brought me closer to God, and I honestly didn't know Christians would care so deeply for me and my kids. In the midst of our family trauma, I found more intimate friendships than I had ever imagined. I have been given to; now it's time for me to take what has been given to me and help others."

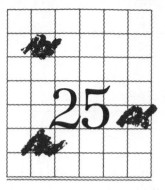

HELPING KIDS
IN CRISIS

The principal told me I would be speaking to the entire student body. They would come in at four different class periods. The public high school was a large, suburban, upper-middle-class school known for its excellent athletic teams, attractive students, and high academic standards. My topic was "Trauma in the Home." As I was being introduced at the first assembly, the principal leaned over and said, "Don't be surprised if you meet some hurting students today." I had asked a psychologist friend of mine to accompany me "just in case we get some problems." The plan was that she could meet with the kids, while I spoke to the next assembly.

After the second assembly I wasn't sure we should continue. I had just heard horror stories of rape, incest, drug abuse, beatings, and a suicide attempt. As I continued to talk about trauma in the home, these hurting students, who looked so together when they walked into the auditorium, continued to tell us story after story of tragedy.

This single experience in my life, more than anything else, reminds me of the fact that we are working with a generation in crisis. All the statistics point to the fact that in every area young people and their families are experiencing more crises in their lives than in any previous generation.

What Is a Crisis?

Crisis is self-defined. What you may view as a crisis I may not see as that extreme. Anytime a person feels that he or she has lost control and cannot effectively cope, then he is in a crisis situation. *Perception* is the key word in defining and dealing with a crisis. A list of crises usually found in youth ministry would be: unwanted pregnancy, eating disorders, suicide, neglectful abuse, death, delinquent behavior, runaway, assault, drug abuse, alcoholism, divorce, promiscuity, homosexuality, truancy, rebellion, or medical problems, to name only the most prevalent crises in the church.

I gave a talk on sexual abuse to a group of youth pastors and made the statement that one out of every four women has been sexually abused by the age of 18. A young man came to me and said, "I have a high school group of 125 young people and we've never had a problem in this area." I asked him if he had ever brought up the subject in the group, and he replied that he had never done so. I challenged him to talk about sexual abuse to his group within the next month and call me back. Two weeks later he called, amazed and a little stunned at the fact that he had already talked to eight people who were traumatized from sexual abuse.

My guess is that if all the people of your church were asked, "Are you or someone close to you going through a crisis?" the majority would answer yes by their own definition.

What Can a Youth Worker Do?

When people are in a crisis, they are often very open to finally receive help. For many who have left the church, when a crisis arises in their life, they turn back to the church for help. The Chinese word for crisis involves two characters, one meaning danger and the other meaning opportunity. The Greeks use the word crisis to mean a decision-making time that could turn out for better or for worse. What can the youth worker do to help people in crisis turn it into an opportunity for growth?

Get education in crisis counseling. There are many excellent books, seminars, and classes available on working with kids in crisis. Realize that you are not a professional counselor but that the kids will often come to you first in a crisis.

Set up a good referral system. Have easy access to phone numbers of professional agencies and counselors who can meet the crisis need.

Work with the family. When a person is in crisis the entire family suffers. Don't neglect the loved ones.

Don't overempathize. Feeling sorry for the person often gets in the way of your ability to give objective and neutral support.

Christian psychologist Gary Collins gives nine practical steps for helping kids in crisis.[1]

1. *Making contact.* This involves going to the young person in need and showing your willingness to be helpful.

2. *Reducing anxiety.* This may involve modeling calmness, listening carefully and sensitively, and giving encouragement and realistic hope.

3. *Focusing on the issues.* Kids in crisis are easily overwhelmed by the sudden events in their lives, and they can be helped by a more objective observer who can determine what needs to be done immediately as well as over the long haul.

4. *Evaluating resources.* It helps to take stock of the young person's individual resources (intelligence, skills, strengths, etc.), interpersonal resources (family, school, church, friends, and other people who can help), and spiritual resources (beliefs, level of spiritual maturity, inclination to pray, etc.).

5. *Planning intervention.* Try to help the kid in crisis make some decisions about what can and should be done to deal with the present circumstances.

6. *Encouraging action.* This gets the youth moving and coping as best he or she can.

7. *Instilling hope.* Instill hope by pointing out the positive, sharing from the Word of God, accepting the kid's need to express anger and grief, and challenging his or her self-defeating thoughts.

8. *Changing the environment.* Get friend and family support, encourage others to pray, give practical assistance, and make referrals where appropriate.

9. *Following up.* Stay in contact with the youth and later discuss both how the crisis was handled and how similar crises could be handled more effectively in the future.

This chapter is meant to be an overview of working with kids in crisis. You will want to do much more to get educated in this important area of your ministry. Three of the biggest need areas for practical information and overview are *substance abuse, suicide*, and *sexual abuse*.

Substance Abuse

If the statistics are true—that over three million teenagers are alcoholics and that at least one out of four young people live in a family where alcoholism is present—then there is a substance abuse problem in your church. The largest segment of our population now experimenting with drugs is in the 9-to-14-year-old age bracket. The sad thing is that kids become dependent on drugs and alcohol more quickly than adults.

With so many people in our churches suffering silently from the problems of chemical addiction, we in youth ministry must begin to meet these important needs. Many Christian families act as if the problem will go away if we don't talk about it. It won't.

Why Do Kids Get High?

The answer to the question of why kids use drugs and alcohol is complicated. Peer pressure, boredom, and poor self-image are all important factors to take into consideration. The vast majority of your students will experiment with drugs and alcohol. The more important question is "Why do kids *continue* to use drugs and alcohol?" Experimentation is normal, but what really hooks them and gets them addicted to these chemicals which they so often put in their body? The answer to this question is easy.

It makes them feel good. When a young person is not coping well in life, the substance dulls his pain. It's a false sense of relief, but nevertheless he feels better and life can go on.

It works every single time. Unfortunately, drugs and alcohol "work." The young person feels a sense of relief. If he is worried about his family struggles, grades, boyfriend/girlfriend loss, or whatever, the substance in his body makes the hurt go away (temporarily).

Stages of Change

The very frightening part of the two reasons listed as to why kids continue to take drugs and drink is to look at what happens when there is continued use and abuse of drugs and alcohol: *Kids stop learning how to cope with stress.* When young people depend on a chemical high to relieve stress, all other stress-reducing mechanisms in the body and mind take second place to the chemical. After all, the chemical works quicker and it works every time. The other thing that happens when kids continue to use drugs and alcohol is that they *change in stages.* It is important for youth workers to understand the stages of use and abuse.

1. *Experimental use.* This often happens in late grade school or junior high. There is an occasional drink at a party or from their parents' liquor cabinet.

2. *More regular use.* Many young high schoolers are in this stage of use. Their tolerance increases (which is dangerous), and there is more than occasional use at parties and social get-togethers.

3. *Social use.* The social-use phase occurs when drinking alcohol or taking drugs is slowly becoming accepted behavior. Now the young person's tolerance is higher. He or she regularly drinks or takes drugs and may even be able to drive less impaired than at an earlier stage because of a higher tolerance.

4. *Daily preoccupation.* The young people are hooked. They may be experimenting with harder drugs. They are getting high a number of times a week. Often their grades will suffer, and to pay for this expensive habit they may begin stealing and lying.

5. *Dependency.* The young person may not realize it, but he has become dependent on a chemical to help him cope with life. He must get high to get through his day. He is addicted. There is a dangerous preoccupation with getting high. Many times the person in this stage will violate his value system and will move from one peer group to the next. Usually there is a loss of control.

Is there hope? *Yes.* Chemical dependency is a disease and it can be treated. We can offer help and hope to people because they can change. Treatment is usually a necessity, but people can and do change. In fact, many students are showing that when you combine God and Alcoholics Anonymous, people have a very good possibility of recovering from chemical dependency.

What Can You Do?

I believe that every youth worker must get as much information as possible. Steve Arterburn's book, *Growing Up Addicted*, has been most helpful to me. I suggest that every youth worker should attend an AA (Alcoholics Anonymous) meeting. By far the greatest percentage of recovery comes when people are actively involved in AA. I also urge people to learn about the various alcohol and drug abuse treatment centers in your area. These centers are very helpful and informative.

Talk openly in your group about alcohol and drug abuse. Never show disgust for the abuser, but continually give your kids the opportunity to talk with you about their problem or how substance abuse of a loved one is affecting them. A number of kids in your group are victims of an abusive alcoholic home. They need as much help as the alcoholic.

The three sections on the issue of substance abuse found in the following pages can be very helpful tools for your ministry.

RECOGNIZING SUBSTANCE ABUSE

A first step in dealing with substance abuse is recognizing its many symptoms. The following signs and changes in behavior don't always mean that there is substance abuse, but they should trigger concern.

_____ secretiveness; withdrawal
_____ disdain for authority
_____ disobedience at home, school, and youth group
_____ withdrawal from youth group functions
_____ drug paraphernalia, incense, seeds, other drugs found on him or her

_____ rise in school absences
_____ violent or noticeably lethargic behavior
_____ wide mood swings
_____ loss of thought process; strange thinking
_____ radical change in school performance; disrespect toward teachers; dropping grades
_____ changes in personal hygiene
_____ increased interest in heavy-metal music and songs with drug-oriented lyrics
_____ unusually late night hours
_____ I-don't-care attitude
_____ tiredness and depression
_____ inability to concentrate
_____ change in appetite; dramatic increase or decrease in weight
_____ lack of coordination; clumsiness
_____ slurred or garbled speech patterns; rapid speech
_____ changes in sleeping habits
_____ periods of hyperactivity
_____ watery, red eyes
_____ drippy nose
_____ loss of interest in hobbies and old friends[2]

QUESTIONS FOR PARENTS

You may suspect that your child or teenager is having trouble with alcohol and other drugs, but short of smelling liquor on his breath or discovering pills in his pockets, how can you tell for sure? While symptoms vary, there are some common tip-offs. Your answers to the following questions will help you determine if a problem exists.

1. Has your child's personality changed markedly? Does he or she change moods quickly, seem sullen, withdraw from the family, display sudden anger or depression, or spend hours alone in his or her room?
   Yes _____ No _____ Uncertain _____

263

2. Has your child lost interest in school, school activities, or school athletics? Have his grades dropped at all?
    Yes ___ No ___ Uncertain ___

3. Has your child stopped spending time with old friends? Is he or she now spending time with kids that worry you? Is your child secretive or evasive about his or her friends, and where they go and what they do?
    Yes ___ No ___ Uncertain ___

4. Are you missing money or other objects from around the house (money needed for alcohol and drugs), or have you noticed that your child has more money (possibly from selling drugs) than you would expect?
    Yes ___ No ___ Uncertain ___

5. Has your child tangled with the law in a situation involving drugs in any way? (You can be assured that if this has happened, there have been other time—probably many— when he/she has been drinking or using drugs but hasn't gotten caught.)
    Yes ___ No ___ Uncertain ___

6. Does your child get angry and defensive when you talk to him or her about alcohol and drugs, or refuse to discuss the topic at all? (People who are very defensive about alcohol and drugs are often hiding how much they use.)
    Yes ___ No ___ Uncertain ___

7. Has your child become dishonest? Do you feel you're not getting straight answers about your child's whereabouts, activities, or companions? A young person may also lie about matters that seem unrelated to alcohol or drugs.
    Yes ___ No ___ Uncertain ___

8. Are there physical signs of alcohol or drug use? Have you smelled alcohol on your child's breath? Have you smelled the odor of marijuana on his or her clothing or in his or her room? Slurred speech, unclear thinking, or swaggering gait are also indicators. Bloodshot eyes, dilated pupils, and imprecise eye movement may also be clues.
    Yes ___ No ___ Uncertain ___

9. Has your child lost interest in previously important hobbies, sports, or other activities? Has your child lost motivation, enthusiasm, and vitality?
    Yes ___ No ___ Uncertain ___

10. Have you seen evidence of alcohol or drugs? Have you ever found a hidden bottle, beer cans left in the car, marijuana seeds, marijuana cigarettes, cigarette rolling papers, drug paraphernalia (pipes, roach clips, stash cans, etc.), capsules, or tablets?

    Yes ___ No ___ Uncertain ___

11. Has your child's relationship with you or other family members deteriorated? Does your child avoid family gatherings? Is your child less interested in siblings, or does he or she now verbally (or even physically) abuse younger brothers and sisters?

    Yes ___ No ___ Uncertain ___

12. Has your child ever been caught with alcohol or drugs at school or school activities?

    Yes ___ No ___ Uncertain ___

13. Has your child seemed sick, fatigued, or grumpy (possibly hung over) in the morning after drug or alcohol use was possible the night before?

    Yes ___ No ___ Uncertain ___

14. Has your child's grooming deteriorated? Does your child dress in a way that is associated with drug or alcohol use? Does your child seem unusually interested in drug- or alcohol-related slogans, posters, music, or clothes?

    Yes ___ No ___ Uncertain ___

15. Has your child's physical appearance changed? Does he or she appear unhealthy, lethargic, more forgetful, or have a shorter attention span than before?

    Yes ___ No ___ Uncertain ___

How to Score the Test

This questionnaire is not a scientific instrument and is *not meant to diagnose* alcohol and drug problems. It is meant to alert parents that problems are likely. The questions are "red flag" detectors and your answers may show a need for further action. Keep in mind that "yes" answers to some of these questions may simply reflect normal adolescent behavior. "Yes" answers to questions directly relating to alcohol and drug use (5, 8, 10, 12) are, of course, cause for concern; they indicate that your child is using alcohol and/or drugs, and action should be taken.

In general, parents should look for an emerging pattern. A couple of "yes" or "uncertain" answers should alert parents to suspect alcohol and drug use, monitor the child more closely, talk to knowledgeable sources, and prepare to seek help.

If you answered "yes" to three or more questions, help is probably needed. Your child may be in the experimental stages or may already be heavily involved in alcohol and drugs. Remember, it is *very, very* difficult to handle this problem without the help of other experienced parents and/or professionals. This is *not* often a problem that passes with time; it may well be a life or death matter. If you are concerned, take action: Call a knowledgeable source, your school counselor or other alcoholism/drug counselors who deal with adolescents, your local council on alcoholism, or other drug/alcohol agency and discuss this questionnaire.

STUDENT INFORMATION

Most young people have used alcohol in one form or another, but few recognize that alcoholism is a disease that can affect the young as well as the old. Take this short test; it may tell you something about yourself.

Yes	No	Question
____	____	1. Do you lose time from school due to drinking?
____	____	2. Is it necessary for you to drink in order to have fun?
____	____	3. Do you drink to build up your self-confidence?
____	____	4. Do you drink alone?
____	____	5. Is drinking affecting your reputation—or do you care?
____	____	6. Do you drink to escape from school or home worries?
____	____	7. Do you feel guilty or bummed after drinking?
____	____	8. Does it bother you if someone says that you drink too much?
____	____	9. Do you sneak drinks from your parents' supply or anyone else's?

——— ——— 10. Do you generally "make out" better when you drink?

——— ——— 11. Do you get into financial troubles over buying liquor?

——— ——— 12. Do you feel a sense of power when you drink?

——— ——— 13. Have you lost friends since you've started drinking?

——— ——— 14. Have you started hanging around with kids who drink?

——— ——— 15. Do most of your friends drink less than you do?

——— ——— 16. Do you drink until you are drunk or the bottle is empty?

——— ——— 17. Have you ever had a complete loss of memory from drinking?

——— ——— 18. Have you ever been to a hospital or been busted due to drunk driving or being drunk in public or in school?

——— ——— 19. Do you turn off to any studies or lectures about drinking?

——— ——— 20. Do you think you may have a problem with liquor?

——— ——— TOTALS

If you answered YES to any one question, this could be a warning that you are becoming a problem drinker. If you answered YES to any two questions, chances are that you might be a problem drinker. If you answered YES to any three questions, you probably are a problem drinker.[4]

Suicide

You could have given me every name in my youth group and the person in my opinion least likely to attempt suicide was Suzanne. Yet here I was talking to Suzanne's mother, who was caught totally by surprise. My mind raced back to the previous Sunday when Suzanne told me her boyfriend broke up with her, but then she was quick to tell me all the "Christian jargon" she was supposed to about it being God's will, there was probably someone else better for her, etc. I missed her hidden pain. I didn't read between the lines. She was a master at hiding her hurt. Now the doctors were struggling to breathe life into her comatose body. She survived, but the shock of her suicide attempt forced me into looking at a very unpleasant topic—teenage suicide.

Our generation of teenagers is killing themselves more regularly than any previous generation. It is a tragedy all across the nation, reaching into the homes of the richest of rich as well as the ghettos. Suicide is the third-highest cause of death among young people. In the United States more than 5000 youth kill themselves annually. That's an average of one every 104 minutes! Besides that, mental health experts estimate that between 500,000 and two million young people attempt suicide every year. That could be as many as 5500 per day.[5]

Common Myths About Suicide [6]

There are common myths about suicide that even people in the helping professions assume to be true. These myths will give you a better understanding of many of the issues surrounding suicide.

People who talk about suicide won't do it. The truth is that about 80 percent of those who commit suicide have talked about suicide, *but most of those they talked to did not take them seriously.* Anyone talking about suicide should be taken seriously.

Mentioning suicide may give the person the idea. Many people are afraid that if they ask someone whether he has contemplated suicide, they could actually cause him to consider suicide even though he had not previously considered it. Not true. If you suspect that someone is considering suicide, check it out. Just plain ask him or her directly. Talking about suicide with someone who is contemplating it actually works as a preventive by encouraging the person to talk about it.

Suicide occurs without warning. Not only do suicidal people give warning, but they usually give lots of warning signs. Hindsight is always 20/20, and after someone has committed suicide, friends and family are usually shocked when they realize how many warning signs they missed. The warning signs can be any combination of moodiness, withdrawal, sudden traumatic event (especially the breakup with a longtime boyfriend or girlfriend), violent behavior, or a history of drugs and alcohol. There are usually more than enough warning signs, but those who are closest to the person simply can't believe that a friend of theirs would actually take his or her own life.

All suicidal people are mentally ill. Too many people believe that suicide happens only to people who are mentally ill, mentally retarded, or very poor. They can't imagine that a *normal* person would want to take his life. The truth is that only about 15 percent of those who take their lives have actually been diagnosed as mentally ill.

Suicidal people are totally committed to dying. Not true. One of the most common characteristics of adolescents who are contemplating suicide is *ambivalence.* They have a strong desire to end their life and at the same time a strong desire to live. Your best approach is to use their ambivalence and encourage their strong feelings about living.

When depression lifts, the suicide crisis is over. Often the lifting of the depression means only that the adolescent has finally decided to take his own life. The depression is replaced with a feeling of euphoria or relief now that the decision has been made. Incredibly, many suicides occur within three months after the people have appeared to overcome the depression.

Suicidal people do not seek medical help. Strangely, research has shown that three out of four people who have taken their lives have seen a doctor within one to three months beforehand.

A Time, A Place, A Method

When someone talks to you about a potential suicide, there is a very effective method to determine how serious he really is. If he is talking about it, then of course it is important and he needs help; however, he may not be lethal yet! Rich Van Pelt, an authority on teenage suicide, says, "There are three things needed to die: 1) a time, 2) a place, 3) a method. If in your discussion with the young person all of the above are present, then the person needs immediate attention."[7]

I vividly remember a late-night phone call from two girls who had been in my high school group and were now in college. Ginny apologized for calling in the middle of the night, but she said Linda was with her and wanted to kill herself. I asked a few questions and discerned that it was serious. She had a time, place, and method. I invited them over to our house. We talked and sought counseling help the next day. The following weekend Linda called me again in the middle of the night. She had just broken up with her boyfriend. I had to discern if she was suicidal. I didn't believe her to be, so I told her I would love to see her the following day. In the middle of the night, she would not have my full attention. I could not let Linda begin to manipulate my time. Van Pelt's formula of time, place, and method will help you make decisions on how serious the potential suicide is.

Keith Olson in his excellent book *Counseling Teenagers* uses an adaptation of a questionnaire originally designed by A. G. Devries in order to make a quick suicide potential evaluation from the person's self-rating.[8]

This questionnaire provides good indicators for suicide potential. However, the weakness is the heavy reliance on the counselor's subjective evaluation. This questionnaire can be a tool to establish a need and then refer the person to a professional who is comfortable in dealing with potential suicidal tendencies.

SUICIDE QUESTIONNAIRE

	YES	NO
1. My future happiness looks promising.	____	____
2. I have recently had difficulty sleeping.	____	____
3. I think I am to blame for almost all my troubles.	____	____

4. When I'm sick, the doctor often prescribes sedatives for me. ____ ____
5. My future looks secure. ____ ____
6. Sometimes I really feel afraid. ____ ____
7. Sometimes I fear I will lose control over myself. ____ ____
8. Lately I haven't felt like participating in my usual activities. ____ ____
9. I go on occasional drinking sprees. ____ ____
10. Within the last few years I have moved at least twice. ____ ____
11. I have someone whose well-being I care about very much. ____ ____
12. I generally feel that I am completely worthless. ____ ____
13. I frequently have a drink in the morning. ____ ____

Suicidal counselees will tend to produce the following pattern of responses:

1. No	4. Yes	6. Yes	9. Yes	11. No
2. Yes	5. No	7. Yes	10. Yes	12. Yes
3. Yes		8. Yes		13. Yes[9]

Sexual Abuse

I almost feel I should put a warning in this section of the chapter that reads *Caution: If you get involved and become knowledgeable in the area of sexual abuse . . . you can never be the same.*

Statistics tell us that one out of four young women have been sexually abused by the age of 18, and one out of eight young men by the same age. Authorities suggest that only one out of 20 sexual abuse cases are ever reported to the police. Perhaps the most frightening statistic is that there has been a 943 percent increase of such abuse in the past ten years.

Our society's conception is that the abuser is a skid row bum, smelling of liquor and brutally forcing himself through violence into a sexual abuse situation. *However, the facts tell us that*

80 percent of sexual assaults on children are by someone they already know and trust.

The Ugly Truth

As I started bringing up the subject of sexual abuse within my own youth group, the stories began to come out of the closet. Janice was baby-sitting for her ex-boyfriend's family. The boy-friend's stepfather came home. He asked Janice to stay. They watched a movie together. He said, "You look tired; let me rub your back." Janice didn't know what to say. He first started rubbing outside her sweater, then under her sweater on her skin. He slowly moved his hand to her breasts. Janice felt paralyzed. The phone rang, and she ran out the door.

Tom went camping at age 11 with his favorite uncle. Seven years later he told me a terrible story of forced homosexual rape which had been going off and on for all those years.

When Debra was nine her father began to fondle her private parts. She didn't like it but thought that maybe she was supposed to let him since he was her father and she loved and adored him. Seven years later (the average length of time for an incest victim), Debra hated her father, was disgusted with her life, and wanted to end it all through suicide.

When Marla's brother would get high on dope he would force himself on her. He always left with the same threat: "If you tell anyone about this, I'll kill you." She believed him. When she finally told her parents they called *her* the liar.

These are not uplifting case studies. If you could meet each one of these people you would never guess that they had such major problems. Their stories are similar to the millions of people in the United States who suffer in silence.

Warning Signs

If you are willing to help people who have been sexually abused, there is hope for them. These victims of one of the most destructive of all human behaviors can receive help, though it takes a great deal of time and a willingness to hurt alongside them.

There are specific signals of sexual abuse. Most victims will not come to you right away with their secret. Teenagers may tell you by their behavior rather than their words.

Listed below are a number of signals of sexual abuse, although the mere fact that a teenager has one or more of these behaviors does not always mean that he or she has been sexually abused.

1. Learning problems in school
2. Poor peer relationships
3. Self-destructive behavior; suicidal tendencies; frequent drug and alcohol abuse
4. Hostility and lack of trust toward adults
5. Major problems with authority figures
6. Seductive, promiscuous behavior
7. Running away
8. Fear of going home; fear of being left alone with the abuser
9. Severe depression
10. Pain, itching, bleeding, bruises in the genital areas
11. Extremely low self-image

If you suspect an incestuous relationship, consider these potential signals for abusive sexual behavior on the part of adults.

1. Demands isolation of the child—discourages friendships, school activities, dates.
2. Enforces restrictive control—allows few social events (actually extremely jealous).
3. Displays overdependence—sometimes the parent will depend on the child to fill needs usually met by the spouse or other adult.
4. Indulges in frequent drinking.

When Someone Confides in You

If you talk about sexual abuse enough times, someone will seek you out for help. You've touched an issue that is never very far from the abused person's mind and heart.

Abused people are dealing with their secret with every sermon, relationship, and activity in their life. When they come to you, here are six principles to help you help them.

273

Believe him. Few people lie about sexual abuse. There are some false stories, but most often they're true. Assume that people are telling the truth until proven guilty.

Listen. Let them tell you their story at their pace. Clarify, but don't interrogate. Abused people need a listening ear. If you have had a similar situation, you may wish to tell them, but do not go on and on with your story. They need to talk.

Be supportive. Sexual abuse victims who tell you their trauma will need your support. They need your verbal support that you believe them and will care for them and help them. They need your time. If God entrusts one of these precious souls to you, you will have to be available to give him or her the priceless gift of your time. At times in listening to the story, we can tend to be critical (saying something like "That was dumb" or "You shouldn't have been so careless"). *Don't be critical.* Abused people do not need to be reminded of their carelessness.

Recognize emotional and medical needs. As someone is telling you his story, do not overlook his medical or emotional needs. He may need to see a doctor immediately.

Find community resources. You cannot handle this problem alone. Have easily accessible phone numbers for rape crisis hotlines, departments of mental health, medical facilities, and women's centers at local colleges and universities.

Don't keep it a secret. One of the biggest mistakes that youth workers make is that they do not report sexual abuse to the authorities. In many states the law requires you to report such abuse. Because of the spiritual nature of church work, youth workers do not enforce the law as a schoolteacher would. However, the secret has already been kept too long, so tell the abused person of your desire to report the crime. Tell him you will walk with him through this. Let the proper authorities handle the legal and psychological problems, but you be a friend and pastoral counselor. If you choose not to report this crime, you are hindering the healing process and perhaps breaking the law.

Usually after you report a case of sexual abuse a detective trained in this field will immediately interview the victim, the abuser, yourself, and family members, and then make the proper decision on what to do.

Where Does God Fit into the Picture?

There is no question about the fact that a victim of sexual abuse can have a badly distorted view of God. Questions like "How can a loving God allow this to happen to me?" are very common and need to be dealt with in a professional manner. Although I am not a therapist, here are a few difficulties I perceive to be evident in the victim's spiritual life.

Fatherhood. There is difficulty in trusting God as a loving Father. This is especially true in the case of an incest victim. The Father image of God is not a positive image to most of these people.

Unconditional love. For victims of sexual abuse the biblical message of unconditional love is a difficult concept to comprehend. There have always been "conditions" for love in their life.

Forgiveness. Unfortunately, many victims feel that they had something to do with the problem. They feel dirty and sinful. Understanding God's forgiveness and forgiving themselves is a difficult task. Along with a difficulty in the area of forgiveness, there is usually an extreme struggle with guilt.

You can help by *accepting* them and their story. These people need *hope* and *reassurance* of your love and God's love. They need to know that the abuse is not their fault, and that God is a loving God. You can even help the long process of *reconciliation*. I'm not suggesting that most sexual abuse relationships will be reconciled to a normal, loving relationship. However, many people I know have become reconciled through prayer. The hate turns to pity and prayer for the condition of the abuser. This does not happen overnight; it may take years.

What Do We Tell Our Kids?

If the statistics at the beginning of this section are true, then we must discuss the problems of sexual abuse within our youth group. We should allow time for the students to talk about the problem.

Often young people will confide in a chosen friend to tell their story. In my *Handling Your Hormones* youth events, I will often have two young girls come arm in arm to share "their secret." Until they chose to talk to me, only those two had known. Help your students help their friends. I've found that the best way to teach on sexual abuse is through case studies and group discussions. Then educate your students thoroughly on this subject.

Another very important point to consider in your youth ministry is to *screen your adult volunteers*. We can't forget that sexual abusers like to stay close to kids. If you see any behavior that seems abnormal, do not be afraid to confront the person. I would rather be overly cautious than to allow permanent change to occur for one of God's precious children. Because of the magnitude of the problem, I believe that not only you but your entire staff should be trained in the area of sexual abuse.

The following is information that I believe should be in the hands of every young person. This information will give kids a better understanding of sexual abuse, of their rights, and of positive steps they can take to deal with this problem. The publisher of this book has given youth workers special permission to reproduce this material for the benefit of their students.[10]

Information on Sexual Abuse

Nobody has the right to touch your body without your permission, regardless of how much he loves you, how much money he has spent on you, or for any other reason.

Anytime a touch makes you feel uncomfortable, you have the right to say no. You never *owe* another person the right to touch you. *Trust your gut feelings*. Pushing, manipulating, pressuring, exploiting, or abusing another person is never acceptable in any relationship.

If someone touches you in a way you don't like, tell the person to stop and get away, and then talk about it with an adult you trust.

If an adult or older teenager has touched you in the past, it is *not your fault*. It is *always* the adult's responsibility.

It is *very important* that you get counseling for sexual abuse *now,* in order to prevent problems as you grow older. If you have never talked with a counselor, seek help immediately,

The sexual assault of a person occurs when a male or female is tricked, coerced, seduced, intimidated, forced into cooperating, or forced into not offering any resistance to sexual activity with another person.

Sexual abuse can be defined as:

Showing children pornographic materials
Taking nude pictures
Adult exposing himself to child or asking him to expose himself
Fondling private areas of the body
Intimate kissing
Genital contact
Intercourse
Rape

Sexual assault includes incest, molestation, rape, and "date rape."

Incest is sexual activity between any relatives.

Usually:	father/stepfather
	grandfather
	uncle
	cousin
	brother
Occasionally:	mother
	grandmother
	aunt

Molestation is sexual activity with someone outside the person's family. Eighty percent of molestations are by someone the victim knows and trusts:

family friend	mother's boyfriend
neighbor	teacher
coach	doctor/dentist
pastor/priest	youth leader
camp counselor	baby-sitter

Only 20 percent of molestations are by strangers.

Rape is forced penetration (by penis or any object) of the vagina, mouth, or anus against the will of the victim.

Acquaintance rape or "date rape" is rape by someone you know or are dating. Date rapists generally use just enough force to gain compliance. A man may use his physical power to coerce intercourse, taking advantage of a situation by using force, pressure, deception, trickery, or teen vulnerability. The date rapist is not a weird, easily identifiable person. He is just like anyone else except that he uses force to get his way.

About 75 percent of teen rapes are acquaintance rapes or "date rapes." What to do if you are raped:

Get to a safe place.
Do not bathe, douche, or change clothes.
Call a rape crisis hotline.
Have a friend or family member go with you to the hospital emergency room (take a change of clothes if possible):

- To preserve the evidence (very important if you decide to prosecute)
- To determine injury
- To check for venereal disease and pregnancy

Reporting the crime to police is a decision that only you can make.

Reasons for Reporting:

Making a police report will benefit you directly.

- Reporting the assault is a way of regaining your sense of personal power and control.
- Reporting enables you to do something concrete about the crime committed against you.
- Reporting helps ensure that you receive the most immediate and comprehensive assistance available.

Making a police report will help prevent other people from being raped.

- Reporting and prosecuting the assailant are essential to the prevention of rape.
- Most rapists are repeat offenders.
- If the rape is not reported, the assailant cannot be apprehended.

Facts About Rape

- In the United States a rape is reported approximately once every six minutes.
- Rape is one of the most frequent violent crimes, and its incidence is steadily increasing.
- Victims range in age from small children to the elderly. They come from all lifestyles and socioeconomic groups.
- Rape is a crime of violence. The rapist uses force or threats of harm to overpower and control the victim.
- Although rape may or may not result in serious physical injuries, it almost always causes severe emotional distress.

PUTTING
THE PUZZLE TOGETHER

MY
AREAS-OF-MINISTRY
MODEL

W hen you are ready to put the pieces of a youth ministry program together, the important question to ask is: How do I do it? How do I organize everything so that it gives me a grasp and focus of my ministry? One way to put it all together is to fill out an Areas-of-Ministry sheet.

If I were asked to consult with you as the youth minister at your church, before I ever stepped onto your church property I would ask you to fill out such a sheet. I would want you to state on paper in a clear and concise manner every aspect of ministry in which your program is involved at your church. Each year you would be responsible to put on paper your goals and objectives for each program and, if appropriate, a calendar of events as well.

Developing an Areas-of-Ministry sheet pulls all your programs together. You know where you are going and how you will get there. This sheet will give the volunteers, parents, and staff at your church the opportunity to see at a glance what you will be doing during the next year. If you are the leader of the youth staff, then the Areas-of-Ministry sheet is an excellent device to keep you in touch with all that is happening in the group.

The next few pages comprise an Areas-of-Ministry sheet from my high school ministry at South Coast Community Church. South

Coast Community Church is a large suburban church with a paid intern staff and a number of volunteers. If you are in a small or average-size youth group, don't expect to put together such a lengthy Areas-of-Ministry sheet.

Remember that the Areas-of-Ministry sheet simply represents goals and objectives of the program, who is in charge, and a calendar of events (if possible).

AREAS OF MINISTRY

High School Ministry

1. Sunday evening celebration
2. High school hour (Sunday school)
3. Area meetings (weekly Bible studies)
4. Mission emphasis
5. Calling and follow-up
6. Contact work
7. One-on-one (discipleship and counseling)
8. Social/special events
9. Retreats and conferences
10. Staff leadership
11. Leadership core (student leadership)
12. Support groups
13. Publicity and promotion
14. Overtime
15. Parents' advisory board
16. Recreation

1. *Sunday evening celebration*
   Director: Jim
   This will be our new program for the fall. The elements of worship, prayer, and praise have been missing in our program, and this Sunday Evening Celebration will hopefully help fill this gap. Sunday Evening Celebration will be open to junior high and senior high students. The evening will consist of praise-oriented singing, special music, a short talk, sharing, and prayer.

Responsibilities: 1) Prepare a short talk or ask someone to speak; 2) make sure that the song leader is there and understands our goals; 3) lead the sharing and prayer time or have a student leader involved.

2. *High school hour (Sunday school)*
Director: Doug
We must put a major effort into making the High School Hour one of our top priority ministries for this year. We have more kids coming to the High School Hour than any of our other programs. We need to upgrade all aspects of this hour and continue high-quality teaching and relational work.

The High School Hour should be a time of *equipping* our people for actual ministry. The atmosphere must be friendly and upbeat. The High School Hour is a perfect time to make appointments for the week and encourage people to come to our other weekly experiences. We always have visitors at the High School Hour; make sure you meet every new person each week.

The program should be upbeat, fun, and affirming, and should have an accepting atmosphere. Student leadership should take an active role in this ministry. All new people should be greeted by the staff and leadership core.

Responsibilities: 1) Lead in the planning of the entire year; 2) oversee each week's responsibilities; 3) Be a "moderator" (M.C.) for the High School Hour.

SAMPLE SCHEDULE

High School Sunday School

Theme: The Issues Around Me (large group)

October	*Speaker or person in charge of program*	*Topic*
2	Doug W.	"Relationships & Me"
9	Jim	"Media & Me"

October	Speaker or person in charge of program	Topic
16	Doug W.	"Communication & Me"
23	Jim	"World & Me"
30	Doug W.	"Music & Me"

Special instructions: Speaker is in charge of curriculum, teaching methods, and any decision to break into small groups.

Theme: Book of Philippians (large group/small group)

November

6	Jim	Chapter 1
13	Katie	Chapter 2
20	Jim	Chapter 3
27	Doug F.	Chapter 4

Special instructions: Speaker will speak for a ten-minute overview of the chapter. Jim will be responsible to put together a weekly small-group Bible study on each chapter of Philippians. The small-group study needs to be in the hands of the small-group leaders one week ahead of time.

December

4	Katie	Student Leadership Seminars (five small groups)
11	Doug W.	Drama Presentation
18	Jim	"The Gift of Christmas"
25		NO SUNDAY SCHOOL

January	Speaker or person in charge of program	Topic
1		NO SUNDAY SCHOOL
8	Doug W.	"New Year Priorities"
15		NO SUNDAY SCHOOL (Great Adventure Winter Camp)
22	Doug F.	Parents' Panel
29	Doug W.	Concert

February		Topic
5		Elective Series
12		Elective Film (Mammoth Ski Trip)
19		Elective Series
26		Elective Series

Special instructions: We will offer three elective series for the month of February. Students may choose any of the electives they want but must stick with the electives for the entire month. New students may attend the "Life at Home" Series.

Elective 1: "Life at Home" (Daryl and Doug W. in charge)
Elective 2: "Spiritual Disciplines" (Doug F. and Katie in charge)
Elective 3: "Serendipity Series" (Jim and Lisa in charge)

Theme: Missions Month

March		
4	Katie	"Servanthood"
11	Katie	"Biblical Missions"
18	Katie	"Peace Child" (Film)
25	Jim	"Involvement"

Special instructions: Katie is in charge of this month.

Theme: Preparation for Easter

April	Speaker or person in charge of program	Topic
1	Doug W.	"Last Week of Christ's Life"
8	Jim	"Crucifixion"
15	Katie	"Resurrection"
22		NO SUNDAY SCHOOL

Theme: Sex, Love, and Dating Series

April

29	Doug W.	"Fantasy Factor"

May

6	Jim	"Sex Ed"
13	Jim	"Love"
20	Doug F.	"Philosophy of Dating"
27	Lisa	Film on Sexuality

June

3	Doug F.	"Creativity" Summer Promotion
10	Doug W.	Concert

3. *Area meetings (weekly Bible studies)*
Director: Jim
   Because of the size of our group and the desire to remain in smaller units, we have decided to work again in areas. The group will be divided into four geographical areas. Each area has an Area Director or Co-Area Directors. Much of the actual ministry of the high school group will take place in the areas.

MY AREAS-OF-MINISTRY MODEL

The following is a diagram of how the areas are divided.

AREA DIVISION DIAGRAM

YOUTH MINISTER (Jim)

Assistant (Katie)

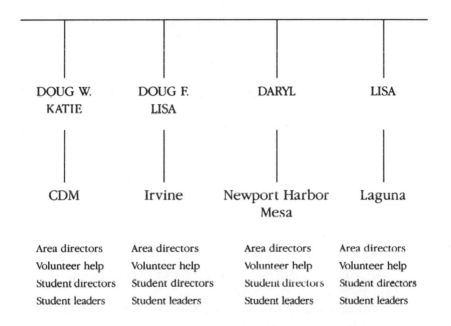

DOUG W. KATIE	DOUG F. LISA	DARYL	LISA
CDM	Irvine	Newport Harbor Mesa	Laguna
Area directors	Area directors	Area directors	Area directors
Volunteer help	Volunteer help	Volunteer help	Volunteer help
Student directors	Student directors	Student directors	Student directors
Student leaders	Student leaders	Student leaders	Student leaders

RESPONSIBILITIES SHEET

Area ministries responsibilities

- Weekly program meetings
- Bible studies
- Contact work
- One-on-one (discipleship)
- Area adult staff
- Area leadership core

Entire high school ministry

- High school hour (Sunday school)
- Mission
- Special events
- Retreats & conferences
- Staff leadership
- Leadership core (monthly)

- Support groups
- Parents' advisory
- Area special events

- Overtime
- Parents' ministry & parents' advising
- Recreation
- Monthly outreach meetings

4. *Mission emphasis*
   Director: Katie

   There are basically two goals in the mission area. First, we must challenge the kids to see beyond themselves and the area in which they live. They need to see the needs of people and be motivated to meet those needs in any way available to them. We must challenge them to develop a lifestyle of servanthood.

   Second, we must bring them to a point of discipleship in which they see mission as an integral part of their faith. We need to create in them a burning desire to serve God wherever He may call them—wherever they can best be used to glorify God and further His kingdom, whether at home or abroad. We will offer a variety of mission experiences to accomplish these goals:

   a. Continue to support Leandro in Brazil through World Vision.
   b. Two orphanage trips—one on October 14-16 and the other over Easter vacation, April 14-20.
   c. 5K/10K Run For Hungry Children, March 3.
   d. Mexicali Outreach, April 14-20.
   e. Hospital visitation—every other week (Pam in charge).
   f. Let It Growl—24-hour fast, January 11.
   g. Fund-raiser for Jim Knowlton—books for Papua New Guinea, November 20.
   h. Mission emphasis in Sunday school, entire month of March.
   i. Finish up the prisoner-letter-writing project.
   j. Short-term summer mission projects.

5. *Calling and follow-up*
   Director: Donna

   Calling and follow-up on visitors or people we haven't seen for a while is a major part of our ministry. Our goals are to let people know we appreciated their visit, to encourage them to come back, and to share our ministry if they are interested. It is important to invite them to come to one of our next events; offer to pick them up if they need a ride.

    a. Adult staff and student leadership must hand our SCCC visitor cards to all new people.

    b. The card will go to Donna (via Lisa in the offering box). Donna will type the new name and phone number on our various lists. She will then hand out the cards according to areas.

    c. The area staff will write a personal note to the new person and give the new name and phone number to a responsible leadership person. This leader will then call or make a personal contact with the new person.

    d. The card is given back to Donna, who will file it and hold us accountable to completing this valuable process.

6. *Contact work*
   Director: Jim

   Our goal in contact work should be to show interest in school and other activities, befriend the kids, and put our caring into action. Lunch is a good time to be on campus. Leave your Bible in your car; this is purely a relational time. The faculty and staff like it much better that way. During the first week of school make an appointment with the school administrator and ask for permission to come on campus. Good contact work events:

   After-school sports
   Assemblies during school
   Drama performances
   Playing tennis, racquetball, etc.
   Going to "hangouts"
   Visit kids at work, but don't be a hindrance

7. *One-on-one (discipleship and counseling)*
   Director: Jim
   EVERYONE IN OUR GROUP SHOULD HAVE A ONE-ON-ONE

AT LEAST ONCE A YEAR! There are four types of one-on-one appointments:

a. *Get-acquainted appointment.* This is a time to build a relationship with someone you do not know very well. He will feel special because you bothered to get together with him. Use this time primarily to begin a base of friendship for the future.

b. *Pastoral or shepherding appointment.* This is an important appointment where you are getting together with a person to let him know you care about him and to "just see how he is doing." It is an important method of follow-up.

c. *Counseling appointment.* This is an appointment for a reason. Someone has a problem that he needs to talk with you about. Be a listener. Most likely he needs your listening ear more than your advice. Also remember that he is trusting you with his problems, so *keep it confidential*. If the problem is over your head, be sure to refer the counselee to someone who has had more counseling experience.

d. *Growth booklet appointment.* There are a variety of growth booklets. Be sure to select one which will hit the high schoolers where they are spiritually. Keep in mind that the purpose of the growthbook is to challenge students to get involved in ministry: "The things you have heard me say in the presence of many witnesses entrust to reliable men who will also be qualified to teach others" (2 Timothy 2:2). Our goal is to bring people into a deeper, fuller relationship with Jesus Christ and prepare them to do the work of the ministry. This is done most effectively in a growth booklet. *This area of our ministry is as important as any other area of ministry within our program.* The growth booklet will bring about:

- More knowledge of God's work.
- Quality time spent with leadership or staff.
- Prayer.

- An opportunity for counseling.
- Relationship-building.

8. *Social/special events*
Director: Doug

Social/special events can be very effective in the areas of outreach, socialization, and just pure fun. We do not need them on a weekly basis; they should not take the place of our Bible studies.

Our goal in social/special events is to play together as a group and give our kids a chance to bring their friends to events. All the events should be well-publicized; staff and leadership core should meet every new visitor.

Special events dates:

September 20:	Youth dedication night; concert & slide show
October 28:	"Overtime" after the football game
November 12:	"Grow For It" (Youth Specialties Student Seminar) 9:00-4:00.
	Scavenger hunt/banana night 7:00-10:00.
December 10:	Bluegrass concert/Christmas party
January 13-15:	Great Adventure winter retreat
February 10-13:	All-area ski trips
March 17:	Car rally & concert
April, Easter break:	Mexicali & orphanage trip
May 19:	Battle of the nitwit stars

9. *Retreats and conferences*
Director: Bernie

Retreats are unquestionably a valuable time to make commitments to Jesus Christ, to spend quality and quantity time with our people, and to give our people a chance to bring non-Christians to a "special experience." All of our retreats should be first-rate and top-quality.

Retreats and Conferences:

a. Grow For It (Youth Specialties): November 12.
b. Great Adventure: January 13, 14, 15.
c. Area ski trips: February 10-13.
d. Mexicali: April 14-20.
e. Summer calendar to be completed by December 31.
f. Fall calendar to be completed by June 1.

10. *Staff leadership*
Director: Jim
   We must continue to develop a sense of community and ministry among our youth staff.

   a. Paid staff will meet Tuesday mornings from 9:30-11:30. The direction of this meeting will be supportive, encouraging, reporting, covering necessary business items, prayer, and some training.
   b. Each area director should be in direct-contact ministry with the volunteer staff in his or her area. A specific time of getting together should be a part of each director's ministry.
   c. Every two months the entire youth department staff will get together for training, support, and a good time together. These meetings will have a fun atmosphere, with a time of training involved in the meeting. Dates for this year are:

   Staff Retreat: September 22-24
   Burns' home: November 4
   Carl's home: January 20
   Place to be determined: May 18

   d. Various youth-ministry training events will be offered to any of the staff who would care to participate. Directors can take their volunteer staff to these workshops and spend some good relational time with them.

   GLASS: September 15, 16, 17.
   (Greater Los Angeles Area Sunday School Convention)

Cornerstone Youth Ministries: November 5

National Youth Ministry Training: January 14, Anaheim
January 16, Pasadena

National Resource Seminar by Youth Specialties:
February 25, North
L.A.
March 3, Orange
County

11. *Leadership core (student leadership)*
Director: Jim
This is the heartbeat of our ministry. Each Area Director is responsible for the Leadership Core in your area. You should develop a special time of input into each other's lives. USE THE LEADERSHIP CORE GREATLY IN YOUR AREA MINISTRIES.

Leadership Core ministry meetings will take place on the second and fourth Sundays of each month. These meetings will be a time of training/equipping, prayer, motivation, and information. The meetings will be held at Jim's home unless otherwise announced.

Leadership meetings:

Oct. 9	Feb. 12
23	26
Nov. 13	Mar. 11
27	25
Dec. 11	Apr. 8
25	22
Jan. 8	May 13
22	27

Leadership Core must be involved in these experiences:

Special retreat
Mexicali

Beginning of summer leadership experience
Short-term summer mission project (optional, but
   strongly suggested)
Freshman/leadership ski trip

12. *Support groups*
Director: Doug
   Support groups should be from 5 to 12 people. There will be
a six-week commitment to the group. After this time they may
get out of the group if they desire. Commitment to each other
for these weeks is very important. If they miss twice, they are
out of the group.
   The support group is not a gossip session or a social meeting.
It is for praying, learning, growing, stretching, and supporting
by one another. Each intern, and hopefully many of the volunteers, will be involved in a support group.

13. *Publicity and promotion*
Director: Donna
a. Keep all mailing lists up-to-date.
b. Bulletin: The staff is responsible to Donna to update her
   each Tuesday by 5:00 P.M. on all events for the bulletin. (She
   will not put in the bulletin what is not reported to her.)
c. Fliers:

   1) We will have a *monthly* bulk mailing (unless there is a
      special need okayed by Jim and Donna). Each area direc-
      tor is responsible for a monthly flier of the area's activ-
      ities and Bible studies.

   2) The all-area flier will be made by:

Oct.	Lisa	Jan.	Katie	Apr.	Daryl
Nov.	Daryl	Feb.	Doug W.	May	Doug F.
Dec.	Doug F.	Mar.	Lisa	June	Katie

   This will include upcoming all-area events and retreats.

   3) Print up a schedule of when these fliers will be due.

14. *Overtime*
Director: Doug

Overtime will be a quarterly event that occurs on a Friday night. This event will follow a local high school football or basketball game. Overtime could be a strong supplement to our high school program.

What is it, and how does it run? Overtime is an upbeat, fun time that has two objectives. The first objective is *outreach*. We desire to reach into the lives of those kids who would otherwise avoid church activities. The second objective is to *divert the attention of the high schoolers from a worldly lifestyle to a holistic Christian lifestyle*.

The tone for the Overtime is, as previously mentioned, *upbeat*. The night will be a rah-rah time with a fast pace, lots of enjoyable entertainment, and a very positive atmosphere!

The program for the evening will be labeled as entertainment/performance. It can include music, drama, skits, film, food, group interaction, mixers, announcements, games, and possibly a light talk.

Overtime schedule: October 28
November 14
Next two Overtime dates to be
announced

15. *Parents' advisory board*
Director: Jim

PARENTS' ADVISORY BOARD

This board will meet four times a year, sometimes in conjunction with parents' meetings. The purpose of the board is to:

a. Provide communication with parents about the youth department.
b. Brainstorm on possible teaching ideas.
c. Receive input on needs of kids and parents.
d. Give parents a platform to voice their opinions and give input to the youth ministry team.

PARENTS' UPDATE

We will publish the *Parents' Update* newsletters six times a year. The *Update* will provide the parents with written information about the youth group, interviews of the staff, schedules of events, book reviews, and a column by Jim on parenting.

PARENTS' MINISTRY (Parent Education)

From time to time we will offer parenting classes relating to parents of teenagers within the Institute of Biblical Studies program in the church. We will sponsor the "Focus on the Family" film series beginning October 14 during the 11 o'clock service.

16. *Recreation*
Director: Bernie
Physical health and play are important aspects of a well-rounded youth program. During this year we will be exploring and developing a recreation program to better minister to our kids.

The recreation program will consist of:

    a. Team sports (e.g. softball league)
    b. Bowling with Carl
    c. Recreation night every two weeks

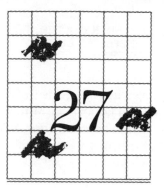

MY RESOURCE REFERRAL LIBRARY

T his section provides a sampling of the many excellent resources available for youth workers today. It is my suggestion that you write these organizations and get on their mailing lists. The better resource library you have, the more well-founded, balanced ministry you can have.

Youth Ministry Training Organizations

The National Institute of Youth Ministry
24422 Del Prado #12
Dana Point, CA 92629
714/240-8414

The National Institute of Youth Ministry is committed to training, equipping, and assisting youth workers to have a more effective ministry with youth and their families.

The Institute sponsors two-week training courses for a maximum of 24 people at a time. The faculty includes some of the finest youth specialists in the world. This can be an unparalleled experience in youth ministry education. The Institute also sponsors "Intensives" across the country. These are in-depth, two-day events geared around one important subject of youth ministry education. The Intensives include Kids in Crisis, Counseling Adolescents, Creative Christian Education, Ministry and Marriage, and Working with Students and Their Families. NIYM has developed an excellent youth worker training video series and sponsors a number of youth events each year.

Youth Specialties
1224 Greenfield Drive
El Cajon, CA 92021
619/440-2333

Youth Specialties is one of the oldest and most respected youth ministry organizations in the world. Their National Youth Worker Conventions and one-day National Resource Seminars for youth workers are attended by over 15,000 people each year. They are also an excellent youth ministry publishing company that is committed to being on the cutting edge of youth work. Their Grow for It Seminars are high-quality, one-day student events. *Youthworker Journal, The Wittenberg Door,* and *Youthworker Update* are all outstanding resources from Youth Specialties offices.

Group Publishing
Box 481
Loveland, CO 80539
303/669-3836

Each year Group Publishing sponsors many top-quality youth-worker training events through their annual Youth Ministry University, one-day training events, and National Christian Youth Congress. Group publishes *Group* magazine for youth workers, *Junior High Ministry* magazine, and very practical books for helping youth workers improve their skills and programs.

The annual Group summer workcamps are very well attended and serve as excellent resources for mission and service projects.

The National Network of Youth Ministries
Box 26146
San Diego, CA 92126
619/578-5155

The Network is a national youth ministry organization committed to bringing together youth workers in different regional areas in the country for mutual support, idea sharing, training events, and combined youth events. The Network has a very healthy emphasis on campus ministry and has an interdenominational outreach.

Curriculum and Program Resources

I am assuming that you know about your denominational material. Therefore, the information presented here is mainly nondenominational.

David C. Cook Publishing
850 N. Grove Avenue
Elgin, IL 60120
312/741-2400

David C. Cook has a number of excellent youth-ministry curriculum resources. The Pacesetter Series is extremely well done. D. C. Cook tends to use professional youth workers to do the writing, which makes their material very practical.

Youth Specialties
1224 Greenfield Drive
El Cajon, CA 92021
619/440-2333

The Youth Specialties "Ideas Library" is one of the finest resources for youth ministry, containing over 4000 ideas dealing with anything from creative communication to retreat ideas. There are also loads of crowd-breakers, skits, and games in the Ideas Series. Youth Specialties' "Talk Box" curriculum resources are excellent for discussion starters.

Harvest House Publishers
LifeSources for Youth Material
1075 Arrowsmith
Eugene, OR 97402
800/547-8979

The LifeSources for Youth material is a series of workbooks

(with leader's guides) geared for junior and senior high school students. The workbooks are on practical subjects and the artwork is enjoyable. Much of the material has been written by Jim Burns, who has put his years of youth ministry experience into making this resource one of America's most widely used for Christian students.

Gospel Light
Life Force
2300 Knoll Drive
Ventura, CA 93003
800/4-GOSPEL

The Gospel Light Youth Division continues to publish excellent resource material for youth ministry. The curriculum material is easy to understand and very creative. *Outrageous Object Lessons* and *A Youth Worker's Book of Case Studies* have been two of the most popular youth worker resources.

Victor Books
Son Power Electives
Box 1825
Wheaton, IL 60187
312/668-6000

Victor Books has recently put out a number of extremely helpful books and curriculum for youth, as well as some great youth-ministry education books. The editors are using some of the finest youth ministry experts in the world, and the new products are some of the finest offered in youth ministry.

Youth Mission and Service Organizations

Youth With A Mission
Box 4600
Tyler, TX 75712
214/882-5591

Youth With A Mission has a wide variety of evangelism and discipleship programs. This is an international organization that has developed an excellent mission training school in Hawaii (Pacific and Asia Christian University).

Teen Missions
Box 1056
Merritt Island, FL 32952
305/453-0350

Teen Missions takes teams of young people all over the world each summer. It offers an excellent training program and a variety of ministries.

Compassion International
Box 7000
Colorado Springs, CO 80933
800/336-7676

This relief and development agency has put together The Compassion Project, one of the finest mission and service experiences available. The Project is an educational tool to help kids understand the devastating pain of poverty. It also gives students the opportunity to raise money and respond to the needs of the poor. The Project is sent free of charge to anyone who asks for it. Do not hesitate to send for information.

Group Magazine WorkCamps
Box 481
Loveland, CO 80539
303/669-3836

Each summer thousands of youth groups work with *Group* magazine in poverty areas of the United States. Group provides the leadership and inspiration and the youth group provides the person power. Group workcamps are known for their high-quality job of ministry and service to the poor.

Habitat for Humanity
419 W. Church Street
Americus, GA 31709
912/924-6935

This great organization gives youth groups the opportunity to build houses for the poor of the world. There is a well-put-together program for churches. Most of the work is in pockets of poverty in the United States.

World Vision, Inc.
919 West Huntington Drive
Monrovia, CA 91016
818/357-7979

World Vision is probably the largest and best-known Christian mission relief agency in the world, offering a variety of special projects for Christian youth groups. The "Let It Growl Planned Famine" is a tremendous opportunity to raise hunger awareness in your youth group as well as to raise money for a truly deserving ministry.

Sexuality Resources

Handling Your Hormones: The Straight Scoop
on Love and Sexuality
Harvest House Publishers
1075 Arrowsmith
Eugene, OR 97402
800/547-8979

Handling Your Hormones is Jim Burns' open, blunt, and Christian presentation on love, sex, and dating. The book covers every subject imaginable in the area of sexuality. It also comes with a Leader's Guide and a Student Growth Guide. There are audio and video tapes of the *Handling Your Hormones* material. This material on sexuality is one of the most widely used resources on the subject. It was awarded the 1987 Gold Medallion Book Award for youth books by the Evangelical Christian Publishers Association.

Why Wait Campaign
Here's Life Publishers
Box 1476
San Bernardino, CA 92402
714/886-7981

Why Wait Campaign is an excellent resource of materials,

including books and films for adults and teens. Internationally known Christian speaker Josh McDowell has put together a team of experts to come up with the latest research available. Their excellent research has paid off in producing a very valuable resource.

Concordia Sex Education Series
Concordia Publishing House
3558 South Jefferson
St. Louis, MO 63118
800/325-3040

This sex-education series is definitely one of the finest available. There are six books in the series, geared for children through adults. The books are relevant and well-planned.

Magazines and Periodicals

Youthworker Journal
Youthworker Update
Youth Specialties, Inc.
1224 Greenfield Drive
El Cajon, CA 92021
619/440-2333

Youthworker Journal is an exceptional quarterly magazine, meeting a real need in youth ministry. The topics are always timely and the writers are the finest in the country.

Youth Specialties also publishes the *Youthworker Update*. This is the best youth ministry newsletter available. *Update* is especially helpful in getting the latest information on the youth culture.

Group Publishing
Junior High Ministry
Group magazine
Box 481
Loveland, CO 80539
303/669-3836

Group magazine is known for its easy-to-read and practical articles, and is especially helpful to lay youth workers. The student section in each magazine is excellent, and the magazine is attractive and always insightful. The publishers of *Group* magazine also publish *Junior High Ministry,* a magazine designed specifically for junior high youth workers. It is put together with the same top quality as *Group* magazine.

Campus Life magazine
465 Gundersen Drive
Carol Stream, IL 60187
312/260-6200

Campus Life is perhaps the finest Christian youth magazine available today. You may order a "leader's edition" of the magazine and get high-quality youth-worker educational material.

Film Distributors

Mars Hill Productions
9302 Wilcrest
Houston, TX 77099
713/879-7777

Mars Hill films are geared strictly for youth. The producers are publishing some of the finest Christian films available today. The films are always excellent discussion starters.

Mass Media Ministries
2116 North Charles Street
Baltimore, MD 21218
301/727-3270

This company does a top-quality job, with numerous films geared especially for youth ministry.

Franciscan Communications (Teleketics)
1229 South Santee Street
Los Angeles, CA 90015
213/746-2916

This Roman Catholic film company has some of the finest discussion-oriented short films available today.

Word Publishing
Box 1790
Waco, TX 76796
817/772-7650

Word produces and distributes films of many of the outstanding youth speakers in the world. Top-quality music videos are also available.

ROA Films
1696 North Astor Street
Milwaukee, WI 53202
800/558-9015

The ROA film catalog is one of the most extensive in the world, including not only religious films but also full-length feature films. The catalog contains a wealth of information.

There are scores of excellent film companies today. I have mentioned a few who specialize in films geared for youth, but in leaving out some of the largest companies I am not implying that these should be excluded from your list of resources. If you do not have a catalog of the Christian films available through your local film distributor, then call and ask them for the latest catalog.

Crisis Resource Hotlines

The following is a partial list of national organizations that can provide crisis information. I strongly recommend that all youth workers gain a working knowledge of information and resources relating to kids in crisis.

Be Sober Helpline	800/BE SOBER
Child Abuse/Parents Anonymous	800/352-0386
National Center for Missing and Exploited Children	800/843-5678
National Institute on Drug Abuse	800/638-2045
National Runaway Switchboard	800/621-4000
Runaway Hotline	800/231-6946
National Rape Hotline	800/222-7273

OUTLINES OF MY 20 FAVORITE TALKS

O ne of the most difficult chores for any youth worker is coming up with new talks week after week or even a couple of times a week. Included in this chapter are skeleton outlines of 20 topical talks for students. Each talk has a Big Idea or main theme, Scripture, and main points.[1]

Building a Strong Foundation

The Big Idea: A firm foundation is essential to living a deeper, more abundant Christian life. Those who have a foundation based on Jesus Christ can withstand even the most difficult trials.

Scripture: Matthew 7:24-27.
Main Points:
1. You need a Cornerstone.
   1 Peter 2:4-8.
2. Build your foundation slowly.
   Philippians 3:12-14.
3. Build on your spiritual foundation daily.
   Joshua 1:8.
4. You must follow the instructions in order to build a strong foundation properly.
   John 14:15,21.

Improving Your Relationship with Your Parents

The Big Idea: Parents are a gift from God; they experience problems and frustrations like anyone else. You can play a major role, and take the initiative to make a difference, in your relating with your parents.

Scripture: Exodus 20:12.
Main Points:
1. God gave you your parents!
   Psalm 139:13-16.
2. Try to walk in your parents' shoes.
3. Spend time with your parents.
4. Communication is a key.
5. The Bible challenges us to honor and obey our parents.
   Ephesians 6:1-3.

Giving the Gift of Affirmation

The Big Idea: Affirmation and encouragement are two of the greatest gifts you can give to anyone. Affirmation makes a powerful difference in the lives of people who give it and receive it.

Scripture: 1 Thessalonians 5:11.
Main Points:
1. Be liberal with praise toward people.
   Hebrews 3:13.
2. Believe in people.
3. Let people know that you are available to be their friend.
   Matthew 19:14.

Dating

The Big Idea: God cares about our dating life. He desires the best for us, including our dating relationships.

Scripture: Colossians 3:17.
Main Points:
1. Establish a friendship before romance.
2. Plan fun and enjoyable dates.
3. Avoid sexual intimacy in a dating relationship.
   1 Corinthians 6:18-20.
4. Choose carefully who you date.
   2 Corinthians 6:14.

Your Mind Matters

The Big Idea: The mind God has given you is a wonderful gift! Dwelling on good and healthy thoughts will glorify God and lead to a happy, fulfilled life.

Scripture: Philippians 4:8.
Main Points:
1. Think about good things.
   Philippians 4:8.
2. Don't dwell on things you have no control over.
   Philippians 4:6,7.
3. Program your mind to think right thoughts.
   Proverbs 23:7 KJV.
4. Keep away from wrong influences.
   Proverbs 13:20.
5. Constantly renew your mind.
   Romans 12:1,2.

Unconditional Love

The Big Idea: God loves you unconditionally—not for what you do but for who you are.

Scripture: Luke 15:11-24.
Main Points:
1. God loves you unconditionally.
   Hebrews 13:5.
2. God loves you sacrificially.
   Romans 5:8.
3. Because of God's love, your task is to *respond* and *accept* His love.
   Revelation 3:20.

Practicing Thankfulness

The Big Idea: Happy people are thankful people. Thankfulness is an attitude which transcends circumstances.
Scripture: 1 Thessalonians 5:18.
Main Points:
1. Make thankfulness an attitude.
2. Make thankfulness a habit.
3. Jesus Christ paid the ultimate sacrifice for our sin; because of this we can be thankful.
   Romans 5:8.

The Call to Servanthood

The Big Idea: The call to Christ is the call to serve. As we learn to imitate Jesus, we will become a more others-centered person.

Scripture: John 13:1-17.
Main Points:
1. Actions speak louder than words.
   1 John 3:18.
2. Treat others as royalty.
   Romans 12:10.
3. Lose yourself in the service of others.
   Luke 9:24.
4. You are the only Jesus that somebody knows.
5. When you serve others you serve Jesus.
   Matthew 25:31-46.

Working Through Loneliness

The Big Idea: At times everyone feels the pain of loneliness. God walks with you through your valley of loneliness.

Scripture: Psalm 23.
Main Points:
1. Risk developing special friendships.
2. Be creative with ideas when you are lonely.
3. Sometimes lonely people are self-absorbed people. Become a more others-centered person.
4. Commit your loneliness to God.
   Matthew 11:28,29.

Handling Peer Pressure

The Big Idea: Peer pressure is one of the most dominant influences in our lives. In God's eyes you are special, and with His help you can win the battle over peer pressure.

Scripture: Romans 7:15-25.

Main Points:

1. Everyone you spend time with has an influence on your life.
2. Choose your friends wisely.
   Hebrews 10:24,25.
3. Remember your uniqueness. You are special in God's eyes!
4. Seek first the kingdom of God.
   Matthew 6:33.

What Is God's Will for My Life?

The Big Idea: The Bible is filled with verses dealing with God's will for your life. Perhaps we should spend less time wondering what God's will is for the future and more time living out God's will for today.

Scripture: Matthew 6:34.

Main Points:

1. Live out God's will for today.
2. You can know the will of God through the Bible.
   Psalm 119:105.
3. Seek the advice and counsel of others whom you respect.
   Proverbs 20:18; 11:14.
4. Prayer is another way of knowing God's will.
   Philippians 4:6,7.
5. At times we can know the will of God through circumstances.
   Romans 12:1,2.

Partying: A Few Practical Guidelines

The Big Idea: Partying strongly influences the life of most American teenagers. Developing Christ-centered standards for our lives will help us make wise decisions about the parties we attend.

Scripture: Colossians 3:1-4.
Main Points:
1. If partying is a weak point in your life, *don't go to parties.*
2. Host "clean parties."
3. As a Christian, if you go to parties, invite Jesus to go with you.
4. Choose friends who will uplift you rather than pull you down.
5. Christians do not live by the world's standards. Matthew 6:24.

Worry

The Big Idea: Worry takes our minds and hearts off God and cripples us from the abundant life we can have in Jesus Christ.

Scripture: Philippians 4:6,7.
Main Points:
1. Yesterday is past.
   Philippians 3:12-14.
2. Your mind influences your worry habit.
   Proverbs 23:7 KJV.
3. Thankful hearts reduce worry.
   1 Thessalonians 5:18.
4. Trust in God is the opposite of worry.
   Proverbs 3:5,6.
5. Live one day at a time.
   Matthew 6:25-34.

Friendship: The Priceless Gift

The Big Idea: Friendship is one of the greatest gifts from God. Your true friends will seek to bring out the best in you.

Scripture: Proverbs 17:17.
Main Points: The qualities of a true friend are:
1. Caring and available.
   Romans 12:15.
2. Encouraging.
   1 Samuel 20:17,42.
3. Willing to sacrifice.
   John 15:12,13.
4. Patient.
   1 Corinthians 13:4.
5. A good listener.
   James 1:19.
6. Loyal.
   1 Corinthians 13:7.
7. Truthful.
   Proverbs 12:19.

Mission

The Big Idea: God does not call every Christian to go overseas for the sake of the gospel. However, He does call each Christian to serve and give to the needs of others as His Son Jesus would.

Scripture: Matthew 25:31-46.
Main Points:
1. God wants you to help in the simple things.
   Matthew 25:31-46.
2. We should give simply for the sake of giving. True giving is with no strings attached.
3. Serving people means serving Jesus.

Do Something Heroic for Jesus

The Big Idea: God has given everyone special gifts, talents, and abilities. We can use those gifts to be heroes for the kingdom of God.

Scripture: 1 Peter 4:10.
Main Points:
1. You are a gifted person.
   James 1:17.
2. You can be a hero for Jesus.
   Psalm 101:6.
3. What are you doing with your life now to make a difference?
   Colossians 3:17.

Building a Healthy Self-Image

The Big Idea: A proper Christ-centered view can turn people who dislike themselves into people who view their life the same way God views them—as special.
Scripture: Ephesians 2:10.
Main Points: How does God view you?
1. You are His creation.
   Psalm 139:1-16.
2. You are loved unconditionally.
3. In Christ your sin is forgiven.
   2 Corinthians 5:17.
4. God's values are different from the world's values.

Steps toward self-acceptance:
1. Thank God for creating and loving you.
2. Accept His forgiveness.
3. You are a part of God's plan.
4. You are a child of God.
5. Fellowship with positive, uplifting people.
6. Reach out to others.

The Resurrection of Jesus Christ

The Big Idea: The facts of the resurrection of Jesus are the cornerstone on which we base our Christian faith.

Scripture: Matthew 28:1-6; John 20:1-8.
Main Points:
1. The significance of the resurrection of Jesus Christ.
   1 Corinthians 15:17-19.
2. The facts of the resurrection.
   a. Jesus foretold His resurrection.
      Matthew 16:21.
   b. The testimony of eyewitnesses and the transformation of the disciples can be logically explained only by the appearance of the resurrected Jesus.
      1 Corinthians 15:3-8.
   c. The resurrection is the only explanation for the empty tomb.
      Mark 15:46; Matthew 27:62-66.
   d. The resurrection is the reason for the beginning of the Christian church and for its rapid growth.
3. How can the resurrection of Jesus affect your life today?
4. What will you do differently because you know the power of His resurrection?

Developing Patience in Your Life

The Big Idea: Patience is an important Christian virtue that is life-transforming. Patience is a fruit of the Holy Spirit.

Scripture: Galatians 5:22-25.
Main Points:
1. View others as God views you.
   Luke 19:1-10.
2. Learn to cope with criticism.
   Colossians 3:13.
3. Use your trials for growth.
   James 1:2-4.

Giving It Away

The Big Idea: God calls all Christians to be wise stewards of their time, talent, and money.

Scripture: 2 Corinthians 8:1-7.
Main Points:
1. Attitude check #1: Give without boasting.
   Matthew 6:3,4.
2. Attitude check #2: Give with a proper perspective.
   1 Timothy 6:10.
3. Attitude check #3: Give sacrificially.
   Mark 12:41-44.
4. Attitude check #4: Give what you have.
   Luke 12:48.

NOTES

Chapter 1—What Is Relational Youth Ministry?

1. This concept is described in much greater detail in Chapter 11.

Chapter 2—Preparing Yourself for Relational Youth Ministry

1. For a list of continuing-education possibilities, see Chapter 27.
2. For more extensive coverage of this subject you may want to obtain Jim Burns' tape *Youth Ministry and Marriage* (National Institute of Youth Ministry, 24422 Del Prado, Suite 12, Dana Point, CA 92629).

Chapter 3—Understanding Today's Youth

1. Zig Ziglar, *Raising Positive Kids in a Negative World* (Nashville: Oliver Nelson, 1985), p. 25.
2. Mike Yaconelli and Jim Burns, *High School Ministry* (Grand Rapids: Zondervan, 1986), p. 17.
3. Myron Harris and Jane Norman, *Private Life of the American Teenager* (New York: Rawson, Wade, 1981), p. 71.
4. Information from the Alan Guttmacher Institute.
5. Denny Rydberg, National Youth Ministry Seminar, 1984.
6. *Saturday Review*, April 1978.
7. *Group* (magazine), January 1986.

Chapter 4—A Brief Overview of Adolescent Development

1. Chapter 18 covers this issue in depth and gives a number of practical ideas for cognitive development.
2. Categories taken from James Fowler, *Stages of Faith* (New York: Harper & Row, 1981). Explanatory comments by Jim Burns.
3. Harris and Norman, *Private Life*, p. 224.
4. Stephen D. Jones, *Faith Shaping* (Valley Forge: Judson Press, 1980), p. 51.

Chapter 5—Learning to Communicate with Today's Youth

1. Wayne Rice, Youth Specialties' National Resource Seminar for Youth Workers, 1985.

Chapter 6—Discipleship—Getting Kids Involved

1. This method of ministry is described in Chapter 13, with the emphasis on the staff putting one-on-one ministry into practice.

Chapter 7—Relational Evangelism

1. Donald C. Posterski, *Friendship: A Window on Ministry to Youth* (Scarborough: Project Teen Canada, 1985), p. 5.
2. This section taken from the Young Life Staff Leadership Manual (Colorado Springs: Young Life). Used by permission.

Chapter 8—Getting Kids Excited About Mission and Service

1. E. Stanley Jones, *Mahatma Gandhi: Portrayal of a Friend* (Nashville: Abingdon, 1983), p. 27.
2. Nelson Bell, *Foreign Devil in China* (Grand Rapids: Zondervan).
3. Dietrich Bonhoeffer, *Life Together* (New York: Harper & Row, 1954), p. 101.

Chapter 9—Camps and Retreats

1. National Youthworkers' Convention, Dallas, Texas, 1982.

Chapter 10—Worship

1. *Growth Unlimited* by Jim Burns is an example of a devotional book that challenges people to read through the entire New Testament in 90 days. Burns' devotional book *Getting in Touch with God* and his workbooks are also practical helps for personal worship.

Chapter 11—Developing Student Leadership

1. A helpful workbook for young people on discovering their spiritual gifts is *Congratulations!—You Are Gifted!* by Jim Burns and Doug Fields (Eugene: Harvest House).
2. Institute of American Church Growth, Pasadena, California, 1983.

Chapter 12—Building Community Through Small Groups

1. Bruce Larson, *Dare to Live Now* (Grand Rapids: Zondervan, 1965), p. 110.
2. Daniel Yankelovich, *New Rules* (New York: Random House, 1981), p. 251.
3. Lyman Coleman, *Encyclopedia of Serendipity* (Littleton: Serendipity House, 1976).

Chapter 15—Building Support with Your Pastor, Staff, and Church

1. *Youthworker Journal*, Fall 1985, p. 29.

Chapter 16—Coping with Finances

1. Paul Borthwick, "How to Design an Effective Youth Ministry Budget," in *Youthworker Journal*, Fall 1984, pp. 23-26.
2. Ibid., p. 25.

Chapter 17—Principles for Strategic Programming

1. National Institute of Youth Ministry, Summer Institute, June 11, 1987.

Chapter 18—Creative Teaching

1. I am deeply grateful to Marlene LeFever of David C. Cook Publishers for her excellent work on learning styles and her practical advice on this section.
2. Marlene LeFever, *Creative Teaching Methods* (Elgin: David C. Cook, 1985), p. 240.
3. Jim Burns, *The Youth Workers Book of Case Studies* (Ventura: Gospel Light, 1987), p. 16.

Chapter 19—How to Plan and Deliver Creative Youth Talks

1. Ken Davis, *How to Speak to Youth* (Loveland: Group Books, 1986), p. 7.

Chapter 20—Building Self-Image in Students

1. Scott Peck, *The Road Less Travelled* (New York: Simon and Schuster, 1978), p. 15.
2. This subject will be treated much more fully in Chapter 23.
3. Statistics taken from Josh McDowell and Dick Day, *Why Wait?* (San Bernardino: Here's Life Publishers, 1987).

4. *U.S. News & World Report*, December 9, 1985.
5. Gary R. Collins, *Give Me a Break* (Old Tappan: Fleming H. Revell, 1982), p. 37.
6. David Elkind, *All Grown Up and No Place to Go* (Menlo Park: Addison-Wesley, 1984), p. 171.
7. Note that we are not talking about New Age thinking, which says we can become infinite by mental imagery. We are referring to achieving legitimate, God-honoring goals in life.
8. Robert Capon, *Between Noon and Three* (San Francisco: Harper & Row, 1982), p. 148.
9. Discussed in greater detail in Chapter 8.

Chapter 21—Counseling Youth

1. H. Stephen Glenn, *Developing Capable Young People* (Lexington, SC: Capabilities, Inc.), session 6, p. 13.
2. From William Miller, *Practical Psychology for Pastors* (Englewood Heights: Prentice Hall, 1985), p. 174. Used by permission.
3. Taken from a seminar given by Dave Rice at the National Institute of Youth Ministry, June 1987.

Chapter 24—Working with Kids from Broken Homes

1. Mike Yaconelli and Jim Burns, *High School Ministry* (Grand Rapids: Zondervan), p. 88.

Chapter 25—Helping Kids in Crisis

1. Gary Collins, *Christian Counseling: A Comprehensive Guide* (Waco: Word, 1980), pp. 51-54.
2. This section taken from *Group* (magazine), October 1986, p. 15. Used by permission.
3. Questions in this section are from the Alcoholism Council of Nebraska. Used by permission.
4. Public Safety Department, Automobile Club of Southern California.
5. Marion Duckworth, *Why Teens Are Killing Themselves* (San Bernardino: Here's Life Publishers, 1987), p. 14.
6. See Blackburn, *What You Should Know About Suicide*; also Yaconelli and Burns, *High School Ministry*, pp. 146-47.
7. Rich Van Pelt, "Kids in Crisis" Seminar, National Institute of Youth Ministry, 1987, Palm Springs, California.
8. G. Keith Olson, *Counseling Teenagers* (Loveland, CO: Group Books, 1984), p. 376.

9. Ibid.
10. For limited local reproduction, use the following credit line: "Taken from Jim Burns, *The Youth Builder* (Eugene: Harvest House, 1988), pp. 276-79. Used by permission." For other reproduction, write for permission to Harvest House Publishers, 1075 Arrowsmith, Eugene, Oregon 97402.

Chapter 28—Outlines of My 20 Favorite Talks

1. Many of these talks are published in greater detail in the *LifeSources for Youth* series of workbooks by Jim Burns (published by Harvest House Publishers).

Other Good
Harvest House Reading

HANDLING YOUR HORMONES
by *Jim Burns*

Frank advice for today's youth on how not to compromise biblical convictions when faced with difficult issues such as parties, drugs and drinking, masturbation, venereal disease, and homosexuality.

HANDLING YOUR HORMONES   GROWTH GUIDE
by *Jim Burns*
A 64-page illustrated workbook with exercises and questions to help youth with their own views and feelings. Companion to *Handling Your Hormones.*

HANDLING YOUR HORMONES   LEADER'S GUIDE
by *Jim Burns*

Practical guidelines for creating an environment in which young people can deal openly and honestly with issues confronting them. For youth minister or lay leader.

GROWTH UNLIMITED
by *Jim Burns*

This 90-day adventure through the New Testament gives youth a deeper grasp of God's Word as they work through each book of the New Testament. Thoughtful questions help develop the habit of a daily meeting with God.

GETTING IN TOUCH WITH GOD
by *Jim Burns*

This daily devotional takes youth to Scripture and provides practical application in such areas as love, prayer, the Holy Spirit, and the promises of God.

CREATIVE TIMES WITH GOD
by *Doug Fields*

Doug Fields, a popular youth minister and author of *Congratulations! You Are Gifted!* and *Creative Dating* understands the adolescent "world" and is committed to helping young people find personal devotions challenging and enjoyable. *Creative Times With God* is a creatively designed and illustrated teen devotional that gives adolescents daily interaction with God's Word in a way that is fresh and relevant. Perfect for junior high and high school age youth.

THE FINAL CRY
by *Greg Laurie*

Every minute one teenager attempts suicide. Every hour one succeeds! Experienced pastor/teacher Greg Laurie provides a sensitive look into the personal lives of today's troubled teenagers. A timely book for teenagers and parents alike.

THE FINAL CRY—VIDEO
by *Greg Laurie*

Greg Laurie, senior pastor of the 6,000-member Harvest Christian Fellowship in Riverside, California, whose teaching is heard throughout the U.S. on his radio program, "A New Beginning," takes the viewer into the personal lives of teens who were saved from becoming another suicide statistic. *The Final Cry* addresses the many profound questions faced by teens and parents whose lives have been touched by this growing national tragedy.

CHRISTIAN LIFE SERIES

PUTTING GOD FIRST
by *Jim Burns*

Designed to help you become a growing Christian. Explores areas such as priorities, peer pressure, and a disciplined devotional life. Discover God's special blessings for those who put Him first.

MAKING YOUR LIFE COUNT
by *Jim Burns*

Make your life count as you serve Him through building a strong foundation, obedience, improving your relationship with your parents, and handling guilt.

LIVING YOUR LIFE...AS GOD INTENDED
by *Jim Burns*

Use this workbook on your journey to learning about prayer, friendship, missions, and how to be more than average. Decide to become all God wants you to be.

GIVING YOURSELF TO GOD
by *Jim Burns*

This workbook will help you get to know God better. Topics covered include getting your spiritual life in shape, enthusiasm, growing in God, and forgiveness.

CHRISTIAN LIFE SERIES LEADER'S GUIDE
by *Jim Burns*

At last—an exciting and invaluable resource guide for working successfully with teens. Fresh ideas and stimulating discussion questions for use with the four workbooks of the Christian Life Series. Material covers an entire year.

CHRISTIAN GROWTH SERIES

COMMITMENT TO GROWTH
by *Jim Burns and Doug Webster*

Through the work of the Holy Spirit, God provides a "spiritual fruit salad" to refresh every believer. Discover how to grow in the fruit of the Spirit.

CONGRATULATIONS! YOU ARE GIFTED!
by *Jim Burns and Doug Fields*

Discover how the Holy Spirit works toward developing your faith and character by empowering you with "spiritual gifts" and find out how to use them.

GETTING IT TOGETHER
by *David Olshine*

Getting It Together takes a close look at the book of Philippians and Paul's desire to know Christ above all else. This workbook will teach you principles on how to read and study the Bible for yourself.

BUILDING RELATIONSHIPS . . . WITH GOD AND OTHERS
by *Jim Burns and Doug Webster*

Based on the 15 "Songs of Ascent" found in the book of Psalms. Find principles for enriching the relationships in your life.

CHRISTIAN GROWTH SERIES LEADER'S GUIDE
by *Jim Burns*

A resource guide to accompany the Christian Growth Series workbooks.

Dear Reader:

We would appreciate hearing from you regarding this Harvest House nonfiction book. It will enable us to continue to give you the best in Christian publishing.

1. What most influenced you to purchase *Youth Builder*?
   ☐ Author   ☐ Recommendations
   ☐ Subject matter   ☐ Cover/Title
   ☐ Backcover copy   ☐ _____

2. Where did you purchase this book?
   ☐ Christian bookstore   ☐ Grocery store
   ☐ General bookstore   ☐ Department store
   ☐ Other

3. Your overall rating of this book:
   ☐ Excellent ☐ Very good ☐ Good ☐ Fair ☐ Poor

4. How likely would you be to purchase other books by this author?
   ☐ Very likely   ☐ Not very likely
   ☐ Somewhat likely   ☐ Not at all

5. What types of books most interest you?
   (check all that apply)
   ☐ Women's Books   ☐ Fiction
   ☐ Marriage Books   ☐ Biographies
   ☐ Current Issues   ☐ Children's Books
   ☐ Self Help/Psychology   ☐ Youth Books
   ☐ Bible Studies   ☐ Other _____

6. Please check the box next to your age group.
   ☐ Under 18   ☐ 25-34   ☐ 45-54
   ☐ 18-24   ☐ 35-44   ☐ 55 and over

Mail to: Editorial Director
Harvest House Publishers
1075 Arrowsmith
Eugene, OR 97402

Name _____

Address _____

City _____ State _____ Zip _____

Thank you for helping us to help you in future publications!